THE
BERLIN
AIRLIFT

THE
BERLIN
AIRLIFT

The Relief Operation that
Defined the Cold War

BARRY TURNER

ICON

Published in the UK and the USA in 2017
by Icon Books Ltd, Omnibus Business Centre,
39–41 North Road, London N7 9DP
email: info@iconbooks.com
www.iconbooks.com

Sold in the UK, Europe and Asia
by Faber & Faber Ltd,
Bloomsbury House, 74–77 Great Russell Street,
London WC1B 3DA or their agents

Distributed in the UK, Europe and Asia
by Grantham Book Services, Trent Road,
Grantham NG31 7XQ

Distributed in the USA
by Publishers Group West,
1700 Fourth Street, Berkeley, CA 94710

Distributed in Canada by Publishers Group Canada,
76 Stafford Street, Unit 300
Toronto, Ontario M6J 2S1

Distributed in Australia and New Zealand
by Allen & Unwin Pty Ltd, PO Box 8500,
83 Alexander Street, Crows Nest, NSW 2065

Distributed in South Africa
by Jonathan Ball, Office B4, The District,
41 Sir Lowry Road, Woodstock 7925

Distributed in India by Penguin Books India,
7th Floor, Infinity Tower – C, DLF Cyber City,
Gurgaon 122002, Haryana

ISBN: 978-178578-240-4

Typeset in Dante by Marie Doherty

Printed and bound in the UK by
Clays Ltd, St Ives plc

CONTENTS

ABOUT THE AUTHOR

Barry Turner is a popular historian whose many books include *Countdown to Victory* (Hodder, 2004), *Suez 1956* (Hodder, 2006), *Outpost of Occupation* (Aurum, 2010), *Beacon for Change* (Aurum, 2011) and, with Tony Rennell, *When Daddy Came Home* (Arrow, 2014). He is also the author of *Karl Doenitz and the Last Days of the Third Reich* (Icon, 2015), described as 'a page-turning narrative' by the *Daily Mail*. He lives in London and south-west France.

LIST OF ILLUSTRATIONS AND MAPS

Plate section

All images from Landesarchiv Berlin/N.N.

Gathering firewood in the Tiergarten district.

Construction workers eat lunch at Tegel airport.

Women construction workers at Tegel.

Runway construction at Tegel.

Berliners watch an aircraft taking off from Tempelhof.

C-47 Skytrains waiting to unload at Tempelhof.

A Sunderland flying boat lands on Lake Havel.

Children from Berlin to be evacuated by flying boat.

A C-54 Skymaster burns at Tempelhof.

Remains of a C-47 that crashed into an apartment building.

Berliners watch as a C-47 comes in to land at Tempelhof.

C-47s being unloaded at Tempelhof.

A young Berliner enjoys Hershey Bars donated from the USA.

Berlin children re-enact the Airlift for a propaganda photograph.

The final flight of Operation Vittles.

US pilot Lieutenant Gail Halvorsen, goodwill ambassador for the Airlift.

Maps on pp. ix, x

Germany and the Allied occupation zones, showing the main air corridors to Berlin

Berlin and the occupation sectors, showing major airports used in the Airlift

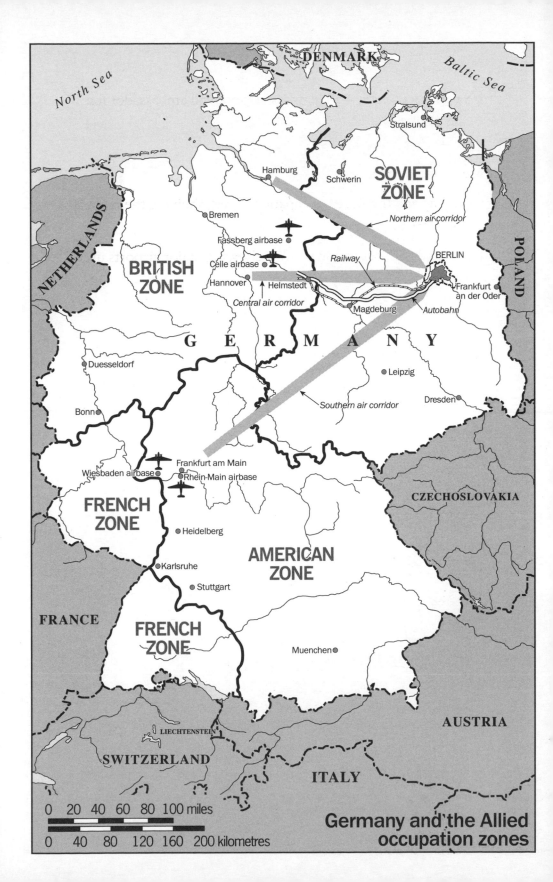

Germany and the Allied occupation zones

Berlin and the occupation sectors

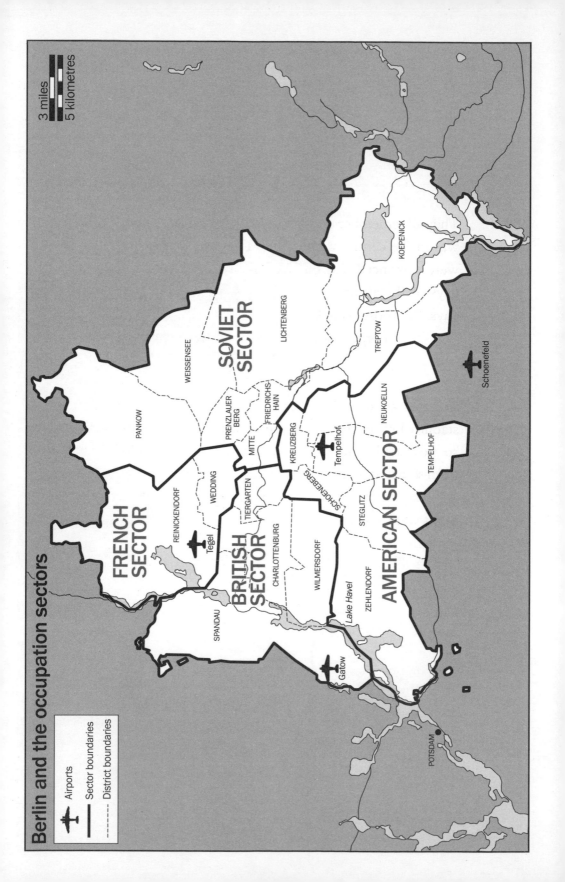

Legend:
- Airports
- Sector boundaries
- District boundaries

3 miles
5 kilometres

FRENCH SECTOR

BRITISH SECTOR

SOVIET SECTOR

AMERICAN SECTOR

REINICKENDORF
PANKOW
WEISSENSEE
LICHTENBERG
KOEPENICK
TREPTOW
NEUKOELLN
PRENZLAUER BERG
MITTE
FRIEDRICHS-HAIN
KREUZBERG
TEMPELHOF
SCHOENEBERG
WEDDING
TIERGARTEN
CHARLOTTENBURG
WILMERSDORF
STEGLITZ
ZEHLENDORF
SPANDAU
TEMPELHOF
Tegel
Gatow
Tempelhof
Schoenefeld
Lake Havel
POTSDAM

They all remember the air-lift with great pride. Then Berlin was in the centre of the world-interest and the Berliners were convinced that the West really cared for them. The days of the air-lift were hard days, exciting days, terrible days. But those were the days.

George Mikes, *Uber Alles: Germany Explored*, 1953

Berlin is all about volatility. Its identity is based not on stability but on change. No other city has repeatedly been so powerful, and fallen so low. No other capital has been so hated, so feared, so loved. No other place has been so twisted and torn across centuries of conflict, from religious wars to Cold War, at the hub of Europe's ideological struggle.

Rory MacLean, *Berlin*, 2014

CHAPTER ONE

For Pilot Officer John Curtiss, it was his second flight to Berlin. The first, in January 1945, had been a mission of destruction. As a Bomber Command navigator he had guided his Halifax through the waving crisscross of blinding searchlights to that night's target, an oil refinery on the edge of the city. He had heard the order for the bomb doors to be opened, seen the orange flashes far below and tried not to think of the devastation and sacrifice. Now, in July 1948, just three years after the end of the war, John Curtiss was flying not over but into Berlin and his aircraft was carrying not bombs but food and fuel for a city under siege. He was just one of thousands of American and British servicemen taking part in the Berlin Airlift, the most ambitious relief operation of its kind ever mounted.

Over eleven months, from June 1948 to May 1949, 2.3 million tons of supplies were shifted on 277,500 flights. Average daily deliveries included 4,000 tons of coal, a bulk cargo never before associated with air carriers. A record day had nearly 1,400 aircraft, close on one a minute, landing and taking off in West Berlin, creating a traffic controller's nightmare at a time when computer technology was still in its infancy. But just about every statistic of the Airlift broke a record of some sort. For those who took part,

1

the sense of achieving something remarkable was to stay with them for the rest of their lives.

John Higgins was an eighteen-year-old dispatch rider when the Airlift was mounted.

> Of my 22 years of service – I was in Cyprus, Kenya and other trouble spots – it was Berlin where I grew up. In eighteen months I changed from a young English hooligan. For the first time I saw the world as a decent human being should see the world.

Fifty years on, John took part in an anniversary veterans' march in Berlin.

> All the schoolchildren were giving us flowers. Then we went up the steps to take our seats and there was an old lady with tears running down her face, just saying 'Danke, danke'. I gave her my flower. And I couldn't talk.

John Curtiss, by then a retired air vice marshal, was also at the veterans' reunion. He was approached by a middle-aged man who was eager to show his gratitude. 'If it wasn't for you and those like you, I wouldn't be here. My parents swore that if the communists took over, they would never have children.'

*

Berlin was a divided city in a divided country in a divided continent. It was not supposed to be like that. Victory over Germany promised a fresh start, a concerted Allied effort to secure a lasting peace in Europe. But it was soon clear that the much-vaunted unity of America, Britain and Russia was based on little more than a joint interest in defeating Nazism. Once the enemy was vanquished, the thin veneer of military and political camaraderie peeled away.

For the more sceptical or more clear-sighted observers, the fragility of the alliance was apparent even while the war was raging. An inter-Allied dialogue on post-war Germany started in mid-1943 when the defeat of the Third Reich, though some time in the hazy future, was judged to be inevitable. In October, a deceptively constructive meeting of Allied foreign ministers in Moscow (Cordell Hull for the United States, Anthony Eden for Britain and Vyacheslav Molotov for the Soviet Union) led to the creation of a three-power European Advisory Commission (EAC) to be based in London. America and Russia were represented on the Commission by their respective ambassadors, John Winant and Fedor Gusev, while the British case was put by Sir William Strang, a long-time government adviser on international affairs.

Their brief was prescribed by decisions already made at top level. That Germany should submit to 'unconditional surrender', affirmed by President Roosevelt and Prime Minister Churchill in January 1943 at their Casablanca conference and subsequently endorsed by Joseph Stalin, was justified as a means of forestalling any inclination, east or west, to negotiate a separate peace. The absence of any flexibility in bringing the war to an end carried with it the message that a defeated Germany would have no say in managing its internal affairs. Unconditional surrender equated with the surrender of sovereignty. It would be up to the Allies to tell the Germans how to run their lives.

But this was to assume that the Big Three could agree on what they wanted for Germany. At no point was this seriously in prospect. The best that the EAC could come up with was a formula for partitioning of Germany into occupation zones under military government with no conditions on the length or terms of occupation. Matters of joint interest were to be settled by an Allied Control Council comprising the commanders-in-chief with their deputies. Berlin was to have its own Interallied Governing Authority (Kommandatura).

These arrangements, so neat and tidy on paper, came with a list of open-ended questions, not least the fixing of the lines of demarcation for the occupation and access to Berlin, which was likely to be in the Soviet zone. The assumption by the western Allies was of free and open transit to the German capital. But the Russians refused to be tied down. Strang noted a disturbing tendency for his EAC Soviet counterpart, 'a grim and rather wooden person'[1] to haggle over insignificant details. In putting this down to bloody-mindedness he failed to recognise the Soviet tactic of playing for time while the advancing Red Army tightened its grip on the territories it occupied.

With his innate distrust of communism in general and of Stalin in particular, Churchill had a clearer idea of what was going on. But priding himself as a realist, he acknowledged Stalin's obsession with security, his own and that of his country. The Soviet leader's resolve to surround Russia with states directly controlled by or submissive to the Kremlin was on a par with his need to be surrounded by underlings of unquestionable loyalty. Given Russia's sacrifice in defeating Nazism, with close on 9 million military and 17 million civilian deaths, Stalin expected more than a share of Germany and was in prime position to get it. Hence Churchill's infamous 'percentages' offer to Stalin exchanging Russian control of Rumania and Bulgaria for British ascendancy in Greece, leaving Hungary and Yugoslavia to be split evenly.

This did not go down well in Washington where President Roosevelt, 'my very good friend' as Churchill liked to call him, was of another school of diplomacy. Having served his political

apprenticeship in the Great War, he was imbued with the ideal-
ism of Woodrow Wilson. The failure of the League of Nations,
Wilson's brainchild, only made Roosevelt more determined to
create a new world order based on mutual trust. This was far distant from Churchill's credo, practical or cynical according to taste,
that the only way to keep the peace was to engineer a balance of
power between leading nations, enabling each to satisfy its territorial ambitions without any one country becoming strong enough
to overwhelm the others.

The cracks in the western alliance began to show at the Big
Three conference held at Yalta on the Black Sea in February 1945.
Neither Roosevelt nor Churchill was at their combative best. The
president, an invalid for much of his political career, was in terminal decline, capable, it was said, of little more than 'talking
situations through to a superficial conclusion'. Churchill was in
better shape but after an arduous journey, he too was often compelled to rest. Stalin alone was buoyant, taking pleasure in the
certainty that the Red Army was bulldozing German forces in
the east.

Three weeks after launching their winter offensive, Russian
spearheads were 300 miles west of their starting point. The
Germans had been swept from Poland, except for the neck of the
corridor leading to Danzig. There was no prospect of a German
counter-offensive. By the end of January, the great industrial region
of Silesia, with its tank and aircraft factories little touched by Allied
bombing, was in Russian hands. But all this paled against a single,
awe-inspiring reality: that from the bridgehead on the Oder river
near Kuestrin, Berlin was little more than 60 miles away.

Meanwhile, to the embarrassment of the western commanders, the deep defences of the Siegfried Line were still intact while
the Rhine, the prime objective of the D-Day invasion, was no

closer to Allied forces than Berlin from the Russians. With Stalin already wielding power over large parts of eastern Europe there was little that Roosevelt and Churchill could say or do to dent his resolve.

The chief bone of contention was Poland. Britain was pledged to secure independence and free elections for Poland; it was, after all, to defend Polish liberty that Britain had gone to war in the first place. But Russia too had legitimate or, at least, irresistible claims to be part of any Polish settlement. Never again must that country's wide open spaces tempt an invader. Stalin wanted the Russian frontier to be moved further to the west, while compensating Poland for loss of territory by allowing it to encroach on Germany. Stalin also demanded a government in Warsaw sensitive to Moscow's wishes. This had no support at all in London where there was a Polish government-in-waiting. Churchill protested vigorously but had no choice but to accept Stalin's handpicked nominees as the core of the new regime. The Soviet leader promised 'free and unfettered elections' at a still to be determined date. Churchill was not taken in but Roosevelt chose to be accommodating.

In late March 1945, fifteen Polish resistance leaders, who might reasonably have expected to be part of the new administration, were arrested and taken to Moscow where they were forced to confess to fabricated charges, including Poland's participation in a British-organised anti-Soviet bloc. A reconstructed government had communists holding all important offices including justice and security. Wounded feelings in Washington that Stalin could act so blatantly against the spirit of Yalta were aggravated by news that a puppet government had been set up in Soviet-occupied Rumania.

Still confident that Stalin was 'gettable', Roosevelt looked to the newly created United Nations to provide the framework for the two superpowers, plus Britain, China and, more problematically, France, to sort out their problems and those of the rest of the world in an atmosphere of mutual regard. But even Roosevelt must have taken a deep breath when at Yalta he put his name to the Declaration on Liberated Europe, a commitment by the Big Three to help freed nations 'to destroy the last vestiges of Nazism and Fascism and to create democratic conditions of their own choice'. The president lived just long enough to recognise the depth of cynicism measured by these words. For the rest, Russia joined the war against Japan in return for territorial and other concessions that, for the time being, were kept under wraps.

On the vexed question of reparations, the general principles were laid down that removals were to take place from the national wealth of Germany within two years of the end of the war so as to destroy its military potential; that there should be annual deliveries of goods from Germany 'for a period to be fixed'; and that German labour should be used in the reconstruction of war-devastated lands. A detailed plan was to be drawn up by a three-power Allied Reparations Commission sitting in Moscow. In the teeth of British resistance, Stalin secured a basis for reparations of a total sum of $20 billion with 50 per cent going to the USSR. Was this a definite commitment? Russia later said it was. Britain and America denied it.

Churchill had his successes. Without too much trouble he saw off Roosevelt's renewed attempt to incorporate the British Empire into the 1941 Atlantic Charter, a high-flown document promising global cooperation and freedom from political repression. It had taken some time for him to realise that when Roosevelt talked of nations having the right to choose their own government, he was including countries under British rule. There was a sharp reaction when Washington mooted the desirability of handing Hong Kong back to the Chinese. At Yalta, Churchill was able to take strength from Stalin's interpretation of the Atlantic Charter that did not preclude Stalin's own territorial demands. The breathtaking effrontery of Stalin speaking in support of an American proposal that all British dependent territories be placed under international trusteeship provoked Churchill to righteous indignation.

Churchill was on a hiding to nothing in standing up for French demands. As the leader of Free France and head of the Provisional Government, General Charles de Gaulle had expected to use Yalta as a platform for national rehabilitation. But neither Roosevelt nor Stalin was ready for that. Both were dismissive of French claims to big power status and Roosevelt had a strong antipathy to de Gaulle as a devious and ungrateful ally. Churchill too was liable to lose patience with the assertive French leader ('Really, France has enough to do this winter and spring in trying to keep body and soul together, and cannot masquerade as a Great Power for the purpose of war'), but stood by his belief in a European future where a strong France balanced a German revival. Attracted to any idea that reduced the pressure on America to take care of postwar Europe, Roosevelt agreed to France having its own German occupation zone and to it becoming the fourth member of the Allied Control Council for Germany. Stalin reluctantly went along on condition that the French zone was carved out of territory designated for Britain and America.

*

As for Berlin, the Big Three approved a broad plan for putting the city under joint administration. By early 1945, the western Allies had accelerated their advance to a point where it was uncertain who would get to Berlin first. It was a prize dear to the heart of Field Marshal Bernard Montgomery. Following the Rhine crossing, he assumed that his 21st Army Group would lead the race to Berlin. But as supreme commander of western Allied forces, General Dwight Eisenhower was acutely sensitive to the rivalry between American and British commanders. Anticipating repercussions in Washington, not to mention threats of resignation from senior officers if he gave Montgomery his head, Eisenhower opted to shift the centre of his advance to General Omar Bradley's Twelfth Army Group with orders to make for the River Elbe, there to meet up with the Russians. The Red Army was offered the chance to be the first to fly the flag over the Brandenburg Gate. It was a paramount decision for which Eisenhower has been much criticised but there were sound strategic reasons for leaving Berlin to the Russians. For one thing they were closer, with a million-strong force ready for the knockout attack across flat, open countryside. The nearest Anglo-American forces were still 250 miles off target. The rate of their advance was impressive but not so great as to guarantee coming in first. Even assuming that the 200 miles to the Elbe could be covered speedily, the other 50 miles beyond was difficult terrain with lakes and rivers to hold up movement. Then there was the nightmare prospect of street fighting in Berlin with no means of distinguishing Russian friend from German foe. What would that do for relations with the Soviets?

Another factor weighed against Berlin falling to forces under Eisenhower's command: the cost in young lives of trying to out-pace the Russians. Bradley, who was content to forgo a triumphant entry into Berlin as long as Montgomery, his deadly rival, did not thereby steal an advantage, calculated that a breakthrough from the Elbe would incur 100,000 casualties, 'a pretty stiff price to pay for a prestige objective'. The warning was not lost on Eisenhower, who was under pressure to conserve manpower against the then probability of the war with Japan outlasting the war in Europe by a year or more. Seasoned troops could expect their services to be in demand in the Pacific war zone.

But it was politics rather than strategy that made the running. At the very least Eisenhower was intent on holding the balance between American and British interests. Also in the back of his mind was the knowledge that his president was keen to foster good relations with the Russians. However naive this may have appeared once Stalin emerged in his true colours, those close to Roosevelt were strongly motivated to treat the Russians as friends and most definitely not as prospective enemies. Roosevelt had his warning voices but they were not loud enough to reach Eisenhower. What he did hear was the opinion of his mentor and army chief of staff, General George Marshall, who backed the Berlin decision as part of the American conciliation policy. For Marshall this had the added virtue of doing down the detested Montgomery.

The reaction from London was predictably hostile but when Roosevelt joined with his generals to deny that Eisenhower's plans involved any far-reaching changes from the strategy agreed at Yalta, Churchill backed off, denying any attempt to disparage the supreme commander or to foster 'misunderstandings between the truest friends and comrades that ever fought side by side'. Eisenhower grasped the olive branch, reassuring Churchill that far from leaving British forces 'in a static condition along the Elbe', it was likelier that 'US forces would be shifted to Field Marshal Montgomery who would then be sent across the river in the north and to a line reaching to Luebeck on the Baltic coast'. The objective was to liberate Denmark and Norway ahead of the Red Army. The destiny of Berlin was left open, though the odds were heavily in favour of the Red Army achieving its dearest wish.

It is just possible that pitted against an ailing president, Churchill could have made more of his chances to influence

Washington opinion. But after his initial protest he went soft on the issue until well after the war when hindsight embroidered his memoirs. Churchill was a realist. He knew above all else that he had to keep in with the Americans who held the whip hand. That made him the loser in more arguments than he cared to admit. As chief of air staff, Sir Charles Portal, observed of his boss, 'Churchill will fight to the last ditch, but not in it'.

The final decision over Berlin was not taken until mid-April. By then, western forces were able to celebrate a much faster progress than originally anticipated. The US Ninth Army, headed by General William S. Simpson, was at the Elbe while Soviet forces were still battling their way through the Berlin suburbs. As Simpson saw it, nothing stood between his troops and Berlin except a wide-open autobahn. But his request to let him go the last few miles was denied.

For Eisenhower the risks were still too high. The Ninth Army was only 50,000 strong. Far ahead of its supply lines, it had a single bridgehead over the Elbe to bring up essential artillery and gasoline. The contrast with the Soviet build-up – 1.25 million men backed by 22,000 artillery pieces – was stark. In any case, whatever interest Eisenhower had once had in taking Berlin was now lost. On the very day that Simpson reached the Elbe (April 11th) Eisenhower dined with General Patton, the abrasive Third Army commander, who took the opportunity to urge an American incursion into Berlin. Eisenhower was not persuaded. The city had 'no tactical or strategic value', he argued. If, as Patton claimed, Simpson could take the city in 48 hours, this, in Eisenhower's view, 'would place upon the American forces the burden of caring for thousands and thousands of German displaced persons and Allied prisoners of war'.[2]

The Berlin garrison, mostly old men and boys huddled in the wreckage of a once great city, surrendered to the Red Army on

May 2nd, 1945. As a young German educated in Moscow, Wolfgang Leonhard was in the Russian advance party.

> Slowly our train wound its way through Friedrichsfelde towards Lichtenberg. It was an infernal picture. Fire, rubble, ghostly starving people in rags. Lost German soldiers who no longer knew what was happening. Red Army soldiers, singing, celebrating and often drunk. Long lines of people patiently waiting in front of water pumps in order to fill small containers. All looked terribly tired, hungry, exhausted and decrepit.[3]

Berlin was a cauldron for the hungry and the homeless. There was no gas or electricity, the gutters were open sewers, the trees had long gone for firewood and the streets were choked with rubble. Dogs were sold for meat and cats for their fur. It was reckoned that over 50,000 orphans were living like animals in holes in the ground. For a typical Berliner, the meal of the day was a bowl of thin vegetable soup, a slice of black bread with a smear of margarine and maybe a scrap of meat.

The Russians were quick to take command of what was left of the civilian population. Four days before the city was formally handed over to the invader, the Soviet commander-in-chief, Marshal Georgy Zhukov, was giving orders for a Soviet-style administration. Berlin was declared a Russian prize of war, irrespective of Allied agreements on its future status. Notwithstanding an orgy of rape and looting, there was hardly any resistance. With the Red Army as the only source of food, obedience was a matter of survival.

A Soviet Military Administration (SMAD), headed by Zhukov, was supported by 'initiative groups' of dedicated German communists trained in Moscow. Anton Ackermann led the way in Saxony,

Gustav Sobottaka in Mecklenburg, while the ten-strong group that found a base in the Lichtenberg district of Berlin was headed by Walter Ulbricht. A 52-year-old exile from Nazism, Ulbricht gave unstinting loyalty to Stalin. Destined to become East German head of state, he was a colourless personality and no orator but what he lacked in charisma was more than compensated, in Soviet eyes, by his value as a dedicated functionary.

Under Ulbricht's direction, politicians with anti-Nazi credentials were persuaded to be part of an anti-fascist coalition, though where Social Democrats and Christian Democrats were appointed mayors they were kept under tight supervision by loyal communists. In quick time Berlin had its own government, the Magistrat, with Dr Werner, a conservative professor of architecture, as Oberbuergermeister and Karl Maron, a communist who had seen out the war in Russia, as his deputy. Trade unions were reconstituted to form a Free German Trade Union Federation (FDGB) under communist control. As too were the police who were now the People's Police, led by Paul Markgraf, a one-time Wehrmacht captain who, captured at Stalingrad, quickly converted to communism. The Berliner Stadtbank, declared a public monopoly, alone was empowered to issue money. News and newsprint were reserved for communist publications while radio pumped out Soviet propaganda. All this and much more was accomplished before the western Allies had even a toehold in Berlin.

Ulbricht and his friends did not have it all their own way. The savagery of the Red Army against the civilian population was hard to erase. Moreover, the systematic destruction of the industrial base (more than 1,000 factories were marked for shipping to Russia) with the consequent loss of jobs led to widespread discontent. But while they were callous in their pursuit of objectives, the Russians were at least consistent in knowing what they wanted.

As the US commander in Germany, Eisenhower was empowered to create a tightly controlled financial and economic structure to allow for heavy reparations. He had no problems with this. With a hatred of Nazism reinforced by his visits to liberated concentration camps, Eisenhower was imbued with the Roosevelt spirit of friendly cooperation with Russia to make Germany pay for its misdeeds. He had public opinion on his side. A proposal put up by US treasury secretary, Henry Morgenthau, to reduce Germany from an industrial powerhouse to a predominantly rural economy, had wide popular appeal though there were snorts of derision from the Washington inner circle. Leading the realists, defence secretary Henry Stimson presaged a more constructive policy when he declared that 'a nation like Germany cannot be reduced to peasant level without creating another war'. The Morgenthau formula, he told the president, was an 'open confession of the bankruptcy of hope'.

Roosevelt was persuaded to distance himself from the Morgenthau Plan. Nonetheless, a watered-down version found its way into orders to American occupation forces. The assumption of collective guilt meant that the German people were to be treated harshly, their living standards kept low and their economic assets used to rebuild the Europe they had tried to destroy. The British military fell into line. All ranks of Anglo-American forces were subject to the non-fraternisation rule and a ban was put on political activity of whatever orientation. The determining factor was the fear of repeating the mistakes of 1918 when, it was said, the Germans had worked hard at being amiable, the better to argue later that they had been misjudged as the aggressors. As a veteran of the first German war, Montgomery was uncompromising, arguing that this time there must be no smokescreen put up by 'appeals for fair play and friendship ... A guilty nation must not only be convicted, it must realise its guilt.'

14

It was soon obvious that the non-fraternisation rule was unworkable. But it stayed in place, causing needless confusion, embarrassment and irritation all round. The Americans were more flexible than the British. GIs could not resist the importuning by small children who draped themselves over jeeps begging for chewing gum, chocolate and peanuts. From meeting children it was a short step to meeting their older sisters or widowed or lonely mothers. Non-fraternisation was wrecked on sex, admitted one senior officer who went on to say that to a young man 'bored and fed up with the company of other men, almost anything in skirts is a stimulant and relief'.[4] Sixty-five dollars was the standard fine for breaking the non-fraternisation rule. Propositioning German girls became known as 'the 65 dollar question'. Many took the gamble. In the Anglo-American zones, up to 70,000 post-war babies were born to unmarried mothers.

*

In April 1945 there was a change of occupancy in the White House. Roosevelt died on the 12th. His successor was his vice president, Harry S. Truman. Two more dissimilar politicians it would be hard to find. Roosevelt was the grand patriarch, on easy terms with Ivy League intellectuals and at home in high society. The short, bespectacled Truman was a farmer's boy from Missouri. He had no college degree and no pretence at sophistication. His favourite relaxation was a game of poker for small stakes. In his climb from local, to state to national politics he presented himself as a plain-speaking, no nonsense, ordinary sort of guy who could be trusted with the cash box.

In 1934, after a succession of minor jobs, Truman was elected to the Senate. Roosevelt backed his nomination for the vice presidency in the 1944 presidential election, judging him to be a safe, middle-of-the-road adjutant who would know his place. With the election out of the way, Truman had few meetings with Roosevelt and made little attempt to participate directly in foreign affairs. However, with increasing signs of Roosevelt's frailty, he could not have been unaware of his likely elevation. His preparation took the form of a heavy reading schedule. But while he kept up with the reports that landed on his desk, when the call came he was still a novice. Diplomacy baffled him and his closest associates saw that he was nervous, uneasy and insecure.[5]

Truman was not short on advice. Most of it came from Roosevelt's former advisers who contrived to push the late president's idealistic notion that despite a deep-rooted antipathy to communism, America and Russia could get along for the sake of world peace. When Soviet demands threatened to derail the United Nations almost before it had got underway, it was Harry Hopkins, Roosevelt's diplomatic guru, who was sent to Moscow to find a compromise. Having overcome the immediate crisis, Hopkins exuded optimism. A sick man in a hurry (he died in January the following year), Hopkins persuaded Truman that the president could do business with Stalin. Of Churchill, he was less sure.

The prevailing wisdom in Washington held that the British prime minister was best kept at a distance. While given credit as the country that had fought longest against Nazism, Britain was now seen, as the poker-playing Truman might have put it, as a busted flush. On paper this was true enough. When Britain went to war in 1939, the economy rested comfortably on its overseas assets and earnings. Six years later, the cushion had deflated. With a balance of payments deficit that had increased fifteen-fold, Britain was the world's largest debtor nation.

By contrast, the economic muscle exercised by America was so mighty as to make all others seem puny. With a gross national product that had doubled between 1940 and 1945, it was now three times that of the Soviet Union and five times that of Britain. As to military strength, America had nearly 12 million men in arms against 5 million for Britain, the latter dependent on American weaponry.

Churchill's counter-argument to raw figures, that Britain still had its empire, did not go down well in a country instinctively opposed to imperialism. Truman could not afford to ignore the impression shared by many Americans that Britain was hanging on to their coat-tails, enjoying the free ride as long as it might last. It was chiefly in response to broadsides from the American press and from Congress that Truman made the arbitrary decision to end Lend-Lease, the programme instituted by Roosevelt in 1941 for supplying America's allies with warships and warplanes, food, oil and other raw materials needed to fight the war. For Truman to cut this lifeline, even going so far as to recall ships already at sea, was a diplomatic blunder. Churchill was aghast, though the strongest protest came from Stalin who, with some justification, called it a 'brutal' act.

The president backpedalled furiously while excusing himself for not having given close enough attention to the relevant documents. Lend-Lease was resumed with the cut-off date left undecided.* But if the slight to Britain was unintended, the feeling in Washington was that it served a purpose in warning Churchill that he could not expect preferential treatment or special regard for his opinions.

For now, Eisenhower and Zhukov took the lead in settling how Germany was to be run. Supreme authority was vested in the commanders-in-chief of the victorious powers. Matters affecting

---

* Lend-Lease finally came to an end in September 1945.

Germany as a whole were to be decided by unanimous agreement between the four occupying countries but when this was unachievable each commander could make decisions for his own zone. Berlin was to be divided into sectors. Though not recognised at the time, except possibly by the Russians, these arrangements made an east–west split almost inevitable.

The approved zonal boundaries required American forces to evacuate territory over a 400-mile front to a depth, in some places, of 120 miles. Churchill warned against the sacrifice of a strong bargaining counter but to no avail. When assurances were sought that Allied forces would retain open access to Berlin by air, road and rail, Stalin prevaricated. The danger signal was ignored, it being taken for granted that settling the details of four-power controls was bound to take time. After visits to London and Paris, where he was met by cheering crowds, Eisenhower flew to Washington for a tumultuous welcome home followed by two weeks of relaxing rounds of golf.

In Eisenhower's absence from Germany, decisions were left to his deputy, General Lucius Clay. One of the most remarkable figures in post-war Germany, Clay was to play a pivotal role in frustrating Soviet ambitions in Berlin. He did not take full command of the American zone until the spring of 1947 after serving as deputy to Eisenhower's successor, General Joseph McNarney. But his elevation was no more than a formality. From the first day he arrived in Germany, Clay was in the driving seat.

A tough-minded soldier administrator who combined managerial talent with the ability to inspire loyalty and enthusiasm, Clay was the first American four-star general with no combat experience. 'He never commanded anything with more firepower than a desk', said a colleague. It was more than enough. With an insider's view of Washington's political hothouse gained from his father, a senator for Georgia, this often waspish chain-smoking organisation man joined Eisenhower's staff when he was 49. At the start he was as anti-German as any of his colleagues but he soon came to see Germany as an incubator for hatching 'our ideals of democracy'. This, he believed, was the best insurance against the spread of communism across Europe:

> I must say with all the sincerity at my command, that 42 million Germans in the British and American zones represent the strongest outposts against communist penetration that exists anywhere.

To support him in his endeavours, Clay had an Office of Military Government (OMGUS) in Frankfurt with a payroll of 12,000.

For most of his time in Germany, Clay's opposite number in the British zone was General Sir Brian Robertson, another soldier administrator but one who had served in the Great War. His father had been military governor in Germany in 1918. Robertson had made his reputation by keeping open the supply lines to Montgomery's Eighth Army, a role he reprised for Field Marshal Alexander in Italy. Deputy to Montgomery in Germany and subsequently to Sir Sholto Douglas, Robertson became military governor in his own right in 1947. With his straight back, clipped moustache and sharply pressed uniform, he was seen by Germans as a caricature of the senior British army officer. Slightly older than Clay, they shared experience as army engineers but otherwise had little in common.

While Clay could be mercurial, ever ready to vent his frustration with Washington by issuing thinly veiled threats to stand down, Robertson, 'whose imperturbability was as solid as the cliffs of Dover'[6], tempered efficiency with a readiness to toe the official line. In their relations with the Russians, both made strenuous efforts to keep on good terms with Marshal Vasily Sokolovsky, the approachable but enigmatic deputy commander of Soviet forces in Germany, who was soon to take over from Zhukov as commander-in-chief.

Food and fuel remained desperately short across Germany as hundreds of thousands of refugees forced out of Soviet-occupied countries to the east, straggled across the zonal boundaries to join the destitute and homeless in the bombed-out cities. Frankfurt's housing stock was down by two thirds; in Nuremberg, scarcely one house in ten was undamaged; over half the buildings of Hamburg had been reduced to 43 million cubic metres of rubble. Cologne, the target of the first British thousand-bomber raid, was almost a wipe-out. Aachen was described as a 'fantastic, stinking heap of ruins'.[7] Yet, in less than a year after the surrender the population of what was one day to become West Germany had jumped by nearly 4.5 million.[8]

For the extent of devastation, Berlin was unique. Willy Brandt, a future mayor of Berlin and West German chancellor, called the city 'a no-man's-land on the edge of the world with every little garden a graveyard, and above this, like an unmovable cloud, the stink of putrefaction'.[9]

The gaunt hulk of the Reichstag, burned out in 1933 and blasted by Allied bombing, shadowed the famous Tiergarten park, now a desert of tree stumps and choked waterways.

George Clare, who had known Berlin in the 1930s, returned in 1945 as a Royal Artillery interpreter.

The absence of the constant roar of city life was more unsettling than the sight of bombed or shelled buildings, of jagged outlines of broken masonry framing bits of blue sky. I had been prepared for that, but not for a city hushed to a whisper. Yet Berlin was not a lifeless moonscape. It lived – albeit in something of a zombie trance – mirrored in the dazed looks of many of the people I passed, more often noticeable in men than women. But then the men were mostly old or elderly, bowed and bitter-faced; the few youngish ones who were about – emaciated shadows of the soldiers who had almost conquered an entire continent – looked pathetic and downtrodden in the tattered remains of their Wehrmacht uniforms. The women were of all ages and, with so many men killed and hundreds of thousands in prisoner-of-war camps, they, not as formerly, the Prussian male, dominated the scene.[10]

A German-American wine merchant turned CIA agent, Peter Sichel, was another whose images of pre-war Berlin were shattered.

Whole areas of the city were totally destroyed; some houses were cut open, with a portion of the house destroyed and a part still suitable for shelter. Apartments that were formerly supplied with central heating could no longer be heated because the fuel was not available. The apartments that were still viable were shared by many families, with one room often accommodating a whole family. Stoves were installed in each room, the stove pipes finding their exit through the nearest window. Food was scarce in spite of rations, rations that did not provide the necessary number of calories ...

You can never forget the devastation and misery that war brings once you have seen it. In addition to the physical misery, there was the complete destruction of a society that, but a short time ago, had provided food and shelter, employment, and social contact. All these things were gone. People were left to their own devices, trying to survive the best they could, using whatever they had to exchange for what would enable them to live another day.[11]

*

American administration in Germany got off to a bad start. The guiding principles were set out in JCS1607, 6-7 which came into force three days after the capitulation. The letters stood for Joint Chiefs of Staff with the numerals at the end signifying the combined sixth and seventh drafts of the directive. An intense programme of denazification and re-education was to be accompanied by a dismantling of industries with military associations (embracing, by some interpretations, the entire economy) and the payment of reparations, chiefly to Russia.

Immediately there were protests from those who were charged with implementing the directive. Lewis Douglas, Roosevelt's first budget director and soon to be US ambassador in London, declared it to be the work of 'economic idiots', adding, 'It makes no sense to forbid the most skilled workers in Europe from producing as much as they can for a continent that is desperately short of everything.' Clay thought the directive to be unworkable but was told to make the best of it. This he did by interpreting it in ways that suited his purpose. The frustration came with trying to get things done.

The early post-war military government was rarely competent. As the western Allies moved into Germany, the tendency of senior commanders was to drop off the least capable of their subordinates. They were tasked with restoring essential services while setting up an administration untainted by Nazism. With little backup (maybe ten or twenty junior officers and other ranks), minimum knowledge of German and fearful of reprisals, the no-hopers saved face by retreating into petty bureaucracy. The majority remained in place after the surrender.

Even after a fresh contingent of civil officers was brought in, standards remained mediocre. In the British zone the Control Commission Germany (CCG), with a staff twice the number of the American complement, was known as Charlie Chaplin's Grenadiers or Complete Chaos Guaranteed. Preparation for the task ahead was limited to a brief and superficial course on German history and instruction on carrying out basic duties. The ability to speak German was deemed desirable but not essential.

The occupying forces did themselves well, starting with accommodation. Of the 1,050 undamaged houses in Munster, nearly half were requisitioned by the British military.[12] The black market thrived on German cameras, binoculars, watches and pistols. The watches were standard Wehrmacht issue and were of higher quality than any that could be found in the Allied ranks. Many were sent home to friends and relatives; others sold or bartered. Cigarettes served as currency. A packet of twenty was liable to pass through many hands before the contents were smoked.

Whenever materials were available, lucky families were allocated prefabricated housing or places in former army camps converted to civilian use. But even so, hundreds of thousands were forced to live rough.

In the cities, water from the tap was no longer fit to drink, the sewers overflowed and gas and electricity cuts were frequent and protracted. Families adapted to make the best of a bad job – for example, getting used to cooking on an upturned electric iron. 'We could even cook pea soup on it. Beetle peas were one of the few things we could get to eat; the peas had to be soaked and then inside every one there was a beetle which had to be removed. This job took ages, but the soup tasted good.'[13]

An outstanding contention between the wartime Allies was access to Berlin which, for a succession of spurious reasons, had been denied to all except Soviet forces.

On June 29th, 1945, Clay led an Anglo-American delegation to Zhukov's Berlin headquarters. Under orders to go gently with the Russians, he made every effort to be reasonable.

> We explained our intent to move into Berlin utilizing three rail lines and two highways and such air space as we needed. Zhukov would not recognize that these routes were essential and pointed out that the demobilization of Soviet forces was taxing existing facilities. I countered that we were not demanding exclusive use of these routes but merely access over them without restrictions other than the normal traffic control and regulations which the Soviet administration would establish for its own use. … We did not wish to accept specific routes which might be interpreted as a denial of our right of access over all routes but there was merit to the Soviet contention that existing routes were needed for demobilization purposes.[14]

Clay accepted a verbal agreement allowing for open access from the west along one main highway, a rail line and two air corridors. This he assumed to be a temporary arrangement that would last only until the Allied Control Council had cleared the way for free movement within and between all four Allied zones. Later, Clay conceded that he had put too much faith in Soviet good intentions. By acceding to Russian control over entry into Berlin, save for four vulnerable routes, Clay had given the advantage to Stalin should he ever decide to make Berlin his exclusive preserve.

The Russians did give way on one point. Self-interest dictated that some accommodation should be found on flying in and out of Berlin. The number of flights had increased substantially since the end of the war and with aircraft of three countries sharing airspace, it was clear that a set of rules had to be devised. In late 1945, the aviation committee of the Allied Control Council proposed six air corridors linking Berlin with Hamburg, Hannover (Bueckeburg), Frankfurt, Warsaw, Prague and Copenhagen. There were Soviet objections to including cities outside Germany but there was agreement on three air corridors, each twenty miles wide: two from the British zone (Hamburg and Hannover) and one, the longest, from the American zone (Frankfurt). As this seemed to be the best deal on offer, the two sides signed acceptance on November 30th. This proved to be the only written compact to emerge from talks on western access to the former German capital.

That easygoing cooperation might lead to Soviet concessions was suggested by the creation of the Berlin Air Safety Centre, where the Russian military was eager to learn from American expertise. When there was something to gain, all was sweetness and light. But it was unsafe to make generalisations. Attempts to establish an Anglo-American base in Berlin proved the point.

An American reconnaissance party to Berlin comprising a convoy of 100 vehicles carrying 500 troops and equipment set off on June 23rd. In command was the ebullient and brash Colonel Frank Howley. It was not an auspicious journey. Entering the Soviet zone at Dessau on the Elbe, Howley heard that there was an upper limit of 50 on the number of trucks that could accompany him. The diminished convoy then moved on to Babelsberg where it was ordered to stop. After more fruitless wrangling, Howley reluctantly decided to return to base. A British contingent was no luckier. Told that the Magdeburg Bridge was closed, they managed to find another crossing but achieved only a token presence.

After two more weeks of inconsequential talks, American and British troops were permitted their official entry into Berlin. It was slow going. The designated overland route, recalled Howley, was 'the highroad to Bedlam'.

It was jam packed with tanks, trucks and other vehicles, all hurrying toward the previously forbidden city. Russian officers, in captured ramshackle cars and trucks, raced up and down our columns to see that we weren't escaping with plunder. The road to Berlin was paved with drunks. Some wanted only to exchange toasts in vodka; others behaved like little commissars. When one particularly obstreperous Red Army officer tried to halt a column at a bridge, an American general jumped from his car and personally deposited the struggling Russian in the ditch to allow our column to pass.

A disagreeable summer rain was pelting down when we finally straggled into Berlin late in the afternoon. The Russians had not allowed us to look over our sector before coming in, and none of us knew exactly where to go once we arrived. As it was, hundreds of officers and men milled around, looking for places to stay in the ruins, and most of them, in Class A uniforms, wound up sleeping on the muddy ground in the rain.[15]

Howley soon discovered that the Russians had dismantled and taken away many of Berlin's industrial resources including the plant of the big electricity firms in the west – Siemens, Borsig, AEG and Osram.

They had dismantled the refrigeration plant at the abattoir, torn stoves and pipes out of restaurant kitchens, stripped machinery from mills and factories and were completing the theft of the American Singer Sewing Machine plant when we arrived. Over in the British sector, they had taken out generating equipment from the only modern plant in the city. Much of the looted equipment was of dubious use or had been wrecked through ignorance.

The Interallied Kommandatura for Berlin opened for business on July 11th, 1945. Responsible to the Allied Control Council, those appointed to the Kommandatura had wide discretionary powers in governing the city, though in practical terms they were constrained by their decision to accept in total 'all existing regulations and ordinances issued by the Commander of the Soviet Army Garrison and Military Commandant'.

What was not known at this time, except by Soviet occupiers, was the power that rested with the Magistrat, the German-run but communist-led administrative body set up well before the arrival of the Anglo-American forces. The Magistrat deserved credit for at least the partial restoration of essential services, though less appealing, from the western point of view, was the assumption of authority to remove whatever industrial fixtures were left in the American, British and French sectors. Western proposals for making life easier for themselves as much as for Berliners were either ignored or vetoed by the Soviet representatives on the Kommandatura.

Howley was not alone in wondering if he and his fellow commanders would ever be allowed more than a toehold in the city. But cynicism was in abeyance while Berlin played host to the last top-level get-together of the western Allies.

CHAPTER TWO

Churchill had pressed hard for a summit. Truman wanted time to consolidate his position but gave way to his secretary of state, James Byrnes, and his chief of staff, Admiral William Leahy, who encouraged him to take the opportunity of a face-to-face exchange with Stalin. For his part, Stalin was ready to engage as long as it was clear to all that he was running the show.

This final meeting of the Big Three was held in late July 1945 in the Schloss Cecilienhof, a Tudor-style imperial shooting lodge in Potsdam, to the south of Berlin. As a masterstroke of one-upmanship, the garden was awash with geraniums, planted to form a huge red star. Nervous of flying, Stalin arrived in a luxury train once reserved for the Czar and his family. Waiting for him in Berlin was a black bulletproof car which carried him the rest of the journey along a road lined with troops. Truman had his convoy of limousines with jeeps and motorcycle outriders. When the president alighted, armed men provided a protective cordon. Churchill, looking old and tired, had just one car. He was accompanied by a plain clothes police officer.

Before getting down to business, Churchill toured the ruined city, stopping off to inspect what was left of Hitler's chancellery. He was stunned by the chaos. Truman shared his sentiments.

'I never saw such destruction', he wrote. Later the same day, the two western leaders had their first encounter. With Churchill in full flow, Truman was not taken with all the 'hooey' and 'soft soap' intended to reinforce the idea of a close and exclusive Anglo-American relationship, though there was 'something very open and genuine about the way he greeted me'. Leahy was less easily seduced. Given the Soviet contribution to defeating Nazism, he found Churchill's rants against communism hard to bear.

> I said that frankly, as I had listened to him inveigh so vio-
> lently against the threat of Soviet domination and the
> spread of communism in Europe, and disclose such a lack
> of confidence in the professions of good faith in Soviet lead-
> ership, I had wondered whether the Prime Minister was
> now willing to declare to the world that he and Britain had
> made a mistake in not supporting Hitler for, as I understood
> him, he was now expressing the doctrine which Hitler and
> Goebbels had been reiterating for the past four years ...
> He heard me through, and with intentness. He said that he
> had been under very great pressure, that he had been just
> thinking out loud, and that the expressions might have been
> stronger than he had intended to convey.[1]

Stalin came over as a straight talker. 'I can deal with Stalin', Truman wrote after returning from Potsdam. 'He is honest, but smart as hell.' Even when his pipedream of universal brother-hood faded, Truman held to his view of Stalin, arguing that he was compelled to reflect the intransigence of the Politburo. As we now know, the reverse was true. But Truman's first impres-sions of Stalin can be excused. When it suited him the Soviet leader could be a good listener and, like Truman, he did not waste words. At Potsdam, he followed his usual practice of ignoring facts that did not suit his argument while relying on ambiguity to win compliance.

Truman's problem was in trying to reconcile conflicting counsel. Byrnes and the US ambassador to Moscow, Averell Harriman, both of whom were at Potsdam, favoured a hard line with Stalin while Joseph Davies, a predecessor to Harriman in Moscow, who was also on hand, proclaimed the purity of Stalin's motives and urged against anything that might antagonise the Soviet dictator.

A recurring topic at Potsdam was the future of Poland and the rest of eastern Europe. The Polish land-grab of a large part of Germany weighed on Anglo-American sensitivities, as did Stalin's refusal to budge on relaxing authoritarian rule. Knowing that the western powers were not prepared to use force, he felt safe in demanding instant and unquestioning recognition of Soviet-sponsored regimes in Hungary, Rumania and Bulgaria as well as Poland.

Truman and Byrnes tried playing the reparations card. Stalin was obsessed by reparations. It was almost as if he imagined that Germany could be made to dedicate itself exclusively to Soviet reconstruction. But the inconsistency was glaring. If, as Stalin wanted, Germany was stripped of its industrial assets, how could it recover sufficiently to pay reparations? But economic logic was never Stalin's strong point. With Vyacheslav Molotov, minister of foreign affairs, as his mouthpiece, the generalissimo (a recent self-promotion) maintained that an agreed figure for reparations had been fixed at Yalta. Not so, ran the counter-argument. Yalta had provided no more than a framework for discussion.

However, the Anglo-Americans were prepared to be flexible. If Stalin cut back on his territorial demands on behalf of the Soviet-sponsored regime in Poland, a generous accommodation on reparations was in prospect. Stalin was not having that. Eventually, the question of just how much Germany was to pay for Hitler's war was left open. A vague compromise allowed for each occupying power to decide on reparations for its own zone while the Anglo-Americans agreed to hand over 10 per cent of 'surplus' industrial equipment and to set aside another 25 per cent to exchange for coal and agricultural produce. Churchill and the hard-liners in Truman's camp were dismayed by the concession. As Harriman icily observed, Russia was becoming 'a vacuum into which all movable goods will be sucked'.

Yet the Soviet gain was marginal. Much of what was expropriated from Germany ended up in railway sidings or in junkyards. Dismantling factories and machinery was relatively easy. The hard part was the reconstruction in Russia. Spare parts were in short supply, as also were managers and engineers to reassemble what was on offer.

Guidelines were laid down for an exodus of Germans from the new Poland. Reluctantly, Truman and Churchill accepted that up to 3.5 million people had to be resettled. The programme was for the entire number to cross the frontier before August 1946. It was plainly a recipe for a humanitarian disaster.

The Soviets and Anglo-Americans agreed on one thing. The occupation zones notwithstanding, there was no call for Germany to be split permanently. But unanimity was lacking on the long-term objective. While Truman and Churchill looked to create a demilitarised but independent democracy that would be no threat to its neighbours, Stalin believed that a tightly centralised and controlled political system was his best chance of instilling communism over all of Germany and beyond.

Though none of this was stated openly it was not hard to read between the lines. As Stalin observed to Marshal Tito, the independently-minded communist leader of Yugoslavia, 'Whoever occupies a territory imposes on it his own social system. It cannot be otherwise.' But he was happy to go along with whatever pious hopes were generated for public consumption. The detail was to come later.

As a cover for irresolution, matters relating to the future of Germany were delegated to a Council of Foreign Ministers. The CFM was told to prepare a peace treaty 'to be accepted by the Government of Germany when a government adequate to the purpose is established'. The first meeting of the Council was held in London in early September 1945. It broke up on October 2nd having failed to settle anything of consequence.

Largely as a test of how far Stalin was willing to bend, Truman took his opportunity at Potsdam to advance his pet project, the freedom of navigation on international canals and waterways. Stalin was instinctively hostile, vetoing any discussion on the subject then or in the future. Even so, Truman remained confident that he had the edge. Shortly after his arrival in Germany he was told that 'the baby has been born', the infant being the atom bomb successfully detonated in the New Mexico desert.

On July 24th, Truman used a lull in the conference to tell Stalin that the US possessed a new weapon of 'unusual destructive force'. With the almost certain advantage of foreknowledge, Stalin showed no surprise. 'I hope you will use it on the Japanese', was his only comment. Truman did just that. An A-bomb was dropped on Hiroshima on August 6th and another on Nagasaki three days later.

But Truman was deluded if he imagined that the bomb gave him a hold over Stalin. While there were fantasists in Washington who cogitated on a pre-emptive strike against Russia, the realists knew that the fallout, literally and metaphorically, from a nuclear attack would be catastrophic for America's European allies.* As a further irony, there was now no need to bring Russia into the war with Japan. But a deal having been struck at Yalta, Stalin was allowed to savour victory over the Japanese in Kwantung while annexing the Kurile Islands and southern Sakhalin. Moreover, the defeat of Japan and the Soviet occupation of Manchuria allowed Stalin to come out openly in support of Mao Tse-tung as his communist forces advanced into northern and central China.

A big talking point in the last week of Potsdam was the absence of Churchill and his foreign secretary, Anthony Eden. Returning to London for the results of the first general election since 1936, it was to hear that they and their Conservative party had been decisively rejected by the electorate. Labour party leader Clement Attlee, Churchill's deputy in the wartime coalition, moved into Downing Street. The demand for radical social reform had proved stronger than the public regard for Churchill who, whatever his achievements as a war leader, was seen as heading a party that was out of sympathy with the common man.

Stalin was confused by events across the Channel. It passed his understanding that Churchill, having had possession of the ballot boxes for three weeks (while waiting for the votes of forces overseas to come in) had not manipulated the election in his favour. Attlee looked to be a poor substitute for Churchill. Physically unprepossessing and with a deceptively mild demeanour, it was not immediately apparent that here was a doughty fighter with a sharp intellect who would not easily give way on British interests.

As the new foreign secretary, Ernest Bevin was a different proposition. The most powerful member of the Labour government after Attlee, Bevin was a blunt, pugnacious 64-year-old who had

---

* The first Soviet atomic bomb was successfully tested on August 29th, 1949.

been schooled in the hard knocks of trade unionism where he had fought off his communist opponents. One of the founding leaders of the powerful Transport and General Workers' Union, he had been an outstanding minister of labour in the wartime coalition government. After the 1945 election he expected to be finance minister but Attlee decided he needed 'a heavy tank' at the Foreign Office. While claiming, as the Labour slogan had it, 'left understands left', Bevin followed Churchill in believing the worst of the Soviet Union. At Potsdam, he came on like John Bull incarnate, intensely patriotic and passionately anti-communist. He detested Molotov and made no secret of it.

Molotov was indeed hard to like. With an enormous capacity for work, he was the perfect understudy to Stalin, performing exclusively to a script written in the Kremlin. 'Naught but an automaton', said Andrei Gromyko, one of his successors as foreign minister; 'obstructive, evasive and insincere', declared a British ambassador in Moscow. But Molotov was also a clever tactician whose sheer persistence in unwavering argument won concessions while giving nothing away. He may, as one commentator noted, have looked 'like an encyclopaedia salesman down on his luck' but he was not to be underrated.

Relations between Bevin and Molotov made Byrnes nervous. Bevin was 'so aggressive that both the president and I wondered how we would get along with this new foreign secretary'. No one was left in doubt that, in Bevin's words to General Ismay, Churchill's wartime chief of staff, Britain was 'not to be barged about'. Bevin saw as his immediate challenge the strengthening of American sinews in response to Soviet bullying. But this could be counterproductive. Truman and his team were disinclined to take their lead from an ally that was too weak to hold its own ground. There was too some resentment against a political grandstander who was so blatantly eager to pull America into European entanglements. On the other hand, Truman no longer needed persuading that Stalin was an opportunist, quick to take advantage of any sign of weakness. The president might well have thought of himself in the same category.

The gloss of inter-Allied cordiality was maintained, though it was a source of puzzlement why, at the last moment, the entire Soviet team was withdrawn from a four-power military athletics meeting. It appeared that the Russians were happy only when they had control over the proceedings. There could be no doubts on this score with the celebrations in honour of Red Army Day. The Schloss Cecilienhof was thrown open to several hundred western senior officers and officials. Anthony Mann was one of the invited journalists.

> We were regaled with caviare, smoked salmon, sucking pig, exotic fruits, ices and limitless vodka and champagne. The exquisite porcelain and crystal, not all of which survived the evening, were emblazoned with the cipher *W* and an imperial crown.
>
> Towards midnight a Red Army orchestra gave spirited renderings of Johann Strauss, and Madame Zhukov revealed herself a talented exponent of the Viennese waltz. The British and American political advisers, Sir William Strang and Ambassador Robert Murphy, observed the proceedings side by side, wearing a slightly dazed expression.[2]

★

After Potsdam, Truman began to reformulate his foreign policy. He put a good face on his first venture into high-level diplomacy, voicing satisfaction that he had made what he thought to be a

realistic downgrade of the Yalta understanding in German reparations. But there was little else to show for his efforts and he
knew it. The Soviet Union was no longer simply a difficult ally,
rather 'a potential enemy threatening America's vital interests
and world peace'.[3]

But Truman had to tread cautiously. American opinion was still
in flux. The voice of isolationism, strong in Congress, was echoed
by opinion-makers in the press. The populist call was for a return
to normality, leaving other countries to sort out their own problems. Alongside the isolationists were those who kept faith in the
durability of the wartime alliance while urging Truman to take the
lead in offering Russia cooperation to achieve an enduring peace. It
seemed inconceivable that Stalin would risk another war so soon
after the last one. Exhausted and lacking a decent infrastructure,
Russia needed all its reserves of energy to build its economy. But as
recent events proved, the advance of communism was less dependent on brute force than on muscling in on vulnerable governments.
Soviet bullying tactics were remarkably successful.

Pre-war Russia was the sole standard-bearer of communism.
Ten years later the hammer and sickle was flying in seven eastern European countries – Albania, Bulgaria, Czechoslovakia,
Hungary, Poland, Rumania and Yugoslavia. Of these, the first six
took their orders directly from Moscow. It was no coincidence that
Yugoslavia, the odd one out, was the only state where the communists held a popular majority, a trump card which enabled its
government to resist Soviet interference.

There were other countries where Soviet-style communism
was making inroads. Having lost 12 per cent of its border territory
to Russia, Finland was being pushed towards a mutual assistance agreement that was very much in Moscow's favour. There
was pressure on Norway to accept a deal on the same lines. The

assumption in both cases was of communists occupying positions of power.

Then there was Greece, where a communist uprising had been suppressed by British troops. But not for long. The restoration of the Greek monarchy led to a campaign of guerrilla warfare as a preliminary to a full-scale civil war. It was an open question as to how long Britain alone could hold the line. The chapter of setbacks for the West seemed to have no end. Despite promises, Stalin delayed the withdrawal of his troops from northern Iran and there was Soviet pressure on Turkey for bases in the Dardanelles. In France, Italy and Finland, the communist share of the total vote was over 20 per cent. In Belgium, Denmark, Norway, Holland and Sweden, the figure was 10 per cent. There was no comfort to be had in Asia, the Middle East or Africa. In Japan 15 million people were homeless and the economy near collapse. China was in the midst of a civil war; left-wing nationalist movements were gaining strength in British, French and Dutch colonies. The talk in Washington was of Stalin aspiring to world domination.

There were fears that he was about to get his way in France. After taking an active part in the last stages of the war, France was counted among the victors but in a semi-detached sort of way. It was a matter of deep resentment for General Charles de Gaulle that he was excluded from the deliberations at Yalta and Potsdam. The war had damaged France physically and psychologically. In Normandy, the worst devastated area, half a million people, nearly one in five, were homeless or living in shells of houses. Road and rail bridges were down, ports blocked by mines and wrecks. Food was strictly rationed, there were few cars on the roads and no domestic heating.

Having been grudgingly awarded the smallest of Germany's occupation zones, consisting of two narrowly connected roughly equal areas (nicknamed 'the brassiere'), France had jurisdiction over some 5 million Germans compared to 22 million in the British zone and 17 million in each of the Soviet and American zones, not counting the multi-million influx of refugees.

But the French zone at least was self-supporting, while the British zone, including the heavily-populated Ruhr industrial region, and the American zone both depended on imports of food and other essentials, either from across the Russian zonal boundary or from further afield. France contributed nothing to the costs of occupation while Britain and America had to pay for supplies. This meant that, in effect, they were subsidising reparations, chiefly to Russia. Germany was said to be a milch cow fed from the west and milked from the east.

With the birth of the French Fourth Republic, the communists emerged as the single largest party in the National Assembly. Their leader was Maurice Thorez, who had spent the war in Moscow. He was under orders to exercise restraint while his party gathered strength. As in Italy, another country trying to find its post-war balance, the policy was to act within the constitution to elect a popular front coalition in which the communists held the critical jobs. As American ambassador in Paris, Jefferson Caffery, reported:

> The Soviet Trojan horse is so well camouflaged that millions of communist militants, sympathisers and opportunists have been brought to believe that the best way of defending France is to identify French national interests with the aims of the Soviet Union.[4]

America responded with dollar loans and tens of millions in unaudited funds for 'objects of a confidential, extraordinary or emergency nature' in an effort to contain if not to roll back the communist swell.

Meanwhile, with each of the occupying powers in Germany giving their own slant to administration, there was a hardening of zonal boundaries. Refusing open access to the Soviet zone, Stalin pressed for four-power control of the Ruhr and other industrial regions in western Germany, responsible for 75 per cent of Germany's coal and 70 per cent of its steel and pig iron. America, and Britain in particular, resisted the incursion. This brought Bevin and Molotov into open conflict. At times the two came close to exchanging blows.

France had some sympathy with Russian demands. It too wanted to bring the Ruhr under joint control, as a means of gaining undisputed access to the coalfields while putting the lid on the revival of German heavy industry. The demand was for a monthly allocation to France of a million tons of Ruhr coal. Though this objective remained out of reach, the coal-rich Saar, straddling France's north-east border with Germany, did come under French control. There was not much to be done on the matter since France was already in possession and was not to be moved. Clay protested, but to no avail, against 'this entirely unilateral action'.

The last thing Truman wanted was an open confrontation with Stalin. But up against Soviet stonewalling, he was prepared to toughen his stance. 'There must be no more compromises', he told Byrnes, though the secretary of state later denied ever hearing the words. 'I'm tired of babying the Soviets ... Unless Russia is faced with an iron fist and strong language another war is in the making.' Whether relayed to Byrnes or not, the sentiments were real enough. In conversation with his foreign minister, Stalin was equally forthright.

In dealing with the Americans and the British, we cannot achieve anything serious if we begin to give in to intimidation or betray uncertainty. To get anything ... we must arm ourselves with a policy of tenacity and steadfastness.[5]

On February 9th, 1946, Stalin addressed the Supreme Soviet. Paraphrasing Marxist dogma, he declared the inevitability of war between the capitalist states. Whoever emerged the victor would then turn their sights on Russia. This would not happen soon. Stalin believed that war between capitalism and communism was unlikely for fifteen to twenty years. But the certainty of it happening at some time was justification for building Soviet power and influence to meet the challenge.

This was not what the western leaders wanted to hear. Even the most leftish conciliators began to think that Stalin had no interest in cooperative peace-making. In Washington there were even those who judged the speech to be nothing less than the 'declaration of World War Three'. This overreaction to what, after all, was fairly standard Soviet rhetoric (if indeed Stalin was threatening world war, he was giving generous advance warning) reflected Stalin's changing image in America from the cuddly Uncle Joe of the war years to public enemy number one.

Two weeks after the pivotal Supreme Soviet, the White House was studying the reaction of one of its career diplomats in Moscow. A noted linguist, fluent in Russian, the combative, 42-year-old George Kennan encompassed within an 8,000-word dispatch, soon to be famous as the Long Telegram, a comprehensive analysis of American–Soviet relations. The wartime alliance with Russia and the back-slapping, all-friends-together sentiment engendered at Yalta was no longer relevant, said Kennan. He portrayed Stalin as a leader obsessed with power which he equated with security, his own and that of his country. It followed that he saw as enemies all countries not under Soviet control.

Kennan was not advocating a showdown. Rather, he favoured a 'containment' of the Soviet Union. This meant a commitment to standing up to aggression, a view supported by Byrnes, but also political, diplomatic and cultural efforts to advance the American way of life. By setting an example to the rest of the world, Kennan expected America to win allies for democracy without the need to take up arms.

He was pushing at an open door. The dispatch so impressed hard-liner defence secretary, James Forrestal, that he sent copies to all his Cabinet colleagues. Truman too was attracted to the Kennan thesis. However, the 'patient but firm and vigilant containment of Russian expansionist tendencies' was likely to be a costly business, implying as it did that America would have to be ready to support any country susceptible to Soviet infiltration. This came to a formidable list, embracing all of western Europe, the Middle East, the Far East and South America. Even if, long-term, the investment paid off (Kennan believed that the 'Soviet power bears within it the seeds of its own decay') there was sure to be strong resistance from American taxpayers.

On March 20th, 1946, Kennan reinforced his message to Washington. 'Nothing short of complete disarmament, delivery of our air and naval forces to Russia and handing powers of government to American Communists' would come close to alleviating Stalin's mistrust, and even then he would 'smell a trap and continue to harbour the most baleful misgivings'.[6]

Kennan was not a lone voice. Less than a month after the delivery of the Long Telegram, Frank Roberts, British minister to the Soviet Union, followed with his own analysis of Russian strategy. Doubting that Stalin would set any limits on Soviet expansion, he predicted 'increasing Soviet pressure in the whole zone vital to British security between India and the Dardanelles'.

The first pressure point was Iran, jointly occupied by Britain and Russia from 1941. It had been agreed that both powers would withdraw their troops when the war was over. The British stuck by the promise but Soviet troops stayed on to support Stalin's demand for oil concessions. Whatever might now be said of Britain's one-time dominance over oil supplies from the Middle East, post-war power politics dictated that Iran fell squarely into the British sphere of interests. The oil refinery at Abadan, an off-shore island at the head of the Persian Gulf, was the largest installation of its kind. It had cost £100 million to build and was Britain's single biggest overseas asset. Moreover, Iran produced more oil than the rest of the Middle East put together. Bevin did not need to be persuaded that British and European economic recovery depended on the free flow of oil. When the Russians refused to budge, Truman responded to 'an outrage if ever I saw one'. The battleship *Missouri* was sent to the Persian Gulf. Stalin took the hint. Soviet forces were withdrawn.

At the same time, Stalin raised the stakes on Turkey by massing troops on the border. His demand was for Soviet naval bases along the straits connecting the Black Sea to the Mediterranean. Bevin was clear as to where this could lead.

The Mediterranean is the area through which we bring influence to bear on Southern Europe, the soft underbelly of France, Italy, Yugoslavia, Greece and Turkey. Without our physical presence in the Mediterranean, we should cut little ice with these states which would fall, like Eastern Europe, under the totalitarian yoke. ... If we move out of the Mediterranean, Russia will move in, and the Mediterranean countries, from the point of view of commerce and trade, economy and democracy, will be finished.[7]

Again, Truman stood firm. Again, Stalin gave way. It was not long before there were American bases in Turkey.

But Soviet treaties with Rumania, Hungary, Bulgaria and Poland closed off their trade routes to the west. Henceforth, their economic energies were to be directed towards Russia's recovery. The consequent shortage of imported food and raw materials to France, Italy and especially Germany could only be compensated by supplies from the US, which meant a drain on European dollar reserves, periodic financial crises and social disruption favouring communism as the universal panacea. None of this suggested that Stalin was working to a preconceived plan, rather that he was on the alert for opportunities to advance the Soviet cause. Signs of weakness were to be exploited while stopping short of gambling on military confrontation.

At this point, in March 1946, Churchill re-entered the fray. Having lost his parliamentary power base, the former prime minister had set about exploiting his popularity as a speaker and as an opinion-leader. Invitations were plentiful. One of the unlikeliest to cross his desk was from a small town in the American midwest, known chiefly for its weekly livestock market. Fulton, Missouri also had a liberal arts college dedicated to exploring 'economic, social and political problems of international concern'. Churchill was offered the chance to deliver three or four lectures on subjects of his choice. The recompense was a modest honorarium and a shared royalty on the published lectures. It was a letter he might easily have brushed aside but for a handwritten postscript. 'This is a fine old college in my home state. If you come out and make a good speech … I'll introduce you.' It was signed Harry Truman.

Though not now seen as anything exceptional, in context, it was a most extraordinary thing for Truman to have done. What did he hope to achieve? At the simplest, a visit from a world celebrity would count as a plus with those who had put him on the path to the White House. But more was at stake. Churchill's anti-Soviet stance was bound to be controversial and Truman was not looking for trouble. On the other hand, the president must have calculated that as long as he was not seen to be in accord with everything Churchill was liable to say, the public reception for the old war leader would serve as a gauge of popular support for frustrating Stalin's territorial ambitions.

Truman made pains to avoid an advance reading of the speech though Byrnes gave him the gist of the content. Also in on the act was Leahy who, amazingly, saw nothing to get excited about in what he judged to be 'usual hands across the sea stuff'.[8] Churchill did indeed stress the importance of the 'special relationship between the British Commonwealth and Empire and the United States' while, on the advice of Lord Halifax, the British ambassador in Washington, adding some mollifying references to the Soviet Union.

> I have a strong admiration and regard for the valiant Russian people and for my wartime comrade, Marshal Stalin. … We understand the Russian need to be secure on her western frontiers by the removal of all possibility of German aggression. We welcome Russia to her rightful place among the leading nations of the world. We welcome her flag upon the seas. Above all, we welcome constant, frequent and growing contacts between the Russian people and our own people on both sides of the Atlantic.

Then came the punch: it was his duty, said Churchill, to place before his audience certain facts about the situation in Europe.

From Stettin in the Baltic to Trieste in the Adriatic, an iron curtain has descended across the continent. Behind that line lie all the capitals of the ancient states of Central and Eastern Europe. Warsaw, Berlin, Prague, Vienna, Budapest, Belgrade, Bucharest and Sofia, all these famous cities and the populations around them lie in what I must call the Soviet sphere, and all are subject in one form or another, not only to Soviet influence but to a very high and, in many cases, increasing measure of control from Moscow. ... The Russian-dominated Polish Government has been encouraged to make enormous inroads upon Germany, and mass expulsions of millions of Germans on a scale grievous and undreamed of are now taking place. The Communist parties, which were very small in all these Eastern States of Europe, have been raised to pre-eminence and power far beyond their numbers and are seeking everywhere to obtain totalitarian control. Police governments are prevailing in nearly every case, and so far, except in Czechoslovakia, there is no true democracy.

If the West failed to heed the warning, disaster threatened: 'I am convinced that there is nothing they [the Russians] admire so much as strength and nothing for which they have less respect than military weakness.'

Churchill was delighted with his reception both in Missouri and in Washington. Writing to Attlee and Bevin, he reported that the president and his circle were 'deeply distressed by the way they are being treated by the Russians and that they do not intend to put up with treaty breaches ... or pressure for Russian expansion'. He anticipated a 'show of strength'.

The predictable response from Moscow, labelling Churchill as a warmonger, came as no surprise. More disturbing for Truman was to find this view shared by sections of the press and by some vocal members of Congress. A British embassy official concluded: 'Profound as the uneasiness is about Soviet policies, there is still a reluctance to face the full implications of the facts and a timidity about the consequences.'[9] However, in mid-1946, though lacking political endorsement, the American and British chiefs of staff agreed on five RAF bases to be made ready to receive B-29 Superfortresses capable of delivering atomic bombs.

The Germany question loomed large when the Council of Foreign Ministers met in Paris in the spring of 1946. Byrnes took the lead in proposing a four-power treaty that would guarantee a demilitarised Germany for 25 years. He had given plenty of advance warning of the American initiative and a lively discussion was anticipated. What was not expected and, indeed, came as a shock to all except the Soviet delegation, was Molotov's flat refusal even to consider a comprehensive settlement for Germany.

To try to break the deadlock, Clay was asked for a detailed study on where he thought Germany should be heading in terms of its political and economic structure. His report was delivered on May 26th. He argued forcefully for central German agencies for all essential services and for preparations for a provisional German government. If this proved to be beyond diplomatic endeavour, a merger of the American and British zones should be considered. The alternative was a 'deteriorating German economy' and 'political unrest'. When, apart from a formal acknowledgement, there was no response from Washington, Clay threatened a press conference to make his views public. When permission was refused he offered his resignation.

It was not the first time Clay had threatened to throw in the towel. In his dealings with Washington he suffered agonies of frustration. An early convert to restoring Germany to a self-sustaining economy with a role in the broader European recovery, his power of decision was limited by a division of responsibilities. While the army was responsible for implementing policy, the policy itself was dictated by the state department, where there was a tendency to keep matters under review while desisting from any move that might upset France or be interpreted as provocative by Russia.

There was broad approval for a compromise plan to eliminate Germany's war potential, to allow for reparations and to develop agriculture and peaceful industries to provide a living standard no higher than that of neighbouring countries, but when it came to action, almost every decision was put on hold for want of Russian and French consent. As a gesture of his determination to press ahead, Clay called a halt to dismantling industrial units in the American zone. No further reparations were to be made 'until the economic unity on which reparations are based has been attained'. It was little enough by way of protest against the crisis that was building up in Germany.

In his last days as commander of British forces in Germany, Montgomery gave his political masters a bleak assessment.

The whole country is in such a mess that the only way to put it right is to get the Germans 'in on it' themselves. We must tell the German people what is going to happen to them and their country. If we do not do these things, we shall drift towards possible failure. That 'drift' will take the form of an increasingly hostile population, which will eventually begin to look east. Such a Germany would be a menace to the security of the British Empire.[10]

Across the western zones food was desperately short. The minimum for daily subsistence was set at 2,000 calories. For the year after the end of the war, civilian rations rarely matched this figure except by resort to the black market. 'The plain fact is', wrote the radical publisher and polemicist, Victor Gollancz, 'we are starving the Germans … not deliberately in the sense that we want them to die, but wilfully in the sense that we prefer their death to our own inconvenience.'[11]

Clay had a strong ally in London where Bevin raged against French objections to building the German economy until their demands for coal and security were met. Bevin threatened to go it alone to promote German exports 'in order to reduce the burden on the British taxpayer'. While diplomatic efforts continued to seek a four-power deal as a level-of-industry plan for Germany, Washington accepted Clay's proposal for a merging of the American and British zones to create a single economic region extending from Hamburg and the North Sea to the Ruhr. The British military governor, General Robertson, was authorised to begin negotiations with Clay.

Much haggling led to an agreement on a common standard of living, a sharing of economic resources and a joint export–import policy with a 50/50 split of administrative costs. The British and American combined zone – Bizonia – eventually came into being on January 1st, 1947. Its capital was Frankfurt. Within six months, German politicians and administrators were appointed to joint agencies for economics, food, transport, communications and finance. An Economic Council, meeting for the first time in June, had delegates elected by state parliaments, the first step on the path to full democracy, if only for the part of Germany controlled by the Anglo-Americans. Among Germans, the prospect of a permanently divided country was hard to accept. Policy debates were soured by the enduring dream of unity, a dream that had to wait for more than 40 years to be made real.

*

Meanwhile, Russia had moved fastest and furthest in putting its stamp on its share of Germany. Stalin loyalist Walter Ulbricht linked the revival of political activity to a predetermined agenda. His first objective was to take over the resurrected Social Democratic Party (Sozialdemokratische Partei Deutschlands, or SPD). This brought him up against Kurt Schumacher, a leader who was not inclined to submit to blandishments or bullying from left or right. Having lost an arm in the Great War and a leg as a result of his treatment in Nazi concentration camps, the tall, gaunt Schumacher compensated for his physical disabilities with an indomitable spirit. His vision was of a united Germany governed by democratic socialism.

This was not at all what Ulbricht had in mind. Free elections were not part of his remit. As he pronounced bluntly: 'Some are of the opinion that elections should measure the relative strength of all parties. ... We regard this concept as false. Elections should be a means of influencing the masses in an anti-fascist direction.'[12]

Ulbricht sought to avoid an electoral division between socialism and communism by engineering a merger between the SPD and the Kommunistische Partei Deutschlands (KPD). Unable to get to Schumacher, who was out of reach in Hannover and was accompanied by a British guard wherever he went in Berlin, Ulbricht concentrated on winning over Otto Grotewohl and other SPD leaders who were closer to hand. When they too proved obstinate, Ulbricht turned to arbitrary arrests and kidnapping. Deaths in prison went unannounced.

The first test of communist electoral strength came in Berlin, where Clay declared that his administration would not recognise the merger unless a genuinely open party referendum produced a clear majority for it. At first, Ulbricht was convinced that he could win a citywide vote for his left-wing alliance, if not by democratic debate then by manipulating the system to produce the result he desired.

Obstacles were put in the way of Social Democrats campaigning against the merger. Communist radio and newspapers harped on the fear that the western powers were about to leave Berlin. Finally, on the Saturday before polling day, those in the east of the city who were not avowedly communist were told that they were to be denied the right to vote. On Sunday, March 31st, 1946 only Social Democrats in the western sectors were able to declare if they were 'for or against an immediate union between the Social Democrat and the Communist Parties'. In the first free and secret election in Germany since 1932, 29,610 Social Democrats voted against a merger. Those in favour numbered just 2,937.

Ulbricht went ahead anyway. In April, across the Soviet zone and in the Soviet sector of Berlin, the KPD and SPD combined to form the German Socialist Unity Party (SED). There is a photograph of Grotewohl and Wilhelm Pieck, the KPD leader, on the flower-decked stage of the State Opera shaking hands on the deal. Grotewohl looks far from happy.

Concurrent with elections in five east German states under Soviet control, elections for a Berlin city council embracing all four sectors followed in October. Though resorting to intimidation and mounting a stronger propaganda campaign than the democratic parties (Social Democrats, Christian Democrats and Liberal Democrats) combined, the result for Berlin's SED, in contrast to the rest of the Soviet zone, was a disaster. It managed to win only 26 of the 130 contested seats. Of the twenty mayoral districts, nineteen were led by Social Democrats, the other by a Christian Democrat. At its first meeting, the city Assembly elected a western-orientated Magistrat with Otto Suhr as president and Otto Ostrowski as mayor, both Social Democrats. When Ostrowski submitted to Soviet browbeating, the new Magistrat replaced him with a man who was to become the undisputed hero of Berlin's regeneration.

Ernst Reuter did not look like a champion. Of diminutive stature, if easily identified by his black beret, he was in poor health and walked with a stick. A devoted communist in his youth, he transferred his allegiance to the Social Democrats having been persuaded by experience that there was little to distinguish between communism and national socialism. Targeted by the Nazis, he escaped to Turkey where he saw out the war. His return to active politics came with his election to the Magistrat, where he was an outspoken critic of the SED and of his arch-enemy Wilhelm Pieck who was now working hand-in-glove with Ulbricht and his Soviet overlords. Nor did Reuter hold back on censuring the Allies for failing to make a determined stand against creeping communist domination. He wanted less talk and more action.

Reuter's first term as mayor was short and violent. When he refused to go voluntarily, the Russians simply refused to accept his appointment. Since all important decisions still depended on four-power agreement, it was a veto the west felt bound to sanction. Reuter was succeeded by Louise Schroeder as acting mayor. She too had a strong independent spirit and though frail, stood up bravely to intimidation. But there was little she or Reuter could do to prevent the tightening of the Soviet hold over Berlin. With each party represented on the Magistrat, the SED, though a minority voice, dedicated itself to disrupting business while agents of the Russian-controlled ministry of internal affairs (MVD) and the ministry of state security (MGB) took the law into their own hands.

To be known as an outspoken opponent of the Ulbricht regime was to risk a beating or worse. Living in one of the western sectors was no protection. George Clare witnessed one of many outrages:

> It was all over in seconds. A car screeched to a sudden halt, hefty men jumped out, grabbed their victim, bundled him into their vehicle and, before those who witnessed it could even begin to comprehend what had happened, they were racing off in the direction of the Soviet sector. There, of course, such dramatics were unnecessary – people just disappeared.[13]

Among those who vanished, never to be traced, were three judges who 'refused to render judgement in accord with the expressed views of communist leaders'.[14]

★

On September 6th, 1946 the US secretary of state, James Byrnes, spoke before an assembly of German politicians and senior officials at the Opera House in Stuttgart. It was intended as a demonstration of American resolution, and the US army put on a grand display with troops lining the streets and armoured cars and tanks blocking off the intersections. The crowd of onlookers was thousands strong.

Much of what Byrnes had to say covered familiar ground. Holding to the undertakings at Potsdam, Germany was to be demilitarised and would continue to pay reparations. After the elimination of industries with military potential, a peacetime economy would be aimed at achieving a standard of living comparable to but not exceeding that of neighbouring countries. While the Ruhr and the Rhineland were indisputably part of Germany, the

US was prepared to accede to the French claim to the Saar and to recognise Poland's annexation of territory in the east. More than anything, the speech was a clarification of existing policy. But there was one dramatic departure from the standard text. At Clay's behest, Byrnes added an American commitment not to withdraw from Germany until it was clear of all other occupying forces.

> I want no misunderstanding. We will not shirk our duty.
> We are not withdrawing. We are staying here.

It was the strongest indication so far of American intent. Unfortunately for Byrnes, he had not cleared his statement with Truman – though, according to Clay and others, he had tried but failed to get through to the White House. The president had no objection to the speech as such; what irritated him was Byrnes' assumption that he was free to formulate policy on the hoof. It was not the first time the secretary of state had failed to consult before acting. Upstaging Truman was not a wise tactic. His days in office were numbered.

Truman's opportunity to make changes in his Cabinet came in November with the Congressional elections. With voters angry at inflation running at 15 per cent and rising, Truman's own Democrat party suffered a heavy defeat. Ironically, however, Republican control of both houses, for the first time since 1929, strengthened Truman's hand in foreign policy. Senator Arthur Vandenberg, one-time arch isolationist, now chairman of the influential Senate foreign relations committee, was among Truman's cheerleaders for closer American involvement in Europe.

At the state department, George Marshall took over from Byrnes. It was a shrewd choice. As wartime army chief of staff, a prime architect of Allied victory in Europe and the first American army general to be promoted to a five-star rank, Marshall came with huge prestige attached to his name. One of his first decisions was to appoint George Kennan as his national security adviser. With relations between Washington and Moscow hardening by the month, the focus of attention was on Germany and its future.

CHAPTER THREE

While Marshall was settling in as secretary of state, former US president Herbert Hoover was preparing to go to Germany and Austria. His mission was to find ways of solving the food crisis. From Truman's point of view the last Republican occupant of the White House was in prime position to attract bipartisan support for a more active policy in Germany. With his reputation as a roving humanitarian and with family origins in southern Germany, Hoover had already spent time in Berlin with Clay, leaving him with the promise that 'the American people will do whatever possible to help ... [looking] to the future and not to the past'. Iis message to Truman was uncompromising. 'You can have vengeance or peace but you can't have both.'

For his latest venture, Hoover was briefed by secretary of war Robert Patterson who was under intense pressure from Clay to get things moving. The two men agreed on an inquiry into a broad range of issues bearing on living standards and security, including reparations, American military strength in Europe and the challenge of reconciling France to German recovery. Jealous of its prerogative, the state department objected. After Truman was brought into the negotiations, a compromise was reached whereby Hoover was to investigate the provision of food and 'collateral problems' along with 'methods ... which will relieve some of the burden on the American taxpayer'.

Hoover left New York on February 2nd, 1947. The timing was propitious. When he arrived in Germany it was in the depths of one of the worst winters on record. Before 1947 was out, Europe had suffered its lowest average temperature, longest period without sun, and the fiercest snowstorms on record. Across the continent as the meteorological horrors multiplied, essential services collapsed while short rations got shorter still as food stocks dwindled to below wartime levels.

Inevitably, it was the shell-shattered Germany that bore the brunt of the punishment. Nutrition was often below subsistence. Instead of meat there was dried fish; instead of potatoes there were turnips. With no domestic fuel, the old and very young found refuge in 'warming rooms' equipped with one small stove known as a 'cannon oven'. The cannon gave off intense heat but only for an hour or two, since a meagre ration of fuel was soon burned up. In the American zone householders were limited to six briquettes to last, who could say how long? And the stench was suffocating.

Travelling in the train once reserved exclusively for Hermann Goering, Hoover was accompanied for most of his tour by Clay, who set up a tight schedule of meetings with those with first-hand experience of the devastation. Some of the worst conditions were in Berlin, where Willy Brandt witnessed life in the ruins.

> In the streets [the icy cold] attacked the people like a wild beast, drove them into their houses, but there they found no protection either. The windows had no panes, they were nailed up with planks and plasterboard. The walls and ceilings were full of cracks and holes – one covered them with paper and rags. People heated their rooms with benches

from the public parks … The old and sick froze to death in their beds by the hundreds.[1]

Ruth Andreas-Friedrich kept a diary of her young life in the city.

No electricity, no water, no coal. And still between 15 and 20 degrees below zero every night. People are freezing to death in their beds. It's impossible to do any work. Countless businesses have been closed due to lack of fuel.

On the black market the price of coal has risen to 95 marks for a hundred pounds. But it is rarely available. At least not to ordinary people. Coal dealers, too, want to be bribed. With cigarettes, butter or other luxuries, it is quite sad how corrupt we have become. No repairman comes without the requisite enticement. No shoemaker repairs shoes, no tailor fixes a coat if you haven't slipped him something. That's only for his work, as nails and soles, thread, needles and sewing kit, solder, gasoline for the soldering iron and whatever else might be needed, you have to supply yourself anyway. We carry our bodily waste in little packages into the ruins; we use forks, spoons or dishes sparingly so as not to waste a drop of water.[2]

Looting and pillaging were commonplace. Victor Gollancz, who was collecting material for his book, *In Darkest Germany*, found that German children were growing up with no idea of morality and with a contempt for government of every kind. The scene in Duesseldorf and other Ruhr towns, where people were living 'in holes in the ground', reminded him of 'a vile Daumier cartoon'. He was especially disturbed by the lack of shoes. Children went out into the snow barefoot. Like Gollancz, Hoover must have seen the cinema newsreels with their standard opening sequence of photographs of emaciated children appealing for news of lost parents. Hoover observed:

> The housing situation in the two zones [American and British] is the worst that modern civilization has ever seen ... Multitudes are living in rubble and basements. The average space among tens of millions is equivalent to between three and four people to a 12′ × 12′ room. ... One consequence is the rapid spread of tuberculosis and other potentially communicable diseases. ...
>
> Over half of the 6,595,000 children and adolescents, especially in the lower income groups, are in a deplorable condition ... In some areas famine edema (actual starvation) is appearing in the children. ...
>
> A considerable part of the 'normal consumer' group of 17,910,000 is likewise in deplorable condition. ... A large part of the group shows a steady loss of weight, vitality and ability to work. ... Famine edema is showing in thousands of cases, stated to be 10,000 in Hamburg alone. The increased death roll among the aged is appalling.

Although he had no way of knowing it at the time, conditions were about to get worse. The hard winter of 1946/47 was to be followed by a summer drought which all but halved the European harvests.

Hoover concluded:

> [Even] those who believe in vengeance and the punishment of a great mass of Germans not concerned in the Nazi conspiracy can now have no misgivings, for all of them – in

food, warmth, and shelter – have sunk to the lowest level known in a hundred years of Western history.

If Western civilization is to survive in Europe, it must also survive in Germany. And it must be built into a cooperative member of that civilization. That indeed is the hope of any lasting peace.

Hoover's recommendations were made public in March 1947. He came out openly in favour of freeing restrictions on German industry except 'for such control as was needed to prevent a return to militarism'. Whatever the views of the Russians and French, the removal and destruction of factories and plants had to be stopped along with reparations that were draining what was left of the German economy. The British and American zones – combined as Bizonia – should move urgently towards a 'self-sustaining economic community'. There was an alternative. 'We can keep Germany in economic chains but it will also keep Europe in rags.' In terms of economic recovery, Germany and Europe were as one. Hoover added some personal advice to Truman.

We can carry on the Military Government of Germany by the tenets of the Old Testament of 'a tooth for a tooth, and an eye for an eye', or we can inaugurate the precepts of the New Testament. The difference in result will be the loss of millions of lives, the damage of all Europe, and the destruction of any hope of peace in the world. I recommend the New Testament method.

Clay and secretary of war Patterson were wholly in agreement, though voices of dissent were heard in the state department where Hoover was attacked for a policy that 'would have recovery rather than security the principal goal in Germany'. Fans of the Morgenthau Plan were also strong in their denunciation of a 'revival of a German colossus'. But with a sympathetic nod from Truman and while Marshall was preoccupied with a CFM meeting in Moscow, Patterson fully endorsed the Hoover Plan, while pushing ahead with a substantial Congressional approbation to meet needs and to restore the raw material and food chain.

*

But there was a weakness that could not easily be remedied. Britain's role in Europe was critical to American policy, not least in the provision of coal, the fuel that accounted for over 90 per cent of industrial and domestic energy. Britain was rich in coal. The problem for the government was in marshalling resources to get the coal out of the ground and to modernise its industry while supporting Bevin in his determination to champion Britain's role as a world power. Military expenditure was five times its pre-war level, slicing nearly 19 per cent off national income, as against 11 per cent for America. The armed forces siphoned off one and a half million men between the ages of 18 and 44, nearly 20 per cent of the age group, who were spread across the world in a diversity of roles which most certainly did not include restoring the nation's commercial strength.

That America would help out financially was never seriously in doubt. Britain believed itself to be a special case. It had stood alone against Hitler while others were bowing in submission to keep clear of trouble. This surely justified a substantial interest-free loan or an outright gift. When, in early 1946, Britain's leading economist and Treasury adviser, John Maynard Keynes, led a high-powered delegation to Washington he set his target at $5 billion – sufficient, it was said, for Britain to return to a trade balance by 1949.[3]

But negotiations proved tougher than expected. There was a thick vein of Anglophobia running through American political life. Partly it was an aversion to imperialism, a sensitive issue in a country that had broken free from the British Empire. There was resentment too at the British air of superiority, the conviction, as a senior Treasury man put it, that however far ahead economically, the Americans would want Britain's 'profound, stabilising influence which would give them just what they need to carry out their responsibilities as world leader'.

Government papers do indeed reveal a breathtaking arrogance in assuming that America relied on Britain more than Britain relied on America. 'I sometimes feel', commented an American diplomat, 'that the Mother Country needs to be reminded that the umbilical cord was cut in 1776.' Differences between the two countries were exacerbated by political divergences. Britain had a socialist government wedded to public ownership of industry and to centralised planning, both anathema to the American way of doing things. Moreover, the recently elected government was committed to a costly programme of social welfare including the much-vaunted National Health Service. Since Britain was patently hard up – why otherwise beg for an American loan? – did it not follow that US taxpayers were being asked to subsidise socialist extravagance?

The loan negotiations dragged out over six months. It was not until July 1946 that a tentative deal was struck on a $3.75 billion credit at 2 per cent interest to be deferred or waived when the trade balance was judged to be seriously out of kilter. In addition, the slate was wiped clean on outstanding Lend-Lease debts. In return, Britain was to comply with US financial orthodoxy by making sterling fully convertible within a year. Restraints on American exports to the British Commonwealth and colonies were to be lifted.

The compact had still to be ratified. On both sides of the Atlantic it came under heavy attack. In Washington, there were fears of opening the floodgates to appeals for aid. What had Britain done to deserve such generosity? The notoriously Anglophobe *Chicago Tribune* ran a front page cartoon of John Bull standing at America's back door, saying: 'Spare a morsel for a poor, weak, sick, hungry, starving man. But make it sirloin, medium rare and if it isn't done just right, I won't eat it.' The opposite view was heard in London. 'We have saved our freedom at a great price', grumbled the *Manchester Guardian*. 'The Americans have, materially, saved theirs at a profit.'

At the Treasury, Hugh Dalton predicted a run on sterling when convertibility came into force. Even if a financial crisis could be averted, the budget was unable to meet the correct level of military expenditure. Bevin was urged to 'make a firm stand against demands that we should foot every bill which anyone presents to us'.[4]

The loan agreement was finally signed off in early December just as the long winter began to bite. At the turn of the year almost every part of Britain reported snowstorms of unprecedented strength and duration. On the weekend of January 24th, 1947, gale force winds built snowdrifts of up to ten feet over most of the south-east. By mid-week, there were high drifts throughout the country. No sooner were they cleared away than the blizzards struck again, whipping the snow into barriers that, given the shortage of snowploughs and the limits to what could be achieved in a raw wind by mere shovel power, were virtually impenetrable. The average temperature for February, the lowest registered for any month for over a century, coincided with the longest sunless period – 23 days – ever recorded by the Kew Observatory.

As the mercury fell so too did Anglo-American relations. Of several contentious issues the most serious was the production of coal or, rather, the lack of it. European recovery was tied to the delivery of coal. Britain had the capacity to satisfy demand but failed to deliver. America had ample supplies but distance and the limited capacity of merchant shipping allowed for only 2 to 3 million tons of coal a month to be divided between the members of the European Coal Organisation (ECO), a British initiative for administering fair shares. The view in Washington was that Britain should live up to its self-styled reputation as a world power by making coal for Europe its first priority. Within living memory, Britain had accounted for nearly half of Europe's entire output. Yet, post-war, production was down 60 per cent on the peak year of 1913. The decline had to be reversed.

The American view of a disabled British economy relying on handouts to delay an inevitable decline was confirmed by the Labour government's handling of the 1947 winter emergency. The argument was summarised neatly in a Foreign Office memo. The Americans, wrote Sir Roger Makins, 'rightly regard the present crisis as one of production, and they find that we are failing to produce'. Makins continued:

> We are not working hard enough. When the future of England depends on a few million more tons of coal we introduce the five-day week, production falls, output per man remains lower than before the war, and absenteeism increases. Informed US opinion looks at the UK today in terms of coal production to an extent which we do not fully appreciate, and we are failing to cope with this vital problem. Americans do not, themselves, think much of a controlled economy, and are confirmed in their view by

their judgement of the results. But they do not want to change it. They just do not feel enthusiastic about putting money into it.

Or, he might have added, putting their trust in Britain as a partner on the world stage.

From the first day of power in July 1945, the Labour government knew that its handling of the coal industry was critical to its fortunes. But unresolved problems were long-standing. Equipment was out of date and there was an acute shortage of technical support to make best use of what was available, management was dismal and its relations with the miners barely functional. All sides agreed that the government had to step in to enforce economies of scale with a 'vast programme of reconstruction of existing mines and the sinking of new ones'.[5] Great things were expected after nationalisation but the legislation was ill thought-out, in fact not thought-out at all, before it became law.

As minister of fuel and power, Emanuel Shinwell had an unenviable job. An MP for a mining constituency* and a doughty cheerleader for workers' rights, he felt unable to demand more from the miners unless they got something in return such as increased rations for underground workers. But his Cabinet colleagues were unwilling to make the industry a special case. There were too many other deserving causes. Faced with a predicted excess of annual coal consumption over supply of anything between 4 and 8 million tons, Shinwell fell back on his trust in the 'new spirit' in the industry to close the gap. But even on the unsafe assumption that his optimism was justified, it was a long-term strategy. To get through the winter of 1945/46, already

---

* Seaham, County Durham.

inadequate coal allocations to householders were cut by 8 per cent from October 1945 but while there was little industrial disruption and no serious domestic hardship, stocks were disappearing at an alarming rate, having fallen from 22 million tons in 1940 to 15 million at the end of 1945. If Britain hit a really hard winter, the reserves would disappear. Then what?

In July 1946, prime minister Clement Attlee recorded his opinion that 'coal is now the most urgent economic problem … and that a disastrous failure can be averted only if it is most boldly and resolutely tackled'. But when he proposed strict rationing to protect essential industries, Shinwell assured him that the projected shortfall to May 1947 of 9.5 million tons would be made up by converting industrial plant from coal to oil. How this was to be achieved went unresolved. By late 1946, of 900 projects, only eighteen were completed. Meanwhile, highly productive opencast mining came almost to a halt for want of machinery and spare parts. A proposal for recruiting Polish exiles and German POWs to boost the labour force was rejected as a potentially disruptive element in tightly-knit mining communities.

The plight of Germany was widely publicised but public compassion was in short measure. In some quarters there was grim satisfaction that Nature had exacted her own penalty for the Nazi years. But even among the more generous-spirited, the problems at home took priority. Government appeals for self-sacrifice to support those in greater need were greeted with contempt. Britain had had enough of self-sacrifice. In this age of austerity everything worth having was meanly rationed or not available at all. Shopping for one person's weekly rations produced not much more than a pound of meat, 1½ ounces of cheese, two pints of milk and one egg. Bread rationing was in force, introduced for the first time in British history, over a year after the war ended.

A 'good' English breakfast consisted of dried egg and soya bean sausages.

A *Picture Post* investigation into the problems of the 'average housewife' found that she spent at least an hour every day standing in queues, that she was sick of the rudeness of shopkeepers and worried by increasing prices. 'Don't you know there's a war on' came back into currency as an excuse for every deficiency and incompetence.

As in Germany and elsewhere in Europe, the black market flourished. It became accepted practice to break the law in minor ways like stealing cups from railway buffets or lavatory paper from public toilets. The spivs traded semi-openly from street corners and dingy alleyways, selling nylon stockings to fashion-starved women. Every shopkeeper and farmer kept a hoard of 'luxuries' to barter against other scarce products – no questions asked. 'It fell off the back of a lorry' was the common excuse for illegal possession.

★

If British feelings for Germany were muted or hostile, appeals from France were greeted sympathetically but with no tangible result. In France where in the winter of 1946/47, snow fell as far south as the Riviera, an appeal was launched for the hunger victims of Provence who, having no agriculture of their own to speak of, were denied supplies from the normally rich farmlands of the north. Even when provisions were made available, a chaotic transport network, with rolling stock down to 10 per cent of its pre-war level, invariably failed to deliver. Early in 1946, Léon Blum, in his final spell as French premier, made an emotional appeal to Attlee ('my dear friend') for help in reviving his country's economy.

One or two million tons of coal or thereabouts per month will decide between our economic reconstruction and our political destruction. I do not in any way exaggerate when I say that the fate of democracy and socialism in France, and consequently in Europe – is at stake for this amount. One or two million tons, that is, a relatively insignificant quantity compared with your global production in Great Britain or with the normal production of the Ruhr.[6]

Blum followed his appeal with a visit to London where he was told emphatically that 'the coal position is such that there is no hope of an early resumption of coal exports'. This left open the possibility of increasing the French share of German coal production, most of which came from the Ruhr in the British zone. But the risk here was a breakdown in the distribution of coal to countries such as Italy, Greece, Luxembourg, Norway and Denmark where there was little or no domestic production. And what of Germany itself, where 'conditions are appalling with people freezing to death, as Monsieur Blum will be aware'?[7] He was also aware, and did not like to be reminded, that France was taking all the coal it could get from the Saar, a region that for all practical purposes was now counted as part of France.

Blum's mission to London did have one positive result. The Dunkirk Treaty, signed on March 4th, 1947, required the two countries to act together to combat any revival of aggressive nationalism in Germany.

When it came to managing a coal industry, British competence was as much in question in the Ruhr as it was at home. Before the war, the region had produced an annual 67 million tons. In 1946, this was down to 40 million tons. As Hoover had noted on his visit to Germany in 1947:

The shortage of coal is, next to food, the most serious immediate bottleneck to both living and the revival of exports to pay for food. Of the present production [of the Ruhr], a considerable amount must be exported to surrounding nations which are also suffering. The shortage leaves the two zones without sufficient coal for transport, household and other dominant services, with little upon which to start exports in the industry. ...

This terrible winter, with frozen canals and impeded railway traffic, has rendered it impossible to maintain even the present low basis of rationing in many localities. The coal shortage and the consequent lack of heat, even for cooking, has added a multitude of hardships.

Clay was frustrated by the British tendency to waste time arguing the virtues of public ownership of the mines instead of concentrating on getting the wheels of industry moving. His view of the British Control Commission was that it took its cue from long practice in colonial administration where slow but steady was the abiding rule. A story in *Fortune* magazine, probably fed by Clay, put it more harshly. 'They [the British] have set up shop in their zone as if they are somewhere in darkest Africa.'

The jibe may have been overstated but the comparison was valid. The Ruhr had indeed reverted to a makeshift society. Food and housing for miners were desperately short. With massive bomb damage still to be rectified, the typical family had no more than four-and-a-half square yards of living space. This, General Robertson pointed out, was less than allocated to prisoners in German jails.

The emphasis on denazification inevitably led to the removal from employment of qualified managers who had served the wartime regime. This had terrible consequences. In February 1946, hundreds of men were trapped underground when an explosion and fire devastated part of the Grimberg-Monopol coalmine in Westphalia. The death toll was 430, including three British supervisors. It turned out that safety procedures had been ignored because the officials who knew about these things had been dismissed. When it was too late, one of them was recalled to direct abortive rescue efforts.

With no increase in coal production, Robertson knew what had to be done. But he came up against the intransigence of a government focused on trying to stabilise a home economy itself heavily dependent on coal. Yet there was no dodging the truth. With Germany having lost 25 per cent of its farmland to the Poles who were now on orders to supplement Soviet rations, the only way for Britain to nourish German miners was to cut food rations at home. Robertson did not baulk at this.

Unfortunately, Robertson's reporting line was not directly to Bevin, who was ready to throw his considerable weight behind the general, but to John Hynd, a junior minister who had been put in charge of affairs in Germany and Austria, a job he coupled with his dogsbody appointment as chancellor of the Duchy of Lancaster. A Sheffield MP and former rail union official, Hynd was judged by Attlee as clever and able, while Victor Gollancz thought 'there is no humaner man in British public life'. His own claim to his appointed task was that he had learned German from a correspondence course. Fiercely independent of the Foreign Office, he set up his headquarters (inevitably tagged Hyndquarters) in Norfolk House in St James's Square. After that it was downhill all the way. Though voluble on matters relating to works councils and trade unions, he had no answer for Robertson when he threatened to show him 'pictures of starving children and dying women'. If nothing was done to stop the rot, 'the economic life of the British zone will stop almost simultaneously. Coal production will stop. The trains will stop. The lights will go out ...' And it would get worse.

> The sporadic looting and unrest which is occurring now would increase. It is not, however, likely that the situation would get out of hand, provided that our own soldiers will be prepared to shoot down starving rioters.[8]

A deal was struck with Washington. 650,000 tons of American grain were sent to the British zone, with a cut of 200,000 tons to Britain. It was a modest palliative. Plainly not up to his job, Hynd was soon moved sideways to become minister of pensions. His successor was Lord Pakenham or, as he was to become, the Earl of Longford, one of the few Labour champions with inherited wealth. A virtuous do-gooder, he was made a deputy foreign minister but without his own department. It was now Bevin who called the shots.

As US ambassador in London, Lewis Douglas witnessed the unfolding economic drama at first hand. A Washington insider, Douglas made it his business to merge in with the political establishment. Before long he was on first-name terms with Bevin, a politician he admired. The feeling was mutual. They shared frustration at the apparent inability of the government to get to grips with the coal crisis. Bevin was wont to declare that with a mere 20 million tons of coal at his disposal, he would be able to shape the future of Europe. The coal shortage 'affects adversely [Britain's] political power in Europe, her authority in the Middle East and, indeed, everywhere throughout the world'.

The ineptitude of business leaders and politicians was hard for

Douglas to comprehend. He had no truck with socialist remedies and saw nationalisation (favoured by Bevin) as a cover for prevarication. He put to Marshall's deputy, Dean Acheson, the idea of importing hard-headed American experts from the coal, steel and textile industries to advise on raising productivity and reducing costs.* Bevin rejected the offer. He felt that Britain has 'little to learn from American management with its "dictatorial" methods of handling staff'. What was wanted was stronger motivation for miners to work harder.

In this regard, if in none other, Bevin and Douglas were as one with Arthur Horner, general secretary of the National Union of Mineworkers. Horner was an old-school communist who, on an orchestrated tour of the Soviet Union, had seen the future. He distrusted Bevin. In his view the foreign secretary was 'pursuing a path which would destroy the possibility of maintaining the wartime friendship [with Russia] and divide the world into two armed camps'. Shinwell, on the other hand, was 'the best minister of fuel and power we have ever had',[9] a double-edged tribute to a minister who accepted all that Horner told him, including excuses for worker absenteeism which increased sharply before and after every sporting event and public holiday.

Business leaders were soon complaining that coal deliveries were so irregular and so far short of undertakings it was impossible for them to plan more than a few days ahead. The Advisory Council on Industry declared the absurdity of 'debating scale of cuts as a percentage of allocations when there are disparities already between allocation and deliveries far greater than the proposed cuts'.[10] As a portent of things to come, several Lancashire

---

* An American Council on Productivity set up in October 1948 found that American steel productivity was 50 per cent to 90 per cent greater than in Britain. Henry Pelling, *Britain and the Marshall Plan*, 1989; p. 52.

cotton mills and the Austin Motor Company shut down for the lack of fuel, while other firms like Rolls-Royce at Derby and Hoover in Glasgow went on to short time.[11]

Barely a week after celebrating the transfer of the coal mines to public ownership ('One of the great days in the industrial history of our country'), Shinwell was forced to admit failure. When the Cabinet met on January 7th, 1947, it was the austere president of the Board of Trade, Sir Stafford Cripps, who took the lead with a demand for an immediate cut in coal deliveries of up to 40 per cent for industry generally and 20 per cent for steel. Appeals to Arthur Horner and the National Union of Mineworkers to demonstrate the 'new spirit of dedication to the public good' promised after nationalisation received a dusty response. Elected to secure better pay and conditions for a militant workforce, Horner demanded a 40-hour week, holidays with pay and much-improved health and welfare services.

Reporting to Acheson, Lewis Douglas gave vent to his frustration.

Only lackadaisical efforts appear to have been made towards providing even temporary housing in the more productive coalfields. No action has been undertaken to increase consumer goods … for the miners and their families. The system of taxation is such that any increased earnings of the miners resulting from increasing individual production leaves but a small residue in the hands of the miners. … Mechanical equipment that is available … is not being installed as rapidly as it might be.[12]

Douglas was equally forthright to John McCloy, recently installed as president of the World Bank.

> The coal crisis ... would have occurred anyway had there
> been no cold weather ... [but] the government has at best
> been lackadaisical and amateurish in its approach to this
> problem. ... Every issue here in England, of whatever kind,
> can be traced back to the original sin – coal.[13]

Intent on maintaining Britain as an international power broker,
Bevin tried hard to keep in with Washington while blaming the
Americans for an 'ungenerous attitude when it gets to business
not talk'. A report from Lord Inverchapel, the British ambassador in Washington, warning that the Truman administration was
losing patience with the apparent impotence of the Labour government, brought a testy response from Bevin. 'There are many
in the Labour party', he wrote, 'not by any means fellow travellers
[who] feel that the US has given us a pretty raw deal.'[14]

There was substance to the complaint. A hefty rise in US inflation (14 per cent or more since the start of the loan negotiations)
had dented purchasing power, while British treasury minister
Hugh Dalton was nervously anticipating the free convertibility of
sterling from July 17th, 1947, when creditor nations were liable to
rush to buy dollars. Closest to the action, or lack of it, Douglas
was inclined to give the hard-pressed government the benefit of
the doubt. With more financial aid Britain would pull through. In
Washington, opinion was less charitable. Robert Lovett, under-
secretary of state, charged that Britain had to show 'far more
managerial competence and more flexibility ... if they are to
operate within the terms and purposes of the loan agreements'.
Treasury secretary John Snyder also hit out:

> The crux of the whole matter is that men will only work for
> incentives, and the British are not producing the incentives

except in the form of dog races, soccer matches and horse racing.[15]

There were sharp divisions within the British government. Dalton complained that Bevin was ever ready to spend money the country did not have, all in the cause of maintaining British prestige. The chancellor and prime minister favoured cutting back on the armed forces and Britain's overseas commitments.

As early as September 1945, Attlee had tentatively suggested a withdrawal from the Middle East, leaving the United Nations to maintain order in the region. Dalton resurrected the idea, arguing for creating a new line of defence across Africa from Lagos to Kenya, putting 'a wide glacis of desert and Arabs between ourselves and the Russians'. It was worth discussing but with the backing of the Foreign Office and the general staff who seemed unable to grasp the fundamentals of economics, Bevin resisted attempts to decrease his bailiwick.

*

By the end of January 1947 the winter still had to do its worst. On the morning of the 29th, the temperature in Manchester fell to below −21°C (−6°F), lower, as the press noticed with perverse satisfaction, than that recorded by an American navy expedition in Antarctica. A week earlier, in response to the news that coal stocks were down to ten days, the government imposed a further 10 per cent cut in deliveries. Snow fell every day in some parts of Britain from January 27th to March 17th.

Ordinary life was reduced to a stultifying grind. In the countryside, cars, trucks and even trains disappeared into the snow, sometimes for days on end before they were located by hard digging. Farm animals had to be left to fend for themselves. Over

4 million sheep and lambs and 30,000 cattle died. Power cuts were long and total. The typical domestic scene suggested a country once again at war, but this time on the losing side. In the gloom of the early morning a candlelit breakfast was the preliminary to a day at the factory or office wrapped in heavy coat and muffler.

After coal allocations to industry were cut by half there was a shutdown of power stations in London, the Midlands and the north-west, and the complete suspension of household electricity supplies for three hours in the morning and two hours in the afternoon. By winter's end over 15 per cent of the nation's workforce was either unemployed or on short time.

An offer from Washington, enthusiastically received by Shinwell, to alleviate the hardship by diverting to Britain coal en route for mainland Europe was politely declined by Attlee. However tempting it was to be given even a brief respite, the prime minister knew that Bevin would resolutely oppose the move. 'Our foreign policy is getting no economic help now and we cannot stand more international difficulties.'[16] Bevin had no need to be told the reaction of France to a proposal for Britain to receive special treatment. In his bumbling style, Shinwell informed the House of Commons that he had tried but failed to obtain a higher import allocation of coal. A furious Bevin retorted that it was 'hardly surprising that our European friends should have drawn the conclusion that we have been doing our best to do a deal behind the backs of the ECO'.

With Britain close to bankruptcy (Douglas Jay, as economic secretary to the Treasury, gave the country three months before it went broke) the government itself seemed to be on the edge of collapse. A heavy legislative programme, a multitude of problems abroad and recurring financial crises had taken their toll. No fewer than three ministers – deputy prime minister Herbert Morrison,

Ernest Bevin and the home secretary, Chuter Ede – were suffering heart trouble, while Stafford Cripps was made tired by the cancer that was to kill him five years on. After a long illness, Ellen Williamson, the education minister, died on February 6th. Senior ministers fell to internecine warfare. Shinwell's scorn for Dalton, 'one of the most disastrous chancellors in Britain's history', was undisguised. According to Shinwell, Dalton was the author of his own misfortunes. 'His estimates of the cost of the occupation forces were wrong as was his optimism about invisible earnings.'[17] He failed to warn the Cabinet that the free convertibility of sterling as part of the deal to secure an American loan courted financial disaster. Dalton hit back. 'Shinwell was the most mercurial of ministers and … a very bad administrator.'[18]

While winter blizzards raged and Britain endured power cuts for up to eight hours a day, Attlee summoned the Cabinet to decide ways to forestall an otherwise certain financial crisis. An exhausted Bevin, already in the advanced stages of coronary heart disease, had to drag himself up two flights of stairs to the meeting because the lifts were not working.[19] He then listened while Hugh Dalton put the case for drastic expenditure cuts, starting with the withdrawal of military support for Greece and Turkey. Bevin gave way.

When the news filtered through to Washington, Marshall was out of town, leaving Dean Acheson, a more combative character, to react. Immediately, he began lobbying hard for America to fill the breach. With hindsight, it can be argued that Acheson overreacted to the perceived Soviet threat. The game plan in Moscow was to play on the fear of war but to stop short of promoting war. There was no immediate risk of Turkey losing control over the Dardanelles. More dangerous was the communist-led insurgency in Greece. The American ambassador in Athens had been sending Acheson alarming accounts of guerrilla fighters infiltrating Greece from Yugoslavia and Albania. But the threat amounted to no more than Moscow making trouble where opportunity allowed.

Acheson's warnings of a dangerous imbalance of power in Europe led to a crucial meeting between the state department and senior congressmen where he succeeded in winning over Senator Vandenberg. The chairman of the Senate foreign relations committee now forced the pace, arguing that concerns over Soviet expansion should be shared with the American voters. The purpose was to win public approval for a more assertive foreign policy. Truman snatched at the opportunity to upstage the left-wing internationalists who were unwilling to acknowledge Russia as an adversary, and the hardline isolationists, outraged at the prospect of signing an open cheque.

The new doctrine, formulated as a message to Congress, was delivered by Truman on March 12th, 1947. Greece and Turkey, though receiving an early mention, proved to be almost incidental to what Truman really wanted to get across. He told his audience:

Every nation must choose between alternative ways of life. The choice is too often not a free one.

One way of life is based on the will of the majority and is distinguished by free institutions, representative government, free elections, guarantees of individual liberty, freedom of speech and election and freedom from political oppression.

The second way of life is based upon the will of a minority forcibly imposed on the majority. It relies upon terror and oppression, a controlled press and radio, fixed elections and the suppression of personal freedoms.

Then came the ringing declaration:

I believe that it must be the policy of the United States to support free peoples who are resisting attempted subjugation by armed minorities or by outside pressures.

An immediate allocation of $400 million for aid to Greece and Turkey was approved by Congress. It was just a first step. Never before had a US leader so clearly committed his country to support subjugated peoples around the globe. The possibilities, and the risks, were endless.

CHAPTER FOUR

When, in March 1947, George Marshall came to Moscow for the latest Council of Foreign Ministers, he retained a faint hope of securing a four-power agreement on the future of Germany. Each delegation had its priorities, but while, broadly speaking, Britain was on side and France thought to be susceptible to compromise on its security and economic claims, the gulf between American capitalism and Soviet communism looked to be unbridgeable.

What chance there was of an accommodation rested on Soviet readiness to trade its advantage in Germany in return for American aid. Marshall knew that while his country thrived as never before, Russia was barely in reach of subsistence living. With famine an ever-present threat, an impoverished people was liable to undermine the Soviet regime. Seeking national and personal security above all else, Stalin was acutely aware of his vulnerability. Might this be the key to a deal? Marshall was in for a disappointment. Stalin's fear of the western powers ganging up against him was far greater than his fear of insurrection. As General Robertson was to caution when the Berlin crisis was building to its height, it was a 'very great mistake to suppose that they [the Russians] will sacrifice their main position on account of their own difficulties.

The trouble about the Russians is that they are quite ready to accept a bad economic position ... and to deal with any disturbance with ruthlessness.'[1]

The diplomatic mood at the CFM was set by the sub-zero temperatures in the streets of Moscow. In relentless monotone, Molotov set out what he must have known were impossible conditions for realising the Soviet vision of a 'united democratic Germany'. These included a strong central government in Berlin, presumably under Soviet domination, and $10 billion in reparations from Germany as a whole, which the western powers interpreted to mean that they would be expected to pump millions of dollars-worth of supplies into their zones to keep the Germans alive while the Russians siphoned off most of the current German production for themselves. Furthermore, Russia demanded the withdrawal of American forces from Germany and repeated their claim to Soviet participation in the control of the Ruhr. The only sign of progress was an agreement that all German prisoners of war should be repatriated by December 1st, 1948. It was a deal that Russia chose to disregard. Six weeks of fruitless dialogue ended with a private conference between Marshall and Stalin that was equally inconsequential.

Free of residual illusions, the secretary of state returned to Washington knowing that if the political and economic impasse in Germany was to be broken it was America that would have to take the initiative. There were powerful voices urging him on. Taking time out from Moscow, Marshall had met Clay in Berlin to agree that Bizonia should be made self-sufficient without delay. From Bevin came an enthusiastic endorsement for a policy he had been advocating for some time, albeit from a weak position. Taking his cue from the Hoover Report and the promulgation of the Truman Doctrine, Marshall made his pitch for popular backing in a nation-wide broadcast on April 28th.

It was time for Germany and the rest of Europe to recognise their interdependence, said Marshall. Critical to any sort of progress was the supply of coal. If Germany was to provide more coal it was essential to restore damaged mines and to revive the engineering industry by raising steel production. With 'the impoverished and suffering people of Europe ... crying for coal, for food and for most of the necessities of life ... the rehabilitation of Germany ... demands immediate decision'. He ended on a chill note. 'We cannot ignore the factor of time. ... Disintegrating forces are becoming evident. The patient is sinking while the doctors deliberate.'

Quick to respond, the two military governors of Bizonia – Clay and Robertson – set to work on a plan for German economic resurgence. A key feature was to double coal production to over 400,000 tons daily by 1948. Miners were to be given special treatment including a daily ration of 4,000 calories (more than two-and-a-half times that of the ordinary citizen) and a 20 per cent wage increase. An emergency building programme aimed at ending the housing shortage. Steel production was to be restored to the 1936 level. The focus was to change from dismantling industrial plants to building new ones. Bevin must have wished that a corresponding plan could have taken shape in his own country where bargaining between the miners' leaders and the government was interminable and futile.

In the event, and despite Marshall's call for urgency, the Bizonia project was put on hold. This was on the insistence of France. Georges Bidault, French foreign minister, warned of his government's collapse, with advantage to the communists, unless there were guarantees that the Wehrmacht would not soon, once again, be marching down the Champs Élysées. Frustration in Germany, where Clay allowed threats of his resignation to resurface, was contained by a fresh round of thinking in Washington that took account of not just the problems in Germany and the worries of France but of the challenge of recovery across the entire continent.

It was Dean Acheson, as under-secretary of state, picking up on recommendations from George Kennan's policy planning staff, who prepared the ground by advocating broad-based financial support for Europe both as a humanitarian gesture and a defence of democracy, thus holding back communism while serving American economic self-interest. Since the end of the war, Washington had handed out close on $15 million in grants and credits to Europe. Yet there was little to show from this largesse except the exclusion of the communist parties from the French and Italian governments. A way had to be found to kick-start a sluggish European economy that would otherwise continue to be dependent on American subsidies.

★

On June 5th, Marshall was awarded an honorary degree from Harvard. He chose the occasion to advance his thinking on the future of Europe. At this stage, he was not in possession of anything that might properly be called a plan. He talked of restoring the confidence of the European people and he declared that the United States should do what it could 'to assist in the return of normal economic health in the world, without which there can be no political stability and no assured peace'. But he did not go into details. Rather, 'the initiative ... must come from Europe. ... It would not be fitting nor efficacious for the Government to draw up unilaterally a programme designed to place Europe on its feet economically. That is the business of Europeans.' He pledged friendly aid and support for such a programme 'so far as it may be practical for us to do so'.

Bevin was quick to pick up on the message. Here was an opportunity to show that despite appearances, Britain still had the muscle to shape events. The story goes that Bevin first heard of Marshall's speech while listening to the BBC news. But advance warning of a major announcement had come via the British embassy in Washington where Acheson had been dropping broad hints. There was also a suggestion that Britain should take the lead in formulating a response. A meeting with French foreign minister Georges Bidault was fixed for June 17th in Paris. Guidance from Washington stressed helping the European nations to help themselves, a caution that while American funding could be expected, it would not take the form of an open chequebook.

The starting point was less about how much money was on the table than about how to bring the Russians into discussions without inciting spoiling tactics. Having agreed to come to Paris for talks with Bidault and Bevin, it was soon clear that Molotov was under orders not to give way to anyone telling Russia how to run its affairs. His opening proposition was to press Washington to be more precise in its offer. What was the size of the aid budget and what conditions were attached?

Molotov argued for each country to put in its own bid on the understanding that it would be free to decide how the money should be spent. 'Any kind of coordinated programme for Europe would mean an infringement of national sovereignties and the domination of weak by stronger powers.'[2] The second part of the sentence was surely said tongue-in-cheek. Even so, he had a point but since neither Bidault nor Bevin wanted the Russians to be involved at all, they made light of Molotov's fears. They were also aware that preconditions would only serve to prolong negotiations and to alienate Washington. 'From a practical point of view', said Bevin, 'it is far better to have the Russians definitely out than half-heartedly in.'

There was still some way to go before Soviet participation was finally ruled out. Meanwhile, there were other critical matters to be settled, notably Britain's role in bringing the Marshall Plan to fruition. Bevin had high hopes of Britain acting more as a financial partner with America rather than as one of a collective of suppliants. Not surprisingly, given Britain's economic fragility, this was not a view shared by Washington.

The crunch came in late June 1947 when, over two days in London, William Clayton, under-secretary of state for economic affairs, said by Acheson to be the 'catalyst' for the Marshall Plan, and Lewis Douglas, US ambassador in London, sat across the table from Attlee, Bevin and Dalton as they tried to impress on their visitors that Britain, as Dalton put it, was 'something more than just a bit of Europe'. Clayton was unmoved. Declaring roundly that no piecemeal solution to Europe was conceivable, he 'did not quite see how the UK problem was different from that of other European countries'.

He had only to turn to the economic indicators to prove his point. Within days, Dalton would be forced to admit that most of the American loan agreed just eighteen months earlier had been spent and that Britain was on a financial precipice. The pain of austerity was everywhere apparent. Food shortages were worse than ever after the bitter cold of the first quarter of the year was followed by widespread flooding which devastated thousands of acres of farmland. Bevin's plea for diplomatic favouritism to compensate for economic weakness to preserve the 'little bit of dignity we have left' went unheeded.

While in American eyes Britain had many faults, not least its faith in central planning, much would have been forgiven if the country had lived up to its potential for meeting the demand for coal. Yet, for all the promises to do better, production consistently fell far short of targets. As a sympathetic observer, Douglas was in turn bewildered and angry. Expressing the hope that he was witnessing a 'temporary phase in the post-war life of a tired nation', a confidential letter revealed his true feeling that 'the British government on the whole is incompetent, blundering and inept'.[3]

Speaking as he said, 'as a personal friend', Douglas warned Bevin that he would have difficulty justifying 'further direct or indirect expenditure of American dollars to support a country which is unable effectively to manage the most important industry it has so far nationalized'.[4] He added that given the disaster that was the British coal industry, America would not go along with whatever ideas socialist dreamers had in mind for putting the Ruhr mines under public ownership.

For all this, even if Britain could not expect preferment over any other country in western Europe, it was the obvious choice for coordinating a multi-nation response to the American offer of economic aid. As the only possible alternative, France was too susceptible to pressure from Moscow via a communist party able to command the vote of over a fifth of the electorate.

With Stalin having decided that the Marshall Plan was a capitalist plot that had to be resisted not only by Russia but by all the countries within the Soviet sphere, invitations were sent from Washington to sixteen nations. These included neutral Ireland, Switzerland and Sweden but excluded fascist Spain, the aim being to meet in Paris for the first step to creating a Conference for European Economic Cooperation (CEEC), the forerunner to the Organization for European Economic Cooperation (OEEC).

By common consent Bevin was made chairman, though on a day-to-day basis the role was taken by Sir Oliver Franks, an Oxford don and wartime civil servant, noted for his imperturbability and fair dealing. He had his work cut out. Each delegation arrived with a shopping list, expecting it to be sent to Marshall with a polite request for a cheque by return.

When reality set in, the CEEC got to work on producing a four-year plan. The ground rules, as made clear from Washington, were increased industrial and agricultural productivity up to and above pre-war levels, monetary reform to provide for financial stability, steps towards economic cooperation between the participating countries, and a correction to the dollar deficit by focusing on exports. Longer-term, and in deference to American doctrine, free trade and unrestricted convertibility of currencies were held in prospect though Britain, with its Commonwealth and imperial markets to protect along with the international defence of sterling, was strongly opposed on both counts.

The work of the CEEC was matched by intense political activity in Washington. Committees of experts and lobbyists were topped off by a nineteen-strong council of economic advisers reporting to Truman and Marshall. While there was general agreement on the basic premise that American security was tied to European recovery, there were worries about inflationary demands on scarce resources such as steel and fears of stimulating competition in American export markets, though the chief concern was reports of ever-escalating costs.

When Clayton heard the total aid figure proposed by the CEEC, he responded angrily. 'It is out of the question', he told Franks. Congress was not a rubber stamp. If the two houses failed to endorse what was now known as the European Recovery Program, what future was there for the bold intent of the Truman Doctrine? As Truman asserted in a characteristically pithy axiom, the Marshall Plan and the Truman Doctrine are as 'two halves of the same walnut'. George Kennan favoured cutting a few corners.

We should listen to all that the Europeans have to say but in the end, we should not ask them; we should just tell them what they will get.

While the talks dragged on into September, growing political and economic disruption in France and Italy, where communist party workers were out of the factories and on to the streets, translated into a $600 million interim aid package. There was support too for an impoverished Britain where, in accordance with the American loan deal of the previous year, full convertibility of sterling came into force in July. There followed the long-predicted and almost inevitable worldwide rush to hand in pounds for dollars. Exchange controls were soon reintroduced but not before Britain had lost most of its dollar reserves. Opinion in Washington was that Britain had only itself to blame for insisting, for reasons of international prestige, on a hopelessly overvalued currency. This was not how it was seen in London, where America was accused of bullying its way to dollar supremacy. What had happened, went the refrain, to the much-vaunted 'special relationship'? It took an independent observer to state the uncomfortable truth. 'It only existed in London. It never really existed in Washington.'[5]

The temper of the times in Anglo-American relations was not improved by differences over Palestine, where Britain held the unenviable responsibility for trying to keep the peace between Jews and Arabs. While the hard-pressed peacekeeping force was fighting a losing battle, the Jewish community was lobbying for unrestricted immigration, opening the way to an independent Israel.

But it was the continuing coal crisis that headed the list of American complaints of Britain failing to pull its weight. The success of the European Recovery Program was said to depend on

Britain committing to exporting an annual 6 million tons of coal to neighbouring countries with limited or no access to the precious fuel. Yet there was no sign of the target being met.

Reporting to a Congressional committee, Douglas spoke wearily of the 'rather squalid history' of an industry noted for the 'failure or, rather, indifference of the old private operators to invest the capital necessary for greatest productivity'.[6] Bevin's frustration at the apparent inability of the coal industry to deliver on its promises spilled over into a series of exchanges with Attlee during the Moscow CFM conference. When Bevin argued that the coal gap could be closed if 'each miner produced one additional hundredweight a day over a period of a year', Attlee replied that even 'pressing ahead with all possible measures' the target of an annual 200 million tons was liable to fail by a margin of 10 per cent.[7] Bevin was in despair. The impression we give to the Americans, he said, is 'that we are decadent'.

There was certainly a feeling that Britain was not to be trusted. Evidence of that came with the American refusal to give practical support for Britain's efforts to develop atomic energy. The ostensible reason was security, the British physicist Alan Nunn May having recently been convicted of espionage. But in an ambassadorial dispatch from Washington, Lord Inverchapel, while noting the 'propensity of Americans to overdramatise' went on to report unfavourable reactions in Washington to left-wing agitation in the Labour party towards 'appeasing rather than resisting Soviet encroachment'. There were those who predicted 'the bankruptcy of the UK and the imminent disintegration of the British Empire'.[8] The normally cool-headed Attlee responded waspishly:

There is rather a feeling here that the Americans, while quite willing to shelter themselves behind us and to expect us to pull chestnuts out of the fire for them, are unwilling to give us real assistance.

In particular,

> We are expected to keep our troops abroad in all kinds of places, whereas the US contribute very little in this way.[9]

But always it came back to the European Recovery Program and the desperate need for coal. From his hot seat in Paris, Franks delivered a blunt warning.

> It was very important that the British Government should remember that the United States attitude to Great Britain would be very much affected by the way Britain carried out its part of the whole Paris Report. Particularly the United States judges Britain by her output of coal and by her export of coal to the sixteen countries and this was to be remembered whenever problems of allocation of coal were under consideration. Again if the plan was to be carried out successfully it would be necessary to keep the confidence of the European nations. While no doubt Great Britain must base its policy on the fundamental necessities of British recovery, there was a marginal area in which for long-run reasons it might be necessary to place the general interests of Europe in advance of immediate short-run British interests. Translating these remarks into a concrete illustration nothing would be more crucial in the eyes of the United States nor more important to Europe than the achievement in 1948 of Great Britain's promise to export 6 million tons of coal to Europe. ... [This is] the most vital figure in the Paris report.[10]

There was, at least, broad Anglo-American concurrence on a policy for Germany where Clay and Robertson were finally permitted to push ahead with economic and political reforms. The target for German industrial production, fixed at about 50 per cent of the pre-war figure in March 1946, was now raised to 90 to 95 per cent. Steel production was to be increased from 5.8 million tons to 10.7 million, the figure Bevin had been advocating for over a year. New administrative machinery delegated legislative powers to the Economic Council and independent authority to a supreme court and a central bank.

Since it was abundantly clear that Britain could not find the dollars to fulfil its share of subsidising Bizonia, the financial burden passed to America, with the British contribution limited to helping provide food and services, chiefly by carrying freight in British ships. The corollary was that Washington would have the greater say in deciding policy.

France remained the odd man out. Bidault put up a strong fight, threatening to resign and to bring down his government unless the announcement of the revised figures for German industry was postponed. Much to Clay's fury, a new date of September 1st was agreed.

With Marshall convinced that German recovery was an essential component of his plan, indeed the chief reason why the plan was mooted in the first place, the pressure mounted on Bidault to submit. Marshall wanted it made clear that while France was entitled to its opinions, America and Britain would not be dictated to on what they could or could not do in Bizonia. When, in August, Bidault demanded that the Ruhr industry should never again fall 'exclusively' into German hands, he was told bluntly that the subject was not open to discussion. The best he could hope for was some sort of international control. But French sensitivities were noted

while behind the scenes, Bidault was assured that his national interests would be taken into account. He and his government had to
make do with that. Marshall was adamant in believing that 'French
security for many years to come will depend upon the integration
of Western Europe including the western German economy'.

He went on:

> Unless western Germany during [the] coming years is effec-
> tively associated with [the] Western European nations, first
> through economic arrangements, and ultimately perhaps
> some political way, there is a real danger that [the] whole
> of Germany will be drawn into [the] eastern orbit, with
> obvious dire consequences for all of us.

The warning to Moscow could not have been clearer.

★

No one yet talked of a Cold War but when Marshall arrived in
London in November 1947 for the latest Council of Foreign
Ministers, the battle lines were plain to see. With the European
Recovery Program close to fruition and Bizonia, soon to be
Trizonia (France joined in June 1948), shaping up to be a separ-
ate state within the wider Germany, any accommodation with
Russia looked to be remote. Privately, Molotov may have regret-
ted his, and Stalin's, early assumption that western democracy
was soft and vulnerable. But it was too late for second thoughts.
In a meeting with Bevin he gave warning of what was to come
by complaining volubly that Russia 'had been threatened by the
United States'. When the CFM met in full session, Molotov quickly
resorted to what Marshall described as 'insulting and undignified
remarks'. Heartily sick of the diatribe, Marshall called for an early

adjournment. Molotov blustered but to no avail. Gathering his papers, Marshall hoped that 'When we meet again ... it will be in an atmosphere more conducive to the settlement of differences'. It was not to be.

Congressional hearings on the European Recovery Program began in January 1948. Marshall put the total cost at between $16 and $20 billion with an allocation of $7.5 billion in the first year starting in April. Fighting Marshall's corner in the Senate foreign relations committee, Arthur Vandenberg, one-time isolationist, spoke powerfully in the cause of 'intelligent American self-interest'. It was by economic rather than by military means that peace and stability were to be achieved.

Even so, there were loud voices raised in favour of trimming the budget. The outcome was in doubt until Vandenberg was unexpectedly handed a trump card. What made it all the more astounding was that the dealer was Joseph Stalin, who chose this moment to mount a communist coup in Czechoslovakia. The overthrow of the legitimate government, culminating in the murder of foreign minister Jan Masaryk who was thrown from a third-floor window, evoked memories of Nazi aggression. Was this a repeat of history, this time with Russia as the villain?

Face-saving for those who had warned of runaway expenditure was provided by a cutback on the first-year appropriation to $4 billion with the total outlay set at $13 billion. In March, the first instalment of Marshall Aid was approved by Congress by a huge majority. Truman signed the European Recovery Act on April 3rd. The two biggest beneficiaries were Britain and France but thanks to the tireless lobbying of Clay and Robertson, Germany came in third and on the same terms. Originally, Marshall Aid for Germany was to be in the form of a loan. Now, four-fifths of the allocation was an outright gift.

Economists have long argued the practical benefits of Marshall Aid, critics pointing out that the money handed over was no more than 2.5 per cent of the combined national income of the recipients. But the relatively modest injection had a huge psychological impact. It restored confidence in western Europe that, with American backing, there was all to gain from taking a stand against Soviet intimidation. If the Marshall Plan had a fault it was to persuade American voters that any international problem could be solved by throwing money at it.

Stalin recognised the Marshall Plan as a defeat and the Truman Doctrine as a challenge that had to be met. Ferocious attacks on American 'openly expansionist' foreign policy and on the Marshall Plan as the first stage in 'the American plan for the enslavement of Europe' led to the setting up of the Communist Information Bureau or Cominform, to coordinate communist strategy across Europe. Strikes and riots followed in France and Italy. Washington responded with authority to the CIA to undertake 'covert psychological operations designed to counteract Soviet and Soviet-inspired activities'. More emergency aid was pumped into the exposed democracies.

The risk of a communist takeover was greatest in Germany. As early as June 1945, Stalin had contemplated a reunified Germany within Moscow's sphere of influence.[11] His ambition had to be modified in the light of tougher than expected opposition from the other occupying powers. But Germany was still vulnerable, with Berlin as the weakest point. It was here that Stalin made his bid to be recognised as the outright victor in the Cold War.

CHAPTER FIVE

In neither east nor west was there any grand plan for Berlin. Territorial logic dictated, sooner or later, a merger with the Soviet zone. But post-war upsets had scuppered a neat solution. The Russians wanted the western Allies out, the western Allies asserted their right to stay. Pragmatically, the Russians had the strongest hand. With control over access to the city except for the three air corridors agreed in November 1945, it was a simple matter to use technical or bureaucratic excuses to interrupt the flow of traffic. It happened in early 1947 when Russian security guards stopped a British military train at the border. Two coaches carrying German passengers were uncoupled and left stranded. A protest note was ignored. A fortnight later, an American military train was held up while German passengers submitted to a body search. The Russians now demanded the right to check identity papers of anyone crossing into their sector, to limit, said the official communiqué, 'the masses of spies coming in from the British and American zones'. Freight trains were held up for hours while every container was opened and checked. Railway and canal bridges were closed without warning for 'urgent repairs'.

There was a paradox here. While the Soviet tendency to harass and obstruct could be seen as a demonstration of strength, it might also be judged a sign of weakness, a heavy-handed reminder to Berliners that whatever their political sentiments, they had no choice but to do as they were told by their Soviet masters. Communism was not popular in Berlin or anywhere in the Soviet zone of Germany. The policy of 'Russia First', the stripping of industrial and commercial assets causing unemployment and poverty, did not win friends. The humiliating defeat for the Socialist Unity Party (SED) in the 1946 Berlin municipal elections rather proved the point. Even the SED itself admitted to 'bleak living conditions' and the 'sinking morale of the workers'.[1] As joint leader of the SED and a former Social Democrat, Otto Grotewohl tied himself into rhetorical knots trying to reconcile contradictory policies while blaming the west for failing to agree to German unity. Disobliging behaviour towards the other powers in Berlin was a way of showing who was boss while making a vain effort to hold back the stream of refugees who were using the western enclave as a staging post for escape to a less oppressive regime.

Tension between east and west was racked up by talk of currency reform in Germany. The need for a stable currency that would serve across the country had been a hot topic for debate in the 1946 session of the Allied Control Council. The practice adopted after the war was for banknotes to be issued separately for the western zones, for Berlin and for the Soviet zone but under four-power control. This turned out to be a bankers' nightmare since the Russians were inclined to print notes as and when needed to cover the costs of occupation.

The result was roaring inflation and the collapse of public confidence in money that changed value dramatically from day to day. In the British zone the exchange rate was liable to jump from 10 to 30 or even 40 reichsmarks to the pound. The Americans set their own rates which were equally idiosyncratic, with some goods such as children's toys sold at bargain prices while spare parts for cars were hugely expensive.

An agreement on a concerted effort to halt inflation seemed to be in prospect towards the end of 1946 but the Russians then decided to make reform conditional on a fixed figure for reparations. Negotiations dragged on for several months until any sort of compromise was ruled out by the Soviet demand to have exclusive control over a duplicate set of banknote printing plates. In other words, back to square one. At an Anglo-American summit in London on December 18th, 1947, Marshall and Bevin, with Clay and Robertson giving counsel, agreed to push ahead with a new currency for Bizonia. In rapid response, Moscow authorised a monetary rebirth for the Soviet zone.

It was clear to all that economic division equated with political division. As the prospect of a united Germany faded into the distant background, the democracies made haste to strengthen their alliance. Smarting from a recent put-down from Washington, Bevin snapped at the chance of getting back into the big game, starting with a rousing declaration of his faith in western unity.

This need not take the shape of a formal alliance ... It docs, however, mean close consultation with each of the Western European countries, beginning with economic questions. We in Britain can no longer stand outside Europe and insist that our problems and position are quite separate from those of our European neighbours. Our treaty relations with the various countries might differ, but between all there would be an understanding backed by power, money and resolution and bound together by the common ideals for which the Western Powers have twice in one generation shed their blood.[2]

This consolidation would include Germany, 'without whom no Western system can be complete'. The alternative 'is to acquiesce in continued Russian infiltration and helplessly to witness the piecemeal collapse of one Western bastion after another'.

At Cabinet meetings Bevin was almost apocalyptic. The Soviet government, he told his colleagues, 'is not prepared to cooperate with a non-communist government'. It was 'actively preparing to extend its hold over the remaining part of continental Europe, over the Middle East and no doubt the bulk of the Far East as well'. It could all happen very quickly, 'leading either to the establishment of a World Dictatorship or, more probably, to the collapse of organised society over great stretches of the globe'.[3]

From February 23rd to March 6th, 1948, the future of Germany and Berlin brought together America, Britain and France along with Belgium, the Netherlands and Luxembourg (now joined in a customs union) in a series of meetings in London. As a result, moves were made towards drafting a constitution for a German Federal Republic to be part of a European defence pact serving as a guarantee against the revival of German militarism and, more significantly, as a bulwark against communist expansionism. The Brussels Treaty was signed on March 17th. The same day, Truman made public his conviction that 'the most serious situation we have faced since 1939' was down to 'the fact that one nation has not only refused to cooperate in the establishment of a just and honourable peace but – even worse – has actively sought to prevent it'.

Endorsement from Berliners came in the form of a mass meeting held in the square opposite the ruins of the Reichstag. March 18th turned out to be a cold and wet day but 80,000 gathered to hear the leaders of the democratic parties declaim against the evils of communism. 'The cry of Berlin is heard beyond our city borders', declared Franz Neumann, chairman of the Berlin

Social Democratic Party, to which Jakob Kaiser, a veteran trade unionist from the east zone, added: 'Berlin is Germany in miniature and Berlin is Europe in miniature. We want a free Germany and a free Europe.'

Ernst Reuter closed the meeting. Soviet advocacy of a 'democratic, peace-loving government for the whole of Germany' was based on a lie since it called for four-power unanimity. If one power could scotch the wishes of the other three, Russia would use delaying tactics to achieve what it most wanted, a Germany under the hammer and sickle. He ended: 'Prague has been overrun, Finland was threatened but if one should ask who will be next, we can answer firmly and confidently, it will never be Berlin.' At this point, Reuter was silenced by an ovation of several minutes. He closed with the words: 'And if the world knows this, then we will not be abandoned by the world.'

*

Much depended on whether America and Britain could maintain a united front in Germany. The signs were hopeful. The breakthrough in European diplomacy represented by the Brussels Treaty raised Bevin's standing across the Atlantic. The welcome boost for the foreign secretary was part of a broader pattern. As anti-Soviet sentiment took hold in America, there was a corresponding gain in Britain's credibility. Its economy was still rocky, with another financial crisis not far ahead, and there were diplomatic squalls over Palestine.* But as the public face of Britain on the international scene, Bevin earned plaudits for his stance against Russia and for injecting a sense of urgency into west European security.

---

* British forces were finally withdrawn from Palestine on May 14th, 1948 when the Jewish People's Council proclaimed the state of Israel.

It helped that Lewis Douglas, doubling as ambassador in London and US envoy in Europe, acted as a cheerleader for Bevin. Briefed by Douglas, the two chief American movers of policy in Europe, Dean Acheson, seen as Marshall's anointed successor, and Averell Harriman, who headed the American administration for Marshall Aid, recognised that Bevin was working valiantly, often in adverse circumstances, for Anglo-American accord. Harriman in particular was strong in praise of Bevin's contribution to laying down the organisation of the OEEC.[4]

Bevin now began to push Marshall for a trans-Atlantic democratic alliance embracing America, France, Italy, Britain and its Commonwealth. Marshall wanted Germany to be settled first but he was attracted to the broader vision. It would eventually take shape in 1949 as the North Atlantic Treaty Organization (NATO).

The pressure on Berlin intensified in the early weeks of 1948. In his dispatches to London, General Robertson reported on an 'intense war of nerves ... against the Germans' who are made fearful that the Western Allies will soon abandon the city'.[5] Restrictions on traffic across the east zone were made more onerous but always with excuses that were more or less plausible. The harsh winter was blamed for the closure of the railway bridge over the River Ems and for lengthy repairs to canal locks. This left a single, overcrowded road starting at the British-controlled crossing at Helmstedt. Even without Soviet interference, the journey east could be a depressing experience, particularly in winter when hazards included fog and black ice.

The British Military Police checkpoint at Helmstedt was marked by a flagpole flying a Union Jack and a sardonic signboard in large letters: BERLIN 117 MILES, AND THE FAR EAST. Forty yards farther on, where Red Army sentries with machine-pistols checked Allied documents, were a similar hut and barrier, and a flagpole flying the Soviet flag. The war-splintered road, the dense black forest lining much of the route, and the sinister absence of any signs of life (because Soviet Zone inhabitants were forbidden to approach the motorway) made the 200 kilometres into central Berlin seem at least double the distance. In the immediate vicinity of the former capital the desolation was total; it was a landscape of anonymous ruins, water-filled craters, and occasional arrows marking emergency road-repairs or unexploded bombs.[6]

A plain indication of Soviet intentions was not long in coming. Following the London meetings of western powers, Marshal Sokolovsky, commander-in-chief of Soviet forces in east Germany and head of the Soviet administration in Germany, with his chief political adviser, Vladimir Semenov, were summoned to Moscow. A plan for disrupting Berlin's communications between zones was agreed as part of a wider policy to frustrate moves towards incorporating Germany into a western defence system. On March 19th, Stalin heard from Wilhelm Pieck, joint leader with Grotewohl of the SED, that the communists could not even come close to winning open elections in Berlin. The western powers were having it too much their own way. 'Let's make a joint effort', said Stalin, 'maybe we can drive them out.'[7]

General Clay was quick to detect the change in the wind. 'For many months', he warned the US army director of intelligence, 'I have felt and held that war was unlikely for at least ten years. But within the last few weeks I have felt a subtle change in Soviet attitude which I cannot define, but which now gives me a feeling it may come with dramatic suddenness.' He admitted to having no firm evidence except 'a feeling of a new tenseness in every Soviet individual with whom we have official relations'.

Later, Clay conceded that he had laid it on rather more thickly than justified to try to persuade Congress to spend more on the military presence in Germany. Troops on the ground gave Clay a negotiating advantage. But along with other realists, Clay knew that a four-power deal on a neutral, democratic Germany was a mirage. Democracy for Stalin and his cohorts was less about free elections than achieving results favourable to communism. To invite Russia to participate in a government for all of Germany would be tantamount to inviting Moscow to replicate the methods employed in eastern Europe. The coup in Czechoslovakia was a potent reminder that Stalin was not to be trusted. Elections were a means to an end. If they failed to deliver the 'correct' result, the means had to be changed.

A glimpse of the truth hidden by Soviet rhetoric for a free Germany came in March with the deliberations of the People's Congress. Said to represent all the democratic elements in the east zone, though in reality communist-dominated, the People's Congress proceeded to elect a council to draft a peace treaty and constitution and to appoint committees to administer economics, justice, culture and welfare. There was no requirement for this government-in-waiting to submit to a popular election.

The opening move to expel the Allies from Berlin called for Sokolovsky to demonstrate his talent for political theatre. Normally an amiable character, he chose a meeting of the Allied Control Council, called on his initiative, to demand a full account of plans for an economic merger of the western zones and to evolve an independent government for west Germany. Clay and Robertson hedged. They were wary of opening a debate that extended beyond their brief. They also felt constrained from sharing classified information though they strongly suspected that Sokolovsky was already in possession of the facts. Putting on a good act, the Marshal read out a prepared statement condemning what he described as a blatant violation of existing agreements. He then declared the session adjourned and marched out. That was it for the Allied Control Council. It never met again.

Five days later, orders were given to begin the shutdown of military and passenger traffic between the west zones and their sectors in Berlin. On March 31st, Sokolovsky demanded that all military trains be opened to Soviet inspection. The next day, the rule was extended to forbid any train to leave Berlin without Soviet permission. At the same time, undisclosed engineering problems disrupted telephone links.

With reports of Russian tanks and troops moving into the city, Clay decided that the time for talking was over. He was ready to give orders to American troops on US trains to refuse Soviet inspection, by force if necessary. Alarm bells rang in Washington. No one needed reminding that Clay, although unquestionably a gifted administrator, had never led the way into battle. It was a gap in his career that perhaps he was over-eager to fill. The word from the Pentagon was to calm down.

Robertson also urged caution. While he had no illusions about the Russians and was even convinced, as he wrote later, that 'we are committed to fight them eventually', he warned against premature action. 'If you send an armed convoy', he told Clay, 'it'll be war; it's as simple as that.' He suggested a concession, allowing the Russians to put unarmed inspectors on trains before they crossed the east–west boundary. This was no different, he argued, from passport control. But as he reported to London: 'Clay is quite adamant against any form of compromise. He feels certain that other Russian moves will follow within a few days and that compromise will only encourage them.' The most that Clay would concede was to provide a list of passengers with their official orders on arrival at entry points.

Robertson concluded: 'I think an attempt to get a clear agreement would be worth trying but, of course, I must stand with Clay. His whole attitude is most pessimistic and bellicose and that is the big difference between us.'[8] Clay had to make do with permission to deploy armed guards but with orders to use their weapons only in self-defence.

The first test of Soviet resolution came on April 1st, 1948. Two Berlin-bound American trains were held up in sidings when inspectors were barred. Eventually both trains returned to the checkpoint at Helmstedt. British and French passenger trains were treated in the same way.

One of the first to be caught up in the confusion was Jean Eastham, a member of the Auxiliary Territorial Service (ATS), the women's branch of the British Army. With three colleagues, she was on her way to the garrison in west Berlin.

> The Russians stopped the train at Helmstedt and we were ordered to get off. I don't know what happened to the other troops but we and some officers were taken to a villa and told we were detained. We were given a meal then we were put on three buses and taken to the autobahn where they kept us waiting for another three hours. Finally, they let us through but they wouldn't release the truck with our kit so we arrived without our luggage. It was all very exciting.

Two days later, the Russians closed the rail routes from Hamburg and Frankfurt, leaving only the Berlin–Helmstedt line open. Consignment notes for commercial traffic to and from Berlin were required to be stamped in the east sector. Few acceptable consignment notes were issued. A protest note reminding Sokolovsky of the verbal agreement with Marshal Zhukov for the 'free and unrestricted use of the established corridors' brought the uncompromising rejoinder: 'There was not and there cannot be any agreement concerning disorderly and uncontrolled traffic and freight and personnel through the territory of the Soviet zone.'

Clay delivered a stark warning to his political masters:

We have lost Czechoslovakia, Norway is threatened ... When Berlin falls, Western Germany will be next ... we must not budge ... If we withdraw, our position in Europe is threatened. If America does not understand this now ... then it never will and communism will run rampant.

He added:

I believe the future of democracy requires us to stay ... This is not a heroic pose because there will be nothing heroic in having to take humiliation without retaliation.

Clay's political adviser, Robert Murphy, spelt out what was at stake:

The charge that the Western powers have destroyed the Control Council constitutes an important element in the Soviet plan to force all three Western powers out of Berlin, in order to liquidate this remaining 'centre of reaction' east of the iron curtain. The next step may be a Soviet ... demand for the withdrawal from Berlin of the Western powers. In view of the prospect that such an ultimatum would be rejected, the Soviets may move obliquely,

endeavouring to make it increasingly impossible or unprof-
itable for the Western powers to remain on; for example, by
interfering with the slender communication lines between
Berlin and the Western zone, taking further action towards
splitting up the city and bearing down on non-communist
political parties in the Soviet sector ...

Our Berlin position is delicate and difficult. Our withdrawal, either voluntary or involuntary, would have severe
psychological repercussions which would, at this critical
stage in the European situation, extend far beyond the
boundaries of Berlin and even Germany. The Soviets realise this full well.

In an attempt to find out just how far the Russians were prepared
to go, Clay sent a train with armed guards across the zonal border with orders not to stop for inspection. After entering Soviet
territory, the train was diverted from the main line onto a siding
where, Clay related, 'It remained for a few days until it withdrew
rather ignominiously'.

In London, Bevin held to his view that Britain 'must stay' in
Berlin. 'An early withdrawal cannot be contemplated.' But he
was only too aware of Allied vulnerability. 'There is nowhere in
the world', he observed, 'where we can make difficulties for the
Russians in the same way as they can make difficulties for
the Western Powers in Berlin without risk of serious damage to
ourselves.'[9]

Acutely aware of budget restraints, the Foreign Office focused
on inexpensive measures to persuade Berliners that they were not
about to be abandoned. These ranged from clearing war damage
('concentrating on re-glassing the windows of dwelling houses')
and a crackdown on communist 'organized hooliganism' to the

restoration of a theatre and the opening of an Anglo-American club.[10] It was little enough. The sense was of doing something, however modest, to keep at bay the fear that a still fragile British economy could not afford open-ended commitments to Berlin. Bevin's advisers agreed with Robertson that the only option was for Britain to 'sit it out and say as little as possible'.[11]

From Washington there were mixed messages. Truman liked Clay's straight talking and sympathised with his assessment that, come what may, the Allies had no choice but to hang on in Berlin. But there were sceptics in the Truman administration, not least the defence secretary, James Forrestal. Though an advocate of a tough line on American–Soviet relations he feared that Anglo-American forces in Germany, below 200,000 in all and mostly poorly trained youngsters dragooned into compulsory military service, were no match for the seasoned million or so Soviet troops backed up by the latest tanks and artillery.

More outspoken was General Omar Bradley who had succeeded Eisenhower as army chief of staff in February 1948. Bradley held to the opinion he had given Eisenhower in the final stages of the war – that Berlin was not worth a fight. Now, he argued that Allied forces simply did not have the strength or the will to stand up to a Soviet challenge in Berlin. He favoured an early announcement of a withdrawal to 'minimise the loss of prestige rather than being forced out by threat'.

As chief strategy adviser, George Kennan proposed settling outstanding questions on Germany with an offer to Russia to accept the withdrawal of all foreign troops. Germany could then be declared neutral territory. Playing down the risk of another European war, Kennan argued that Russia had neither the naval nor air power capable of challenging the West.

Marshall felt himself caught in a pincer movement. The flaw

in Kennan's plan was plain to see. The withdrawal of American troops in Germany implied withdrawal across the Atlantic, whereas for Soviet forces, the fall-back was no further than the Oder–Neisse line marking the border between Germany and Poland. But Marshall was also nervous of giving Clay his head. More than once he considered putting the pugnacious general on the retirement list.

Where was Truman in all this? His record fixes him as a fervent anti-communist, a politician who was determined to uphold American values. But foreign policy was not exclusively about Germany and Berlin. A bigger worry was China where the civil war looked set to end with an overwhelming communist victory (the People's Republic was declared in October 1949). At home, the president had to juggle competing claims on the federal budget while facing down the Pentagon, for which money was no object when it came to modernising the national armoury. With a presidential election due in November and with polls showing him trailing his Republican rival, Thomas Dewey, Truman had no desire for any move deemed reckless or premature. As to Germany, the supreme pragmatist chose to wait on events.

*

Tensions eased a little in Berlin. Though traffic restrictions were still onerous, essential supplies were allowed through, albeit intermittently. The shortfall was made up by increasing the amount of airfreight over which, diplomatically speaking, the Russians had no control. What became known as the Little Lift, from early April through to early June 1948, was a very modest affair – 80 to 100 tons of army rations delivered daily to the 30,000-strong Allied garrisons in Berlin. The British contribution – three Dakotas on daylight round trips – was etched in memories by its unlikely codename, Operation Knicker. One army driver at the Berlin end identified his mission by fixing the appropriate garment to his wing mirror. Reserve stocks were built up, especially of coal brought in by rail. But at best, power stations had only sufficient fuel to last 45 days. Food was reckoned to run out even faster. A cut-off of supplies would leave Berlin on the edge of starvation within 36 days.

West Berliners were said to be 'in a highly nervous state'. They would have been yet more apprehensive had they known of Russian confidence, relayed to Stalin, that 'our control and restrictive measures have dealt a strong blow at the prestige of the American and British in Germany'. The Little Lift had proved 'futile', with the Americans reportedly admitting that it was too costly to continue.

Even allowing for the tendency of Russian intelligence to embellish their dispatches for Stalin's consumption, the Soviet action had undeniably caused consternation in the western camp. The Little Lift was derided by the press. 'Talk of an air bridge is merely picturesque', insisted *The Times*. 'It would be foolish to suppose that, if the worst came to the worst, the Allied community and forces here could be maintained by this means alone.' The implications were spelt out by the *New York Times*: 'Should the Russians maintain transport restrictions the city, which requires 2,000 tons of supplies daily, could not be fed by air. In that case a western Allies' decision to leave could be explained as a diplomatic sacrifice in the interest of the Germans.'

Anxieties intensified when, on April 5th, a Viking passenger aircraft on a scheduled flight from London via Hamburg to Gatow in the British sector encountered a Russian Yak fighter. As the Viking made its approach, the Yak pilot went into a steep climbing turn close to the British plane. Too close, as it happened. In the head-on collision, fifteen lives were lost.

Having immediately ordered fighter escorts for all British passenger planes, Robertson made a protest to Sokolovsky who expressed deep regret along with an assurance that no interference with passenger flights was intended. The fighter escorts were stood down. But a day later, Sokolovsky reversed his position. The accident was entirely the fault of the British pilot who had failed to abide by air safety directives. Could this be true? Robertson was put on the defensive but was vindicated by the subsequent British inquiry which Sokolovsky boycotted. Said Bevin, in the Parliamentary statement: 'We had the wing of the Viking with the Yak's wing embedded in it. We had the undercarriage of the Yak which was locked in the "up" position, thus disproving the Soviet story that the Yak was about to land. We knew that the Berlin Air Safety Centre had no knowledge of the presence in the air of the Yak fighter.' There was no suggestion that the action was deliberate. But the blame rested squarely on the Soviet pilot 'and the foolhardy manner in which he was handling his machine'.

The incident left Sokolovsky in the uncomfortable position of having to explain why he had been unable to fulfil his pledge to protect the air corridors. This he did by calling for a stoppage of all commercial flights and for Soviet approval of all flights through the corridors 24 hours in advance. The Soviet report on the Gatow crash even questioned the existence of a four-power agreement by referring to the corridors as having been 'designated by the Soviet authorities'. A robust response from Clay and Robertson was met by silence, confirming that the Russians were not ready for a showdown that might lead to war. Though there was comfort in this, the odds had shortened on another maverick Russian pilot causing an international crisis.

The Gatow incident strengthened Robertson's resolve.

Temperamentally inclined to be accommodating in the hope of a lasting settlement, his latest public statements took on a harder edge. His speech in Duesseldorf on April 7th made him sound like Clay in one of his more assertive moods: 'We must accept it is a fact that an Iron Curtain splits Germany.' He called for German support for the ideals of west European civilisation in the face of a 'common enemy': 'Make up your minds to stand together against these gentlemen' (he refrained from mentioning their nationality) 'who, with democracy on their lips and truncheons behind their backs, would filch your German freedom from you ... The prospects are good. Go forward and seize them.'

*

Having secured the Brussels Treaty, a second phase of the six powers in London ended on June 7th, 1948 with a clearer idea of where the participants were heading in Germany. The western zones were to be embraced by the Marshall Plan, there was to be a new international control authority for the Ruhr and, in September, an elected assembly was to be called to draft a federal constitution for all of Germany but, failing that, for the west only. Russian claims to share in the Ruhr were rejected and there were to be no more reparations. America, Britain and France pledged to keep troops in Germany until peace was secured.

The weakest link in this united front was France, where fears of Russian aggression were secondary to opposition to any plan that looked to restore Germany as a European power. With no clear government majority in the National Assembly, foreign minister Georges Bidault was inclined to put off firm decisions in a vain attempt to pacify his critics. But delaying tactics proved self-defeating as Anglo-American sympathy turned to irritation. Pushed hard to make up his mind and that of his government,

Bidault survived an acrimonious debate in the Assembly with approval for the London agreements by a vote of 300 to 286.

Stalin took his revenge in Berlin. On April 25th, the Soviet administration had introduced revised and more complex rules for rail freight. Two weeks later, 26 rail wagons of Berlin mail for the west were seized by Russian officials. Next, five coal trains were held up because their documents were 'not in order'. On June 12th, all rail freight from the western zones was suspended over a dispute about the labelling of containers. Later in the day, a Russian commander took direct control of the Klingenberg power station, located in the Soviet sector, but supplying electricity for all of Berlin. Ominous warnings of power cuts were accompanied by propaganda accusations that the Allies were deliberately holding back on food supplies for the city. And so it went on.

Throughout May and early June, the Berlin press reported on new curbs on the movement of goods and people almost on a daily basis. Interruptions in freight traffic were usually justified on grounds that shipments were improperly labelled. Crossing in to or out of the Soviet sector was a gamble on having the relevant papers correct, by Soviet interpretation, in every detail. Delays were interminable.

A political flashpoint was the closing, allegedly for urgent repairs, of the autobahn bridge over the River Elbe near Magdeburg. The only alternative crossing was fifteen miles down-stream where a hand-operated ferry allowed for just two vehicles to cross at a time. A survey by British engineers showed that while the Magdeburg bridge needed patching up, the work did not jus-tify closing the entire highway. Coming on top of all the other bureaucratic irritants, it stretched the short temper of Colonel Frank Howley, American commandant in Berlin, to breaking point. After a long, acrimonious and inconclusive meeting of the

Kommandatura, the four-power administrative authority for the city, Howley announced that he had had enough. 'I'm going home to bed. My deputy will take over.' This caused Colonel Yelizarov, Russian deputy commandant, to jump to his feet. In view of Howley's 'hooligan action', he shouted, it was impossible to continue the meeting. With that, the Russian delegation walked out. As they departed there was an appeal from the chairman: 'But we haven't settled the date of the next meeting.' Yelizarov shot back: 'As far as I'm concerned there won't be a next meeting.' That was the end of four-power control in Berlin.

Meanwhile, preparations for implementing currency reform were gathering pace. Deutschmarks printed in America had been shipped to Germany in sealed containers bearing the cryptic inscription 'Bird Dog'. The terms for exchange were set in Frankfurt where German technicians handling the operation were confined to a small administrative quarter known as the 'Frankfurt cage'. The reichsmark would cease to be legal tender at midnight, Saturday, June 19th. The deutschmark was to be introduced in stages. At the start, every German citizen in the west zones was entitled to exchange 60 reichsmarks for 60 deutschmarks of which the first 40 were paid out on Sunday at local food offices. The remainder was promised within two months. Every employer was to receive 60 new marks for each employee so that wages could be paid at their current level. It was a tightly organised plan, implemented efficiently, though the design of the notes caused irritation.

> The buxom girl on the 50-mark note carried a basket of oranges and tropical fruit, which had not been seen in Germany for years, and a female figure on the 20-mark note seemed to be wearing the Phrygian Cap of France's

Marianne. The male in a loincloth on the 5-mark note was studying a navigation chart and was flanked by a fine ocean-going merchantman of the kind forbidden to Germany by the Potsdam Agreement.[12]

However, these were minor issues. More to the point was the question of what was to happen in Berlin where the overlap between east and west was such as to risk the chaos of two rival currencies? When, on June 18th, the three western military commanders, Clay, Robertson, and the French general Marie-Pierre Koenig, gave notice to Sokolovsky of the imminence of currency reform, they made a point of excluding Berlin from their undertaking, at least for the moment. However, the next day the Soviet authorities announced that 'banknotes issued in the western occupation zones will not be allowed to circulate in the Soviet zone or in Greater Berlin *which is situated in the Soviet zone and is economically a part thereof*.[13] This was followed by a specific threat:

> We give notice to you and the German population of Berlin that we shall apply economic and administrative sanctions which will ensure that only one currency will circulate in Berlin – the currency of the Soviet zone.[14]

If this did not go down well with the Allies, it was received with even less favour by Louise Schroeder, who was standing in for Ernst Reuter as mayor of Berlin. Rejecting the Soviet directive, Schroeder proposed that the two currencies should be circulated on an equal basis throughout the city. She was supported by the Magistrat. On June 23rd, when the city Assembly met at the Rathaus in the Soviet sector to debate the issue, a demonstration by communist agitators brought violence to the streets. That night, power supplies from the eastern sector were cut off and large areas of the city blacked out.

Despite the hostile mob outside the city hall, the Assembly voted overwhelmingly to approve the compromise. As the meeting dispersed, members came under physical attacks, with Jeanette Wolff, a Social Democrat and former concentration camp inmate, suffering severe injuries. An east sector policeman who tried to intervene on the side of law and order was discharged the following day on orders of the Soviet military.

That the challenge would not be allowed to pass was anticipated in Moscow. Despite a warning from the French of 'incalculable consequences' the introduction of the new deutschmark went ahead for all three western sectors of Berlin on June 23rd.

Clay gave the go-ahead without reference to Washington. At the same time, in expectation that the Russians would try to 'force us from Berlin' he held in readiness his armed convoy of 6,000 troops prepared to test a Soviet blockade. Nor was this all. At his headquarters in Wiesbaden, General Curtis LeMay, American air force commander in Europe, prepared for a much tougher reaction to Soviet obduracy. Architect of the infamous firebombing attack on Japanese cities, the cigar-chomping LeMay was known to favour a pre-emptive strike against Soviet airbases in Germany. He was convinced that the neat line-up of aircraft on airstrips in the east sector would make a perfect target.

Western deutschmarks for Berlin, identified by the addition of a large 'B', found favour in the east where the Soviet-approved notes were poorly produced and easily forged. The confusion caused by two competing currencies added yet another complication to the struggle for day-to-day survival. Elsewhere the deutschmark was an immediate success. Products not seen for years began to appear in the shops. The black market retreated as free market confidence took hold.

The Soviet response was to close all land communications between the western zones and Berlin, 'for technical reasons'. Supplies to west Berlin of coal and food, including fresh milk, were stopped. At the same time, electricity was cut off by the Soviet-controlled power stations. The power stations in the Allied sectors had capacity to provide for German homes and factories for only a few hours daily. The Berlin press carried an appeal from Sokolovsky to the people of Berlin. Denouncing the western powers for refusing to agree to reasonable Soviet proposals in the Allied Control Council, for trying to ruin Berlin's economic life by introducing western marks and for trying to split Germany, the Marshal made clear that four-power government of Germany had ended, at least for the time being.

The west countered with a blockade of the entire Soviet zone. An embargo was put on all rail traffic from the west until normal communications with Berlin were restored. This brought to an end monthly deliveries of 250,000 tons of coal and 30,000 tons of steel from the Ruhr. The official reason given was the Soviet failure to return empty railway wagons.

Despite Sokolovsky's announcement that the Allied Kommandatura had 'ceased to exist for all practical purposes' there remained a diplomatic loophole. As Robertson pointed out, by making no formal demand for the Allies' departure from Berlin and by not excluding the possibility of the Control Council and the Kommandatura resuming their duties, the Russians had 'left themselves a line of retreat'.[15] Moreover, the Soviet and satellite foreign ministers' meeting in Warsaw on June 24th confounded expectations by not demanding the dissolution of Bizonia as they had done at earlier gatherings.

Though it was difficult for Bevin to talk directly with Robertson by telephone ('because all lines are tapped by the Russians') he gathered from the military governor that 'stocks are in some respects better than we had anticipated' and that there was 'no cause for immediate alarm'. The British garrison had food for 37 days and the German population for 27 days. Petrol reserves would stretch to ten weeks and coal to six weeks. Still, 'the German population will suffer considerable hardship while industry dependent on electricity will come virtually to a standstill with resultant large-scale unemployment'.[16]

A frantic search began for a solution to the crisis before it deteriorated into a shooting match. From Washington came an appeal to Clay to slow down or even abandon currency reform in Berlin to avoid armed conflict. Clay made a snappy response. 'If the Soviets want war it will not be because of Berlin currency but because they believe this is the right time.' The people of Berlin had demonstrated their hostility to communism. The Allies could not let them down. As the other pacemaker, Bevin was ready to contemplate military action but knew well enough that Britain could only follow in America's wake.

Bevin rejected a much-touted let-out, that of allowing the Russians to feed the whole of Berlin. 'It would not be possible for us to acquiesce in this since we might as well evacuate Berlin to allow the Russians to act in our sectors.' Meanwhile, 'we should put into service as many transport aircraft as possible'.[17] Was this the seed that germinated into a full-blown airlift? Not a bit of it. Relaying his master's voice, Ivone Kirkpatrick, head of the German section of the Foreign Office, made it clear that Bevin 'realises it would not be possible to hope to supply the needs of two million civilian inhabitants of the western sectors by air transport alone'.[18]

So what was to be done? It seemed that no one in the high reaches of government on either side of the Atlantic had a clue.

CHAPTER SIX

Bringing in supplies by air for the Allied garrisons along with a few extras for the Berlin citizenry was a well-established if irregular practice. But while the short-term tighter schedule of deliveries known as the Little Lift served as a morale-booster for the occupying forces, it also suggested that to attempt anything more ambitious was to enter the realm of science fiction. The logistical challenges were simply too great.

One who challenged this consensus was a senior RAF officer, a 47-year-old flying boat veteran who had served on Eisenhower's planning staff for the D-Day invasion and latterly had presided over the inquiry into the mid-air collision between the British Viking passenger aircraft and a Russian Yak fighter. For Air Commodore Rex Waite, success in military planning called for bold thinking. Everybody was telling him that west Berlin could not be sustained by an air bridge. He set out to prove otherwise.

The result was a brilliant exercise in forward planning. Waite identified eight airbases that could be used for loading, six of them, including a flying boat base, under British control and two in the American zone. At the receiving end, west Berlin had only two airports, Gatow and Tempelhof, both of which would need radical upgrading to bear the extra load of traffic. But that was only the start. Waite had to plot a schedule that would allow convoys of aircraft to land safely, unload and take off with precision timing.

Nobody asked him to take on the job. It was just something he felt he could do, like a crossword puzzle. And he did it without assistance. When a journalist saw Waite 'his head bowed over a tiny pocketbook, making drawings and calculations with the stub of a pencil' he had no idea that history was in the making. On June 23rd, he took his draft plan to General Herbert. The commander of the British sector was not impressed. There were too many unanswered questions. Undeterred, Waite returned to his slide rule to produce a more detailed proposal. This time, Herbert was sufficiently taken with the idea to arrange for Waite to make his presentation to the military governor. It gave Robertson pause for thought. While he had no faith in the long-term viability of an airlift, there was certainly a case for a stop-gap measure that would buy time for a negotiated settlement with the Russians. He decided to consult with Clay.

Clay, too, was sceptical but he was short on ideas for breaking the blockade. What he really wanted was to be given a free hand to embark on Operation Truculent, an armoured breakthrough on the ground deploying up to 6,000 troops with artillery backup.

> I am still convinced that a determined movement of convoys with troop protection would reach Berlin and that this might well prevent, rather than build up, Soviet pressures which could lead to war. Nevertheless, I realize fully the inherent dangers in this proposal, since once committed we could not withdraw.

Precisely so. The prospect of another European war caused nightmares in Washington where army secretary Kenneth Royall remained disinclined to accept Clay's assurance that the Russians were bluffing. An armed convoy with orders to shoot its way through was not to be contemplated.

Frustrated by inaction and realising that he was within his rights to act on Waite's initiative without permission from above, Clay ordered General Curtis LeMay to focus exclusively on flying supplies to Berlin. The job went to General Joseph Smith, commander of the military base at Wiesbaden, who was told that he could expect to be relieved of this particular responsibility within 45 days. Twenty-four hours later, the first C-47 Skytrain arrived at Tempelhof. The date was June 26th, 1948. By the end of the day, 25 flights had brought in 80 tons of flour, milk and medicines.

'It was a pretty modest start', as LeMay admitted later. When access to Berlin was relatively trouble-free, the daily delivery of freight by land and water routes was around 13,500 tons. The survival level for the city was reckoned to be around 4,500 tons daily. The carrying capacity of a Skytrain was just 3 tons. For Truman's closest advisers the figures could not add up to anything but an embarrassing fiasco. George Marshall dismissed the Airlift as 'obviously not a solution' while Walter Bedell Smith, US ambassador in Moscow, had 'little faith in the ability of the airlift to supply Berlin'. As a leading commentator, Walter Lippman saw the Airlift as a 'spectacular and temporary solution' which could 'only be carried on ... in the summer months'. Come the fog and rain of a Berlin winter, the 'cost in lives of pilots and crews ... and of money, would be exorbitant'.

The Soviet advantage was strengthened by the absence of any formal agreement on free access to Berlin, except by air. A frantic search of the Allied Control Council files revealed a vague understanding on the movement of passenger and freight trains and there was a British record of talks with Marshal Zhukov which seemed to procure a deal on road traffic. But in the absence of a watertight legal case, the claim to right of entry to Berlin rested on its 'unchallenged continuance over the past three years'.[1]

In Germany, the communist press reported gleefully on the discord and uncertainty in the Allied camps. But in direct communications with Clay and Robertson, the Soviet Marshal Sokolovsky adopted a more conciliatory tone. While insisting on closing the Helmstedt–Berlin autobahn to prevent the 'illegal conveyance of the currency of the western zones', he gave cosy assurances that 'all measures … are being taken' to reopen the railway. He stoutly denied a British claim that 30,000 freight wagons had been expropriated by the Soviet authorities.[2]

The Russians took heart from the gloomy prognostications circulating between the western Allies. The received wisdom in Moscow was of weeks, not months, before the American-led coalition would be forced to choose between using force to break the blockade (which they were almost certain not to do) or accepting Russian terms for keeping a toehold in Berlin, terms which included ditching plans for an independent west Germany.

On Sunday, June 27th, James Forrestal met with Kenneth Royall and under-secretary of state Robert Lovett to agree on the options to be put to the president. Their deliberations produced little that was constructive. Truman was presented with the choice of abandoning Berlin, fighting for the right to stay, or holding on in the short term while looking for a face-saving get-out. The reaction from the White House was Truman's now familiar double act. Having refused even to consider withdrawal ('We are going to stay – period'), he rejected even a partial mobilisation to prepare for the worst, choosing instead 'to deal with the situation as it developed'. Clay was told not to say anything that suggested the possibility of war over Berlin. Bevin was less inhibited.

The abandonment of the many Germans who have stood by us in Berlin would cause such lack of confidence in the Western Zone that we should find it almost impossible to maintain our position there. With the loss of Western Germany we should face not only the collapse of our whole Western system, but the complete domination of Europe by Russia reinforced by a Communist controlled Germany.[3]

Having secured Cabinet backing for staying in Berlin come what may,[4] Air Marshal Sir Arthur Sanders, commander of the British Air Forces of Occupation, was told to allocate 50 aircraft to the supply route. With the promise of more to come, Bevin spoke of building up the Airlift to 'really sensational proportions' at the same time pressing ahead with the London proposals to create an independent government for west Germany. As a deterrent to Russian aggression, he now urged that two squadrons of B-29 Superfortresses, capable with modifications of delivering atomic bombs, should be based in Britain, in easy range of Moscow, to 'persuade the Russians that we mean business'. On Bevin's behalf the request was made via the American embassy to secretary of state Marshall, who wanted assurance that Bevin had fully explored the effect on British public opinion. The assurance was given on Bevin's say so. Meanwhile, Marshall agreed in principle to an easing of diplomatic communication by using London as a clearing house for dispatches that needed to be shared between the Allies. This made Bevin central to decision-making on Berlin. There were wider implications. The Airlift afforded Bevin an opportunity: to bind America closer to the defence of western Europe and to secure Britain's role as essential partner in a trans-Atlantic alliance.

Truman approved the British request for joint military planning on June 29th. An Anglo-American military meeting was held the next day. After Bevin won Cabinet approval on July 13th the National Security Council signed off the dispatch of 60 Superfortresses to British airbases. B-29s were also sent to west Germany. Those landing in England were reported as being on a 30-day routine training mission. Their stay was soon extended to 60 days, then to 90 days before eventually their long-term presence was taken for granted.

How far the Russians saw these manoeuvres as a serious threat is open to question. Even if the B-29s had been adapted for atomic weaponry, America did not yet possess the number of atomic bombs needed to destroy the Soviet war machine, or indeed the scientists capable of assembling a stockpile. It is almost certain that Stalin knew this but he could not ignore the long-term implications. Nor indeed could the British government. Bevin had taken the first critical step towards delegating to Washington the right to decide if and when to press the atomic button. While prior consultation was assumed, in no way could it be guaranteed. But for now there were more immediate concerns for Bevin to worry about.

*

Before Britain could engage fully in the Airlift there were practicalities to be overcome, starting with the shortage of aircraft and aircrews. Briefed by Sir William Strang, head of the German section of the Foreign Office, Bevin refused to be downhearted. 'Get me some figures I can lean on', he ordered. Strang did so by leasing or buying back planes, mostly Douglas Dakotas, that had been sold off at the end of the war, including a fleet from the American west coast.[5] A York Avro, technically obsolescent but still the chief transport plane for the RAF, arrived in Berlin on June 28th with 8.5 tons of provisions reserved for the British garrison. The operation order for the air supply of west Berlin was signed on

June 30th. The following day British C-47 Dakotas (Skytrains by another name) carried 311 tons of food for German civilians. The Airlift was originally codenamed Operation Carter Paterson after Britain's leading removal firm, but the Russians were quick to pick up on the inference that Britain was preparing to exit Berlin. Carter Paterson became Operation Plainfare. The American share of the action was dubbed by General Smith: 'Hell, we're hauling grub. Let's call it Operation Vittles.' Between themselves, Berliners spoke of Operation Cowboy. It was an apt description.

The great majority of Berliners were unattracted by communism; a majority was almost certainly opposed to communism, a sentiment reinforced by a deep-rooted hostility to Slavic people in general and to Russians in particular. The experience of occupation had done nothing to mitigate gut prejudice. Popular thinking strongly favoured western values. This proved to be so whenever elections were held. In west Berlin, mass meetings to support democracy were a regular feature of daily life. In January 1948, a survey of west Berlin radio listeners showed 68 per cent favouring American radio (RIAS) and north-west German radio over the communist-controlled Radio Berlin.

But anti communism did not necessarily equate with open defiance. A precarious existence made for caution. If the western powers pulled out of Berlin, as well they might, those who had stood up to be counted would be the first to be shot down. One who was prepared, even eager, to take the risk was Ernst Reuter, the elected mayor of Berlin who had been pushed out of the job by the Russians even before he had started. This arbitrary rejection of a popular vote had the reverse of the intended effect by boosting Reuter's authority. He was the undisputed champion of political freedom. If the Airlift was to gain momentum, Clay needed Reuter's backing. The meeting was in Clay's office. Not speaking German, the military governor usually worked through interpreters. But Reuter was fluent in English. It helped that the two leaders could exchange views openly without the otherwise inevitable pauses for translation. Clay did not pull punches. 'I want you to know this', he told Reuter:

> No matter what we may do, the Berliners are going to be short of fuel. They are going to be short of electricity. I don't believe they are going to be short of food. But I am sure there are going to be times when they are going to be very cold, and feel very miserable. Unless they are willing to take this and stay with us, we can't win this. If we are subjecting them to a type and kind of treatment which they are unwilling to stand and they break on us, our whole lift will have failed. And I don't want to go into it unless you understand that fully, unless you are convinced that the Berliners will take it.[6]

Though like many others, Reuter found it hard to believe in the Airlift, he was quick to offer his blessing. 'General, I can assure you and I do assure you that the Berliners will take it.'

The commitment was mutual. Clay's public statements were unequivocal. 'Thousands of Germans have courageously expressed their opposition to communism. We must not destroy their confidence by any indication of departure from Berlin.' Appeals to him to evacuate the dependents of the US garrison were given a dusty answer. American servicemen who were concerned for their families were told that if they sent home their wives and children they too would have to leave. Almost all applications were promptly withdrawn. Among the few who took up the option was General Bradley's son-in-law who was brought home along with his family.

To have exposed them to the risk of falling into Soviet hands, said Bradley, would have clouded his judgement.

What of the third partner in the western administration of Berlin? Though central to the alliance, France, for the most part, was a bystander of the Airlift. Its military carriers, JU-52s, were slow and small but, in any case, were fully allocated to colonial duties in North Africa and South East Asia. Even supplying the French garrison in Berlin was dependent on American deliveries. Then again, the language barrier complicated air traffic control. The occasional JU-52 was soon phased out of the operation.

Until late June with the arrival of the more capacious C-54 Skymasters, capable of carrying up to 10 tons, the Airlift had all the makings of a boy's adventure. For those directly involved, in the air and on the ground, it brought back the wartime spirit of working together for a common cause. In the profusion of memories and anecdotes in the early months it is hard to find examples of doubt or resentment at being pulled in to an enterprise that was fraught with risk. This in large part was because most of the American and British aircrews were professionals who quickly caught on to the excitement of a heroic mission that was more humanitarian than belligerent. But aircrews were in short supply. Many had been demobilised, others were doing duty in the Pacific, mopping up after the Japanese surrender.

Among those for whom service in Germany was an unexpected break in routine was Flight Lieutenant, later Air Vice Marshal John Curtiss, a navigator with 5 Squadron in Abingdon near Oxford. Having been transferred from the now disbanded Bomber Command to Transport Command, Curtiss had spent the early part of his peacetime career with the RAF dropping unwanted bombs over the North Sea and then ferrying home Indian troops. Now he was looking forward to his posting to Singapore. It was not to be. Instead of the Far East, he was told that his journey's end had been changed to Wunstorf airbase near Hannover. He could expect a short stay. 'You'll soon be back', he was assured. 'Take kit for ten days.' As it turned out, Curtiss was at Wunstorf for a year, recording 263 round flights to Berlin.

Built in 1924, Wunstorf had seen out the war as a Luftwaffe training base. Conditions were primitive. For Hammond Innes, who visited Wunstorf to research a novel, the aircrews' quarters were like an enormous jail.

> Long concrete corridors echoed to ribald laughter and the splash of water from communal washrooms. The rooms were like cells, small dormitories with two or three beds. One room we went into by mistake was in darkness with the blackout blinds drawn. The occupants were asleep and they cursed us as we switched on the light. Through the open doors of other rooms we saw men playing cards, reading, talking, going to bed, getting up. All the life of Wunstorf was here in these electrically-lit, echoing corridors. In the washrooms men in uniform were washing next to men in pyjamas quietly shaving as though it were early morning.[7]

Meals were taken at odd times and for most of the day crews had to exist on NAAFI buns. 'Added to which', says John Higgins, another Airlift veteran, 'NAAFI buns were notorious. If you got hit by one it could kill you.' When Dickie Arscott, a flight lieutenant with 46 Squadron, arrived at Wunstorf he was told that his bed for the first night was a billiard table. 'It was sheer chaos. When I woke up, I simply joined a queue for the first available aircraft. The loading party was an army platoon led by a second lieutenant.

Learning on the job there was always a risk they would overload.'
After two weeks of flying three return trips to Berlin every day,
Arscott was recalled for interview for a permanent commission.
His medical revealed that the Wunstorf experience had cost him
two stone (28 pounds) in weight. He was sent home for a week
to recover.

It didn't help that the June weather for 1948 was typified by
persistent rain and high winds. Wunstorf and mud were synonymous. On July 2nd, it rained solidly for eighteen hours. As a result,
26 Dakotas were put out of action by electrical troubles. To taxi
his York out of the glutinous mess that was his parking space,
Squadron Leader Best had to rev all four engines at half power.
Immediately he hit the perimeter track he shut the throttles and
clamped the brakes to stop the aircraft from skidding into the mud
on the far side of the runway.

When the fleet of Dakotas at Wunstorf was reinforced by heavier four-engined York aircraft taken off the routes to Singapore
and India, the base was close to bursting point. With an operations room equipped with nothing more than a Perspex board
for plotting incoming and outgoing traffic, it was every pilot for
himself. 'It was by guess and by God', recalled Air Vice Marshal
Larry Lamb, then a flight lieutenant. Loading for a quick take-off,
he had to climb along the fuselage over tightly packed cargo to get
to the front of the aircraft.

Learning on the job brought some useful advice for pilots of
converted bombers designated for carrying flour. 'Just stack the
sacks from front to rear until she drops back on her tail. Then start
the engines so that the plane can thrust forward on to its nose. It
will level itself off without trouble.'

Sorting out the confusion at Wunstorf was not made easier
by a divided command. Technically in charge was Group Captain

Wally Biggar who was responsible for all air transport resources allocated to the British Air Forces of Occupation (BAFO). But he shared authority with Group Captain 'Hetty' Hyde representing Transport Command. To complicate matters, the army took care of the loading and unloading of aircraft. There were even civilian administrators representing the Control Commission getting in on the act. It was not until the lines of responsibility were clearly defined that a start could be made on upgrading Wunstorf. Eventually, Biggar was sent off to Fassberg, another airbase in urgent need of renovation, while Hyde gave the orders at Wunstorf.

The conversion of Fassberg from a former Luftwaffe fighter station to a base for Transport Command was an ambitious project. Living quarters were of a reasonable standard but a new pierced steel planking (PSP) runway had to be built, together with hard stands and five miles of railway sidings, involving the clearing of five acres of forest. While the work progressed, Fassberg was operational by July 27th. First shared with the USAF, the base was soon to be turned over entirely to Operation Vittles.

The two USAF bases – Rhein-Main, outside Frankfurt, and Wiesbaden – were better prepared. Rebuilt after the war, Rhein-Main boasted a 6,000ft concrete runway with most of the supporting infrastructure. But since no one had anticipated the Airlift, the inadequate loading dock came in for criticism. And Rhein-Main was not waterproof. Aircrews knew it as Rhein-Mud. At Wiesbaden, another former Luftwaffe fighter base, there was a 5,500ft concrete runway and a loading dock served by mechanical loading equipment.

The chief drawback to both American bases was their distance from Berlin. Rhein-Main was 280 miles from the city, while the British base at Fassberg was half the distance and could thus

Gathering firewood in the Tiergarten district of Berlin. Few trees were left standing.

Photo: Landesarchiv Berlin/N.N.

Construction workers at Tegel airport take time off for a potato soup lunch.

Photo: Landesarchiv Berlin/N.N.

Most of the construction workers at Tegel airport were women.

Runway construction work at Tegel.

Berliners watch an aircraft taking off from Tempelhof.

Photos: Landesarchiv Berlin / N.N.

C-47 Skytrains waiting to unload at Tempelhof. In the background, B-17 Flying Fortresses.

(*this page, above*) A Sunderland flying boat lands on Lake Havel with a cargo of salt.

(*this page, below*) Children from Berlin are taken to a flying boat on Lake Havel, to be flown to the West.

(*opposite, top*) After suffering brake failure, a C-54 Skymaster burns after running off the end of the runway at Tempelhof.

(*opposite, bottom*) The remains of the C-47 that crashed into an apartment building on the approach to Tempelhof.

Photos: Landesarchiv Berlin / N.N.

Berliners watch as a C-47 comes in to land at Tempelhof.

C-47s being unloaded at Tempelhof.

With chocolate an expensive rarity, a young Berliner enjoys Hershey Bars donated from the USA.

Photos: Landesarchiv Berlin / N.N.

Suspiciously well dressed Berlin children re-enact the Airlift for a propaganda photograph.

The final flight of Operation Vittles, showing the total amount of freight moved in the operation.

US pilot Lieutenant Gail Halvorsen, who dropped candy to the children of Berlin and became a goodwill ambassador for the Airlift.

provide for more round trips a day. Assuming, of course, that planes were in a fit state to take off. More often than not, they were in no condition to fly. Maintenance crews had to work round the clock. With near-continuous flying, technical faults were unending. The shortage of spares was such that some of the older aircraft had to be cannibalised to keep the rest in the air. Geoff Smith remembered:

> A Dakota had navigation light problems because a bulb had failed. We had no spare bulbs, so what could we do? We had to push him to one side because he couldn't fly in the dark. The next aircraft to come in with a minor problem, whatever it was – the flight sergeant told us, 'go and pinch a replacement off that one, he's not going anywhere!' You pinched off one to get the other working.
>
> That Dakota was a perfectly serviceable aircraft apart from one bulb; within three weeks it looked like a wreck – everything had gone – wheels, undercarriage, all the navigation lights, instruments were all taken out.

Pre-flight inspections with engineers working on twelve-hour shifts were not unusual. The least favoured, known as the 'graveyard shift', extended into the small hours with maintenance by torchlight. Fear of a rushed job causing an accident could weigh on a young man's conscience. Gordon Westwell recalls a fatal crash at Wunstorf.

> It was an aircraft I'd serviced. The crew said there was a small cable they thought wanted changing, so I changed it. I also found that the plane needed a wheel change. The tyres on an aircraft spin so fast when it lands there's a chance

the tyre will move round the rim – there are two white lines and once it moves beyond that you change it – that's the type of problem it was. I reported it and the work was done but the York crashed on take-off and all the crew were killed. It was a worry because we didn't know what the problem was. It turned out to be engine failure, but when you're 19, it's a big worry.

The Americans flew into Tempelhof, close to the city centre; the British used Gatow, an airfield set among pine trees in a south-west suburb of Berlin, a short walk from the Russian boundary. Berlin's most visible reminder of the Airlift, Tempelhof was built to match Hitler's grandiose schemes for making the German capital the world's eighth wonder. With its limestone cladding, the crescent-shaped terminal, over a kilometre end to end and still one of Europe's largest buildings, has a lightness rarely associated with totalitarian architecture. Tempelhof was unfinished at the beginning of the war. Designs for a broad tree-lined boulevard leading under a triumphal arch towards a great hall, close to the city centre, remained on the drawing board. The architect's models gave Hitler one of his few pleasures as he pictured the excitement of thousands of his followers gathered to marvel at Luftwaffe displays.

But however kind on the eye, Tempelhof was not best suited to heavy traffic. Surrounded by five-storey apartment blocks, it was also often fogbound. At the start of the Airlift, the airport had not a single concrete runway. A new PSP runway was quickly in place but this began to give way with the arrival of the first C-54 Skymasters, a much heavier version of the Skytrain. As the Airlift gathered pace, work started on a concrete runway which opened to traffic in September. A second runway was finished a month later.

To reduce the risks of an approach in bad weather and to avoid an encounter with one of the apartment buildings, a flare path was erected across a neighbouring cemetery. The church spire had to be replaced by a flat roof. With jaw-dropping hypocrisy, the communist press railed against this 'sacrilegious act'.

Gatow was also in need of an upgrade. Neither of its two runways, one concrete, the other steel planking, were suitable for anything but small light aircraft. A new half-constructed concrete runway was scheduled to open at the end of the year. The sense of urgency occasioned by the Airlift reduced the work time to six weeks. At the same time, the steel runway was extended to 2,000 yards and high-intensity lighting was installed.

With the scarcity of equipment and building materials, improvisation was called for. The Russians had purloined much of Berlin's railway track but had left the rock ballast. Lorry load after lorry load was taken to Gatow. A factory producing tarmac was found just inside the Russian sector. Sympathetic east Berliners worked at night to roll barrels through the wire. When demand outstripped supply, the gap was filled by salvaging the road surface in districts worst hit by bombs.

George Newman was responsible for the construction equipment at Gatow.

We had bulldozers, graders, cranes, stone crushers, rollers and dumpers. Some of these machines had to be flown in and they had to be weld cut to get them into the plane. Once in Berlin they were either riveted together again or welded together using fish plates.[8]

The call went out for steamrollers, however old and dilapidated. One patriotic driver brought his roller from Leipzig at the centre of the Russian zone. At each checkpoint he explained that he had work to do just a few miles on. Who could have doubted him? Among the first to fly into the upgraded Gatow was John Curtiss.

> Setting course for the first of three radar beacons, we normally flew at 1,500 to 2,000 feet. When we were some 60 miles from Gatow we called up to give our landing time and load. From then on it was quite straightforward though it could be a trifle nail-biting in bad weather. The worst moments were before we had parallel strips for takeoff and landing, particularly when the aircraft taking off in front of us was a bit slow.
>
> I overheard an American pilot who was on the approach when a civil airline Halifax, painted bright red, was taking its time before rolling. Over the radio came his heartfelt words, 'If that goddam flying fire engine doesn't haul his ass off the runway pronto, he's going to get 80,000 lbs of pulsating aluminium up his backside.'

It was quickly resolved that no aircraft should remain on the ground at Gatow for more than 50 minutes, whatever the cargo, or stand on the unloading apron with its doors open for more than 30 minutes. With its excellent ground control approach, it was not long before Gatow was the world's busiest airport, handling three times the traffic of New York's LaGuardia.

*

It came as a surprise to many that the Russians, having declared a blockade, did not immediately bring down all the barriers to make it fully effective. But short of building a dividing wall, which had to wait until 1961, it wasn't easy to split east and west Berlin into watertight compartments. There were strong economic, social and service links between the sectors. It was odd, for example, that electricity for the Russian radio station, which spewed out anti-western propaganda day and night, was supplied by a power station in the west. Then again, electricity for Gatow came from a power station just over the Soviet boundary.

The railway system took no account of artificial barriers. Over 80,000 Berliners crossed the city each day on their way to work. Because canal barges had to pass through the British sector, goods said to be for Soviet consumption were often dropped off before they crossed the checkpoint. The black market revived. There were even Free Shops in the east that accepted the very deutschmarks the Russians were supposed to be intent on outlawing. Truckloads of foodstuffs bearing Soviet-zone destination papers were unloaded in the west.

Allied forces with rations to spare were quick to pick up on opportunities to supplement their pay.

> There was a bombed-out road near an old army barracks and there was just one house left. It belonged to Frau Schmidt who was our local black market lady. She'd tell us the current price of goods like coffee and cigarettes and if we wanted to sell to her we could. She had connections everywhere.

There is much anecdotal evidence of pilfering by Allied soldiers. Products with a high price tag on the black market such as sugar were liable to go missing from storage. Offences were rarely punished or reported in the press. One GI with an enterprising German girlfriend made a small fortune. When caught he was let off with demotion and a fine.

There were also more formal economic ties between east and

west that were hard to break. In late June, Marshal Sokolovsky was at a meeting of the East German Industrial Committee where he heard, apparently for the first time, of the impact on the Russian zone if the west decided to retaliate by cutting off trade between west and east Germany. Sugar refineries would suffer if western steel piping was not delivered, canneries would fall idle without western raw materials, the Baltic fishing fleet depended on spare parts from the west, and heavy industry, including steel, would be crippled if imports were cut off.

When the Russians stopped milk deliveries to the west the retaliation was to suspend meat sales to the east. After the Berlin Food Agreement was cancelled by the Russians on June 20th, food from the Soviet zone was reserved for the east sector of the city. There again, American-supplied flour was moved to secure ware-houses in the west.

The Russians did their best to frustrate the movement of goods within the western sectors.

When the planes at Gatow had been unloaded onto trucks, the trucks then drove along the Ritterfeld-Damm to the junction at the Potsdamer Chaussee where they turned right and proceeded to Spandau storage depot at Eiswerder. It was at this junction that the Russians erected a road barrier to prevent the trucks from proceeding along the Potsdamer Chaussee. A platoon of infantry troops were readily sent out and under the cover of riflemen, removed the barrier.

A few days later another attempt was made by the Russians to hinder the transport. This time, they mounted two searchlights about 1,000 Watts endeavouring to blind the truck drivers as they approached the road junction.

As soon as we received notice of this, we transported a 35 kW generator to the site, rigged up a couple of 2,000 W lamps and positioned them so that they counter-blinded the Russian lamps. This game went on for a few days and I visited the site every morning about 10 o'clock. Just in time for the canteen wagon which arrived about 10.30 to provide tea and wads [buns] for the troops who were dug-in on the opposite side of the road to the Russians. The WVS [Women's Voluntary Service] ladies who served us, also offered tea and cake to the Russians and so we finished up, the Russians on their side of the barrier and us on the other side, drinking tea and sharing fags.[9]

There was as much disruption in the air as on the ground, as Frank Somers experienced.

We were flying into Berlin three times a day, and on at least one occasion we were buzzed by Russian aircraft who tried to force us down. A squadron of Russian fighters – LA5s. There were about ten of them. It was frightening. We had nowhere to land   the weather was very bad. But they broke off their engagement and we carried on as if nothing had happened.

Soviet fighters straying into the air corridor induced extra caution into the Airlift. Pilots were told to stay well within the designated air lanes and fly higher than 5,000 feet. This was not enough for the Soviet representatives at the Air Safety Centre who protested against the 'rupture of traffic regulations' by American planes. Since the rules of the air over Berlin were almost entirely an American initiative, this took some swallowing.

A few counter-hits helped to raise Anglo-American morale. US Colonel Frank Howley was quick to find ways of needling his Russian opposite number. When he discovered that Sokolovsky's house was serviced by a gas main from the west, he switched off the power. Compelled to find alternative accommodation, Sokolovsky had to bear another indignity when, citing a boundary violation, Howley confiscated his removal van.

With other tricks up his sleeve, the American commander would have played a rougher game had he been allowed. Instead, Russian soldiers caught on night-time foraging expeditions, stealing anything they could carry, were merely sent back to their own lines. Anglo-American forces had to be more careful. Investigating a hold-up of traffic at Wittenberg in mid-July, John Sims was arrested as a spy and thrown into a damp cell. He was there for three days. 'A Russian major did everything he could to humiliate me in front of some Russian soldiers.' A long statement, in Russian, was read out to him. Did he agree to it? Sims had not understood a word but he nodded assent. After that, a fellow officer was allowed in to see him and he was escorted back to the British sector.

Germans who worked with the British and Americans were given even less consideration. Policemen who strayed over the Russian boundary were liable to be arrested and beaten up. Some of them were never accounted for. Potsdamerplatz, where the American, British and Soviet sectors met, was not a place to hang around, particularly at night.

The make or break for the Airlift was the delivery of coal, the essential source of commercial and domestic power. As with every other aspect of the Airlift, there was no scarcity of pundits ready to declare, without fear of contradiction, that it could not be done. Carrying significant quantities of coal by air was a fantasy that even Jules Verne would have scorned. But Clay was ready to give it a try. There are various accounts of his telephone conversation with LeMay but they agree on substance. Clay came quickly to the point.

'Have you any planes there that can carry coal?'

'Carry what?' asked LeMay.

'Coal', repeated Clay.

'We must have a bad connection', said LeMay. 'It sounds as if you are asking if we have planes for carrying coal.'

'Yes, that's what I said – coal.'

LeMay rallied. 'The air force can deliver anything.'

And it did.

The first load of airborne coal, 10 tons in 200 bags, landed at Tempelhof on July 7th. It was unloaded in fifteen minutes.

Among aircrews, coal was not a favoured cargo. They complained of headaches and breathing problems. Moreover, coal dust corroded control cables and electrical connections. A suggested alternative was to pack the coal in strong sacks which could then be heaved out of planes on a low flypast. Unfortunately, there were not that many safe open areas. In any case, a few trial runs revealed that the coal turned to dust when it hit the ground.

In the short run, canvas navy-surplus duffel bags were judged the best coal sacks. These were eventually replaced by multi-ply paper sacks, said to be virtually dust-tight. Aircrews tell a different story. There were those who found wheat growing under the floorboards of their aircraft, the result of a potent mix of coal dust, flour and rainwater. Twenty years after the Airlift, what had been coal-carrying planes gave off puffs of black dust when they landed. Since the coal came from the Ruhr in the British zone, from July on, it was British planes that did most of the carrying.

A less bulky cargo than coal but one equally challenging was salt. Though essential for a minimum diet, salt corroded cables and attacked the airframe. The solution was to enlist the Sunderland flying boats of RAF Coastal Command which had airframes treated to resist corrosion and control wires in the roof where salt could not get to them. Based at Finkenwerder on the River Elbe near Hamburg, the Sunderlands flew to Lake Havel, west of Gatow, delivering up to 30 tons of salt a day. The cargo was taken into Berlin by a fleet of some 40 barges that had been left moored on the lake at the end of the war. With a total load of 15,000 tons, the canal traffic between the Havel and Berlin was more economical in fuel than any other transport. In charge of the operation was an eighteen-year-old Royal Service Corps second lieutenant, Courtenay Latimer.

> I only got the job because I'd been a naval cadet for four years and was supposed to know all about nautical things. The Havel lake, shaped like a giant boomerang, was partly in the British, partly in the American sector. At the elbow of the boomerang, under the trees of the Grunewald, was our Water Base. The Engineers had built us a hut, like a large rabbit hutch, on the deck of a derelict barge. This was our office, containing a desk, telephone, three chairs and a stove.

To unload the Sunderlands, a ramshackle fleet had been gathered consisting of a launch, two diesel tugs ('noisy, smelly little steel bathtubs'), one elegant motor cruiser and 26 pontoons.

The Anglo-German workforce was on duty from 4.30 in the morning, ready for the first flying boat of the day to arrive at 5.00.

We were ferried across to our barge by Herman who had charge of the launch. The lake was beautiful at that early hour – silent, misty and mysterious. And every morning, as we made our crossing, we bobbed a solitary fisherman in a black skiff anchored in the reeds. He never so much as turned his head.

Courtenay Latimer never tired of watching the approach of a flying boat, 'skimming along the water before settling heavily and taxi-ing like a great swan to its mooring'. It was met by the tugs with the pontoons lashed to their sides. As they went in under the Sunderland's wings the doors opened for the unloading, 5 tons of salt to each aircraft. 'Speed was essential. A Sunderland could be unloaded and off again in twelve minutes.'

When, late in the year, Lake Havel froze, the new Handley Page Haltons, the civil version of the Halifax bomber, were able to carry salt in panniers slung under the fuselage and land conventionally.

A priority was to maximise carrying capacity. By jettisoning excess equipment, the average load of an RAF Dakota was increased from 2 to just over 3 tons. But more was achieved by giving closer attention to cargo weight and content. There was to be no more fresh bread, which contained 30 per cent of its own weight in water. Instead, bags of flour were brought in, even though this meant finding coal for baking. Fresh potatoes gave way to the dehydrated variety, much less tasty but also much lighter.

The first package of Pom [dried potato] was like a magic show. Will it really turn into something or will it be all lumpy? Three neighbours watched. They didn't really dare try it. Mother was more resolute. 'It's getting thick! Look! It's getting good and thick', cried Frau Schulze, and the first dehydrated potato soup with mother's green vegetables cut up in it tasted wonderful to all of us.[10]

Certain goods, such as newsprint and cigars made from German home-grown tobacco, were given a high rating as morale-boosters. Under the same heading came a grand piano for the Berlin Philharmonic and the regimental goat of the Royal Welch Fusiliers. And, of course, space had to be found for medical supplies. These included 2,000 rubber hot water bottles for the sick and aged. Packaging, normally 25 per cent of total weight, was reduced to 6 per cent by replacing tins and wooden boxes by sacks and light cardboard containers.

The Airlift was led and managed by the Anglo-American military but the hard labour – loading and unloading, runway and road construction, fetching and carrying – was carried out by thousands of Berliners working round the clock.

'No sooner had the aircraft come to a standstill and our engineer had opened the door, there were three or four Berliners standing right in that door', says George Newman. 'The truck was already backing up to the plane before our props had even stopped turning. The men looked at those sacks of flour and you could tell what they meant to them. I think that this was their ticket to freedom, that if enough of those sacks came through, they'd be able to stay in Berlin, they'd be able to stay free.'

When coal bags were unloaded, women sweepers gathered up the spillings; even an ounce of coal was precious in Berlin. Children were keen to get involved. Horst Molkenhuhr was allowed out of school every third day to join the workforce at Tempelhof, but only for the first month of the Airlift. Seventeen minutes were granted for unloading the largest aircraft. A Dakota could be cleared in ten minutes.

Workers were given a midday meal – hot corned beef, dried potatoes, bread and margarine. Later in the year, restrooms with baths were built.

Though contact between aircrews and ground workers was sporadic, the shared experience of making history inspired a mutual respect, a notable achievement so soon after the end of the war.

Having lost two brothers to fighting in the Aegean in 1943, John Huggins, a dispatch rider in Berlin, was not easily given to charitable impulses. Yet the sheer determination of Berliners to survive and to recreate their city caused him to change his outlook.

I saw women clearing bombsites with their bare hands. At the back of a restaurant I saw a mother with two young children waiting for the scrapings to come out. These people didn't ask for a war any more than my family who lived through the London blitz.

John decided to do something about it.

I used to fill my pannier bags with NAAFI cakes, vile things though they were, then ride to a place just off the Kaiserdamm where I doled them out to the kids. They would wait for hours for the English airman to turn up on his motorbike to give them these cakes. Later, it got better when I collected our lads' chocolate rations to hand out.

Courtenay Latimer still recalls with affection his team of German helpers who met the Sunderlands on Lake Havel.

Karl-Heinz Heinig, the foreman, was everywhere, manifests fluttering on his clipboard. He wore, probably illegally, the sand-coloured peak cap of the Africa Korps; he had been one of Rommel's men though he never talked about it. Herr Schmidt, the interpreter, was an older man, probably about 45, but he seemed old to me. Pop, the driver of the motor cruiser, was the noisiest member of a very noisy workforce. An old man with a battered, pugnacious face, he was fond of jokes. I never understood his quick wit or the reasons for the gusts of laughter from the stevedores as they toiled with the bags of salt. When I asked Schmidt to translate, he became evasive. Probably the jokes were at my expense. These fellows were half starved, yet they were always cheerful, crackling with repartee.

One incident stands out in the memories of a young subaltern in 1948 Berlin.

It was a warmish day when Schmidt turned up with a great woolly scarf wound round his neck. I teased him. 'It's not that cold. What will you wear in winter?' He smiled bleakly, a droplet gleaming at the end of his nose, then said, 'We feel the cold because we don't have enough to eat, Mr Latimer. It will get much colder and perhaps the airlift will fail. This lake will freeze. How do you think it will be for those of us who work here when you have gone back to England?'

July got off to a bad start with a fruitless exchange between the Allies and the Soviet Union. America, Britain and France offered open-ended negotiations on Berlin on condition that the blockade was lifted. After two weeks of silence, the response was a blunt refusal to accept any preconditions. The idea that four-power talks could be limited to Berlin alone was dismissed as 'laughable'. 'Talks could be effective', said Molotov, 'only if they were not limited to the administration of Berlin since that question cannot be severed from the general question of four-power control of Germany.' For good measure and to avoid any misunderstanding, he added: 'Berlin lies at the centre of the Soviet zone and is part of that zone.'

On July 2nd, General Smith announced his latest target for the Airlift. Four hundred and fifty flights daily to Berlin by a fleet of 52 four-engine C-54 Skymasters and 100 twin-engine C-47 Skytrains would carry 'substantially more than 1,000 tons' for every round trip. The British contribution was predicted to be around 750 tons. This was still a long way short of target. Truman stood by his press statement of July 1st, describing Berlin as a 'beleaguered garrison' that would be sustained by all possible means, but he held back from spelling out what this meant in practical terms. Only Bevin, who spoke in the same defiant terms in the House of Commons, openly declared his faith in the success of the Airlift. But the figures did not add up. West Berlin needed 2,000 tons of food plus 3,000 tons of coal and other essential supplies on a daily basis. Operations Vittles and Plainfare combined rarely exceeded 1,500 tons.

Still, it was a measure of Bevin's stature in his party and in government that the normally disruptive far left gave him its full backing to persevere in Berlin. Only two years earlier, when the Social Democrats in the east zone had been dragooned into a merger with the communists, 24 members of the British Parliamentary Labour party had sent a telegram of congratulations to the leaders of the newly formed SED, praising what they then believed to be a 'victory for democracy'. How times had changed.

Meanwhile, the Russians were still holding to the fiction that there really was no blockade, that it was simply 'technical difficulties' on roads and railways that had led to the stoppage of traffic. But at a meeting between Sokolovsky and the Allied military governors on July 3rd, the Soviet commander came clean. Once the current problems had been solved, there could be no guarantee that they would not recur elsewhere. There could be no misunderstanding. The western sectors of Berlin would remain under siege until the Allies gave up on plans to create an independent west Germany. A note of protest at the continuation of the blockade produced the repetitious offer from Moscow to 'secure by its own means adequate supplies for all greater Berlin', in other words, a Soviet takeover of the city.

Despite all that was being achieved by the Airlift, this still seemed to be the likeliest outcome. As an American defence official remarked, 'If you're damned fool enough to let somebody slam a door on your finger, the first thing you do is to pull your finger out'.

CHAPTER SEVEN

B erlin was a machine for churning out rumours and lies. In newspapers, cinemas and on radio, reporting and propaganda were synonymous. For the first few weeks of the blockade, the Soviet-controlled media had the edge. While few were deceived by mob tactics dressed up as 'spontaneous' demonstrations of popular opinion, repeated efforts to portray the Airlift as a capitalist enterprise destined to fail, though none too subtle, were persuasive.

A free press on both sides of the Atlantic cultivated uncertainty. With little else to go on, reporters in pursuit of a story were liable to give credence to claims of Soviet invincibility while opinion leaders took the side of war-weary readers who had no desire to provoke the Russian bear. As to the logistics of the Airlift, the received wisdom held that a plane was most emphatically *not* designed for bulk cargo. In Germany as in Russia, memories of the siege of Stalingrad were still fresh. Having pledged to relieve German forces by air, the Luftwaffe came nowhere near to achieving its objective. There was no reason to expect the Anglo-American air forces to do any better.

At cinemas, Soviet newsreels shown before the main feature rarely passed up the opportunity to vilify Allied efforts to support west Berlin.

Here we see a close-up of the Anglo-American airlift. A Dakota landing with 4 tons of coal on board. Shortly afterwards it takes off again – also loaded with a 4-ton payload. We'd love to have seen what they loaded up for their return flight. [It was a recurring Soviet contention that the Allies were using the Airlift to clear Berlin of incriminating evidence of plots to overthrow the communist regime.]

In Berlin's eastern port from 1–20th July alone, 26,000 tons of coal and briquets were delivered from Poland and Saxony. A single barge can carry 600 tons – the air lift needs 150 planes to carry the same amount.[1]

A *Neues Deutschland* report on August 12th was of so much coal shipped to east Berlin there was scarcely enough room to store it all. Believable? No. But Soviet propaganda could always be relied upon to over-egg the pudding.

Since the Soviet government announced that it would take charge of feeding Berlin to compensate for low rations, freighters loaded with corn have been arriving in Rostock non-stop. Freight trains are standing ready to rush the goods to Berlin. A steady supply of flour has been meeting the needs of the city's one million inhabitants since August 1.

Thanks to a further agreement between the Soviet and Polish governments, Poland has been delivering cattle to cover the city's meat requirements. Czechoslovakia has committed itself to delivering potatoes to Berlin.

Every Berlin housewife can hand in her ration cards in the Soviet sector, where she will receive her full allocation, no matter in which sector she lives. Thanks to supplies from the Soviet Union, Poland and Czechoslovakia, Berlin's millions can be fed – including those in the sectors where the Western forces have been reducing their daily supplies.[2]

If west Berliners were disinclined to change allegiance, they were swayed not so much by faith in the Airlift as by the certainty that Russian promises were made to be broken. It was a stock joke that things could only be worse if the Americans were blockading the city and the Russians were running the Airlift.

The war of words escalated in the summer with an American-inspired blueprint for undermining Soviet power across eastern Europe. What was in effect an open cheque to groups of political activists that supported American values was endorsed by the National Security Council on August 18th. This robust approach found favour with Bevin who had long been calling for a propaganda offensive. In a Cabinet paper circulated in January 1948, he recommended 'a small section in the FO [Foreign Office] to ... provide material for our anti-communist publicity through our missions and information services abroad'. This led to the setting up of the Independent Research Department (IRD) to promote the idea of social democracy with a European slant.

'It is for us', declared Bevin, 'and not the Americans, to give the lead in the spiritual, moral and political sphere to all democratic elements in Western Europe which are anti-communist and, at the same time, genuinely progressive and reformist, believing in freedom, (social and economic) planning and social justice – what one might call "The Third Force".'[3] Russia's pretence to be a 'Workers' Paradise' was to be exposed as a 'gigantic hoax'.

Funded through the secret service, the IRD kept up a steady stream of briefing papers for newspapers and radio stations hungry for material. Friendly journalists on German newspapers were particularly favoured with insights into Soviet machinations.

The American programme was more ambitious. 'Whereas in the past we have confined our efforts to presenting the advantages of democracy', Clay told the War Department, he was now proposing a full-frontal attack on communist pretensions, embarking on what he described as a 'cultural cold war'. In Berlin, Clay's chief instrument for striking back at Soviet propaganda was the Radio in the American Sector (RIAS). As 'the free voice of the free world', RIAS was on the air 24 hours a day and when fully powered could reach into Poland and Czechoslovakia. If, as frequently happened, service was interrupted by electricity failures or Soviet attempts to jam broadcasts, RIAS vans with loudspeakers were sent out on the streets where crowds gathered to hear the news. Censorship was minimal and German performers were free to satirise officialdom of whatever political persuasion. Essential listening was *Die Insulaner* (The Islander), a comedy programme created by Guenter Neumann who ridiculed heavy-handed bureaucracy and made the uniformed functionary an object of fun. 'Next to the Airlift', said Clay, 'RIAS was the strongest weapon in the Cold War.' He might have added that Voice of America and the BBC also did their bit to lift morale. Licences were granted to newspapers and publishers known to favour Allied policy. *Der Monat*, a journal on international affairs, was designed to win over German intellectuals to American policy.

Information centres, clubs and libraries were set up offering lectures and discussion groups. Young people were immersed in political education. Some of the well-meaning efforts of the British Council came in for ridicule. When the Cambridge University Madrigal Society arrived, it was to perform with 'traditional Elizabethan water music'. A stage was built near Gatow. 'Undaunted if inaudible, they sang catches and roundelays from boats moored at the bottom of General Herbert's garden as Yorks,

Haltons and Dakotas roared back and forth overhead.'[4] Of a more practical nature, political lectures and debates were nearly always oversubscribed.

★

But the success of the Airlift depended less on feeding the mind than on sustaining the body. Hope was kept alive by the increase in the number of planes on the aerial convoy. Though little noticed for a time, the game-changer came with the appointment of General William Tunner to take command of Operation Vittles. He landed in Germany on July 28th, 1948.

Like many of the new generation of American pace-setters, Tunner was imbued with the spirit of Frederick Taylor, the pioneer who made time and motion study the core of scientific management. Taylor's insight was to recognise that workers could be made more efficient, and thus more productive, if manufacturing was broken down into standardised and closely supervised segments. Henry Ford made his fortune by adapting Taylorism to the mass production of affordable cars. The output of military hardware also benefited from the Ford touch. Ford's mammoth factory for B-24 bombers turned them out at the incredible rate of one an hour. Tunner argued that the same level of tight planning and management could revolutionise military transport.

The epitome of American 'can do', Tunner was not blessed with sensitivity. One of his closest colleagues described him as 'very demanding and sometimes just impossible'. His critics, of which there were many, found him humourless and socially inept. A self-confessed workaholic, once he fastened on to an objective he was not to be deflected. Everyone agreed that Tunner was intensely ambitious. His lobbying for the Berlin posting left no room for doubt that by his own estimation it was Tunner alone who could succeed in the job. He may well have been right.

A graduate of West Point, Tunner gained his wings in 1929, the same year as Curtis LeMay. His chance to prove his worth came early in the war when he was responsible for delivering aircraft from American factories to collection points in Canada, Bermuda and other bases, the first leg en route across the Atlantic. With long-distance air travel still in its infancy, Tunner started from scratch in recruiting and training pilots. In 1942, Air Transport Command (ATC) was created to move 'men and material wherever needed'. Tunner, now a full colonel, was made head of the Ferrying Division, the largest unit of ATC, which itself was expanding into a major force. The biggest challenge so far for air transport, and what turned out to be Tunner's dress rehearsal for the Berlin Airlift, came with opening supply lines from India to Chinese forces fighting to hold back the Japanese invasion.

The route was over the Himalayas, soon to be known as the Hump, to Chungking, at 500 miles the longest supply chain of the Second World War. It was also the most hazardous. With few aircraft able to fly above 30,000 feet, crossing the world's tallest mountains was a daunting prospect even in good weather which was rare. High peaks and deep valleys created draughts that could drop a plane 5,000 feet or more in less than a minute. Rain, snow and ice further lowered the odds against a successful run.[5]

Though losses were high, the airlift over the Hump was marked as a great success. Much credit went to the organisational brilliance of Tunner who, by late 1944, had built up the operation to a strength of 287 planes and close on 20,000 personnel. In all, the airlift carried 650,000 tons of military equipment and munitions. Tunner was determined that this should not be the end of the story. 'From the Hump on', he wrote, 'airlift was an important factor in war, in industry, in life.' The first priority was a new fleet of bigger, more efficient planes. Tunner spent the early part of the post-war years campaigning for 'transport aircraft based at airports throughout the country, ready for instant duty'.[6]

Inevitably, his interest focused on Berlin. Now deputy commander of the Military Air Transport Service (MATS), he spoke out for 'the only organisation qualified to run a huge airlift'. For the first month of the Berlin crisis his voice was drowned out by a combination of politics and logistics. The hope in Washington was for the Airlift to be wound down as soon as the Russians could be persuaded to back off. Putting Tunner in charge was liable to be interpreted by Moscow as a hardening of intent.

Tunner also came up against General Hoyt Vandenberg, air force chief of staff, who had more to think about than Berlin. Understandably worried about having too few aircraft to meet commitments in the Pacific and in Europe, Vandenberg was liable to lose patience with what he regarded as Tunner's obsession. In any case, it was a brave man who would question the ability of Curtis LeMay to do whatever was necessary to provide for Berlin.

Tunner did have one friend in high places. General Albert Wedemeyer, deputy chief of staff for the US army and a veteran of the war in China, had first-hand experience of what an airlift could do. To adopt the same strategy for Berlin was to Wedemeyer no more than common sense. So too was the assignment of the most experienced air transport commander. But acute sensitivities were involved. It was less than a year since the US air force had been hived off from the army. While Wedemeyer was on good personal terms with Vandenberg, he was aware that unsolicited advice on how best to marshal air services was not welcome. Even so, as the weeks passed and demands on the Airlift intensified, Wedemeyer pressed his advantage. It was time for fresh thinking.

Tensions were raised in mid-July with the Soviet rejection of the Allied offer to reopen negotiations on Berlin if, first, the blockade was lifted. Stalin could see no virtue in conciliatory gestures. Russian and east German intelligence supported his conviction that the Airlift was bound to fail. 'The American mood has changed from warlike to dejected', said one report that landed on Sokolovsky's desk. 'The many American aircraft arriving in Berlin are taking out documents and other property of the American administration.'[7]

On July 22nd, Clay was at the White House to argue the case for holding on in Berlin, come what may. 'If we move out', he told the National Security Council, 'we have lost everything we are fighting for.' And again, 'The future of democracy requires us to stay ... Berlin ... had become a symbol of American intent.' The military governor touted the achievement of the Airlift in the short time he had been operating. Fifty-two C-54s and 80 C-47s were flying 250 round trips daily, bringing in to the city over half of the necessary 4,500 tons of daily supplies. He called for another 75 C-54s and a new airport in Berlin.

Vandenberg voiced his doubts. If the air force was to pull its full weight in Berlin it could not be expected to respond to a crisis elsewhere. Moreover, if Russia decided to shoot first, many planes would be destroyed, thus making it impossible to supply troops and hold outlying bases.

It was Truman who revived the idea of sending an armed convoy to reopen the road and rail links to Berlin. What odds did Clay give to the chances of this starting a war? Clay was optimistic. The Russians were liable to set up road blocks but they could be removed. Secretary of war Kenneth Royall was not convinced. He would support a convoy only if the troops were unarmed. At this point, Clay's short fuse detonated. 'But that's ridiculous. If they stop us we shall have to move backward. I'll never order troops of mine to run from the Reds without a fight.' Clay felt that he was losing the argument but Robert Murphy, his political adviser, was more hopeful. He detected in Truman an understanding of what was at stake. When Vandenberg stuck to his line, Truman asked what he would do if it came to a choice between the Airlift and convoys. If Russian aggression led to war, wouldn't the air force have to play its part in defending Berlin? Clay recalled:

> As the meeting ended and as we were walking out of the door, the President said to me and Ken Royall, 'Come into my office.' We went into his office and he said something like this: 'You're not feeling happy about this are you, Clay.' I said 'No, Sir, I'm not. I think this is going to make our efforts a failure and I'm afraid what will happen to Europe if it does fail.' He said, 'Don't you worry, you're going to get your planes.'[8]

Eight squadrons of C-54s were to be assigned to Operation Vittles. A little later, at a Pentagon meeting, Vandenberg submitted with good grace. Since the president was backing the Airlift, no effort would be spared 'to make it an operation worthy of the name'.

Wedemeyer took the opportunity to put in a word for Tunner. His colleague was still not sure about that. 'Any of my senior officers can handle it. If I just tell LeMay to step up the organization, it'll be done.' But within 24 hours he had changed his mind. Tunner was called in. 'Well, Bill, it's all yours', said Vandenberg. 'When can you take off?'

Tunner's reception in Germany was frosty. LeMay owed loyalty to General Smith who was now to be summarily replaced by a task force commander who demanded a free hand in planning and personnel. LeMay was not inclined to ease the way for Tunner. The newcomer was allocated staff quarters in a derelict hotel and a war-damaged apartment block. No desks, chairs or telephones were provided.

Brief meetings between Tunner and Smith were marred by mutual hostility. Tunner did not rate his predecessor and made no secret of his opinion. The Airlift was a 'wing and a prayer operation' that had to be got into shape. This was unfair to Smith who had made strides in the brief period of his command. It was he who had raised the efficiency of the Airlift by introducing the 'block system' to allow for different types of aircraft to fly in groups so that they could be spaced according to cruising speeds. Planes were scheduled to take off every five minutes, flying 1,000 feet higher than the flight in front. The pattern began at 5,000 feet and was repeated five-fold. In July, before Tunner arrived, a start had been made on tightening air traffic control to end the congestion of planes backing up for miles as they flew in ever-expanding circles waiting for permission to land.

Unfortunately for Smith, though he knew what was wrong, he lacked the muscle to get things done. Tunner took over with army and air force backing and with the political establishment in Washington willing him to succeed. He made the most of his opportunity. Within days, he had his own people in the critical jobs. Smith and his team were no longer required. Having secured his headquarters in Frankfurt, Tunner flew to Berlin to see what could be done to save time and effort at the receiving end of the Airlift.

He did not have to look far for signs of overstretch. A not unusual schedule for an aircrew was nine hours flying followed by eighteen hours on ground duty followed by eight hours blessed sleep. Tunner was quick to spot that the strain could be lifted by streamlining the timetable with shorter turnarounds. An early decree was for crews to stay close by their planes. The new routine was for unloading and loading to take place immediately the engines were switched off. Simultaneously, an operations officer would be alongside with orders to the crew for their next trip and an updated weather forecast. But most important and most welcome was the mobile snack bar with pretty girls recruited by the German Red Cross to serve sandwiches, doughnuts and hot coffee. There were complaints from those who wanted to sightsee in Berlin. Tunner was unsympathetic. 'If they want to see ruins, there are ruins in Frankfurt.'

The latest C-54 Skymasters started arriving three weeks after Tunner took control. It was a plane with great Airlift potential. Stripped of 'excess equipment', it had a loading capacity of over 10 tons. With cruising speed of 170 mph, it could cover 3,900 miles before needing to refuel. Veterans testified to its manoeuvrability and light controls which meant less fatigue on long flights.

Picking up on an idea first raised by Smith, Tunner argued for the Skymaster to fly out of Fassberg and Celle, both in the British zone and much closer to Berlin than Wiesbaden. 'Two planes at Fassberg could do the work of three at Wiesbaden', said Tunner. Celle had to be upgraded before it could cater for the 'big birds' but Fassberg was ready for immediate USAF occupation. Bevin was quick to give approval. Work started on a new runway at Celle. The base was handed over to the USAF in early October.

Tunner learned much by experience. Two weeks into his command he flew from Wiesbaden to Berlin. Ahead of him, just three minutes apart, was a line of heavily loaded Skymasters. Another queue was on his tail. As the procession neared Tempelhof the weather turned hostile. Low, dense cloud and blinding rain cut out the radar and, in Tunner's words, 'everything went to hell'. One Skymaster missed the runway and crashed. Flames from the wreckage brought the next arrival to an emergency stop which blew its tyres while a third Skymaster averted disaster by landing on an auxiliary runway still under construction. Meanwhile, at increasing risk of collision, banks of aircraft were circling from 3,000 to 12,000 feet.

With patience, the muddle could have been sorted out. But patience was not Tunner's strongest suit. Shock treatment was more his style. In radio contact with Tempelhof he made his decision. 'Tunner speaking and you'd better listen. Send every plane in the stack back to its home base.'

There was a moment of silence. This meant wasting hundreds of hours of flying time and holding back hundreds of tons of cargo. There had to be some mistake. An incredulous voice was heard from Tempelhof. 'Please repeat.' 'I said, send everything in the stack below and above me home. Then tell me when it's OK to come down.'

What became known as Black Friday led to an addition to the rule book. Never stack; any aircraft that missed its approach was to return to base through a central corridor and then be rerouted back to Berlin. Radar was upgraded and night flying was introduced.

Tunner thought in terms of a conveyor belt (another reminder of his debt to modern business methods) which could be slowed down or speeded up as circumstances dictated. Standardisation was now the rule. His dream was of landing one plane and dispatching another every three minutes of the day and night; in other words an aircraft movement in or out every 90 seconds. Though there was some way to go before the target came within reach, on August 12th, for the first time, the daily delivery to Berlin of food and other supplies exceeded the 4,500 tons, enough for west Berlin to survive at a tolerable, if not comfortable level of subsistence.

CHAPTER EIGHT

A n attempt to restore Berlin to the diplomatic agenda started
in Washington. The idea was to make a direct approach to
Stalin. Cutting out the middle man appealed to Truman who held
to the belief that straight talking at the highest level produced
the best results. This was not the view in London, where Bevin
objected to this 'weak way of doing things'. He had not forgotten
an informal American contact with the Kremlin earlier in the year.
An assurance that 'as far as the United States is concerned, the
door is always wide open for full discussion and the comparing of
our differences' had been interpreted in the Soviet press as a go-
it-alone break between America and its allies. Bevin had not been
best pleased at this unintended slight. Now, buoyed up by a positive
meeting with the signatories to the Brussels Defence Treaty, he
was more than ever confident that the West could afford to take a
hard line with Stalin.

From his ambassadorial base in London, Lewis Douglas worked
hard to persuade Bevin to be conciliatory. What harm could there
be in an open discussion on Berlin with the offer to consider other
German matters 'in the appropriate place in the appropriate manner'? If Stalin refused the bait, there would be strong grounds
for an appeal to the United Nations.[1] Douglas conceded only that

France should be given time to resolve its latest political crisis before contact was made with Moscow. Bevin gave way reluctantly while remaining convinced that the advantage was being handed to Stalin to decide what should be discussed and to set the timetable for further discussions.

Bevin was also averse to leaving the initiative to the three Allied ambassadors in Moscow. How would Stalin react to an invitation that could be seen as patronising? On the international scene, the Soviet leader was not used to dealing with those who did not aspire to his exalted status. Incapable of accepting anything at face value and acutely sensitive to criticism, he might easily assume a deliberate put-down. The point did not seem to have occurred to anyone in Washington. It was Douglas himself who regretted the 'note of arrogance which has crept into our dealings with other countries'.

On July 26th, 1948, Bevin agreed on a note to be handed to Molotov setting out Allied rights in Berlin, the intention of the Allies not to be coerced, together with their willingness to discuss all outstanding matters. 'Our object', said Bevin, 'should be to try to get the Russians back to the River Oder. If we left Berlin now the Slavs would settle on the Rhine and that would be the end of Western Europe.'[2]

The three western ambassadors – Walter Bedell Smith, Yves Chataigneau (who was new to the job and uncertain of his political base in Paris where a new government was still in the making) and Frank Roberts, Bevin's private secretary and an old Russia hand, standing in for Sir Maurice Peterson, absent on sick leave – were received by Stalin and Molotov on August 2nd. The mood was optimistic. Roberts was 'very much struck by the affability of their hosts'.[3]

As the senior spokesman, Bedell Smith set the tone. Having ended the war as Eisenhower's chief of staff, a job that entailed stage-managing the German surrender, he was a tough-minded and forceful character who was sent to Moscow in the expectation that his record in fighting Nazism would weigh in his favour. If Smith had a weakness it was his tendency to play down Soviet duplicity. Schooled in Roosevelt's image of world power, he saw a future in which America and Russia would cooperate to keep the rest of the world in order. He was convinced that a deal with Stalin was there for the making. Disillusion was slow to set in. it had barely surfaced when the opportunity came to lead the Allies in direct negotiations with the Soviet political elite.

After an exchange of pleasantries, judged to be a good sign by the visitors, Stalin came to the point. There was a single way to end the blockade. All the Allies had to do was to accept the Soviet mark as the legitimate currency throughout Berlin and to suspend plans for a west German government. He added that since the Allies had moved towards a separate west German state with its capital in Frankfurt, they had conceded their judicial right to be in Berlin. He proposed a joint statement providing for the removal of all transport restrictions in Berlin simultaneously with the withdrawal of western currency from the city and the resumption of four-power talks on Germany.

It was an offer that was bound to be rejected. The Allies were as one in demanding recognition of their right to be in Berlin. This had to be accepted before there was any talk on the future of Germany as a whole. If Stalin was adamant, there seemed to be nothing further to say.

Optimist though he was, even Smith was at a loss 'for new avenues of approach to the same old question'. Then, as he recalled:

Stalin threw himself back in his chair, lighted a cigarette and, smiling as he looked directly at me, asked:

'Would you like to settle the matter to-night?'

I replied of course that there was nothing I would like better.

'Very well,' Stalin said, 'I can meet you on this proposal. There should be a simultaneous introduction in Berlin of the Soviet zone Deutsche mark in place of the Western B mark, together with the removal of all transport restrictions. Second, while the Soviet Government will no longer ask as a condition the deferment of the implementation of the London decisions for setting up a Western government in Germany, this should be recorded as the insistent wish of the Soviet Government.'[4]

A concession that appeared to give the Allies a free hand in west Germany had Smith hooked. The meeting ended with Smith agreeing that 'the three of us would present his (Stalin's) proposals to our respective governments for action'.

Smith was too precipitous in assuming that Chataigneau and Roberts were on side. It is likely that Chataigneau said little since he was feeling his way into an unfamiliar role but Roberts certainly had reservations. To relegate the currency issue to 'technical questions', as Smith was inclined to do, was to throw away one of the strongest cards in the Allied pack. Bevin too was quick to raise objections.

'As I feared', he telegraphed Roberts, 'we made a mistake in not facing Stalin squarely at the outset with the question of ... Soviet currency in Berlin ... [this] lies at the very heart of our difference with the Russians ... As I now see it, Molotov's object is to ... control the currency position so that the Russians will be masters of the whole city and our writ will not even run to our own sector.' He added: 'We are not and will not consent to be in

Berlin on sufferance. Nor are we going to allow ourselves to be squeezed out.'[5]

The message was for Roberts to get Smith to toughen up and not allow himself to be browbeaten. Bevin took the same line with Washington. But he recognised the weakness of his position. He had to hand a gloomy report from General Robertson, who could see no way out of the impasse in Berlin.

'Our position is fundamentally weak because we cannot stay in Berlin indefinitely in defiance of the Soviet', Robertson wrote. The Airlift was better than nothing but not by much. 'I see no reason to change the opinion I have always held, namely that it is not possible to keep Berlin supplied by air through the winter.' Meanwhile, 'We have no effective means of protecting members of the Magistrat. Large-scale abductions are always within their [Soviet] power. Sabotage by German henchmen of power stations could do us great damage.'

Robertson concluded: 'It would be better to accept a half-way house than admit to a breakdown.'[6] He held to what was becoming a favoured view in Washington and London, that the efforts to save Berlin would be better directed towards building a strong and independent state in west Germany.

Bevin had no objection to making west Germany central to European defence. But Berlin was not to be given away. He refused to believe that 'the situation is as bad as General Robertson suggests'.[7] He noted that General Clay was consistently bullish. While pressing hard for more aircraft to be designated for the Airlift, the US military governor made no secret of his insistence on a written guarantee of Allied rights in Berlin as the prerequisite of any broader agreement. But it was for Truman and Marshall to take the lead. There was only so much Britain could do to bring pressure to bear on Stalin. In a message to the Combined Chiefs of Staff,

Bevin warned that 'if there is war with the Soviet Union in the near future, it is bound to be primarily a United States undertaking'.

> The role that the United Kingdom could play would be bound to depend on the extent and timing of the United States assistance. Without such assistance, our economic situation would deteriorate to a degree which would not only interfere drastically with our present economic recovery programme but would gravely impair our war effort. In particular a rearmament programme would involve a major reorientation of our production and could only be carried out if the United States could provide us with sufficient assistance to support our economy including adequate supplies of raw materials and food. Further it would be necessary to face the problem of assuring our overseas financial position. I therefore wish to impress on Mr Marshall that in considering any recommendations of the Combined Chiefs of Staff we shall be bound to have these factors in mind and are ready to discuss them in greater detail with the United States Government as soon as may be necessary.[8]

It had not yet come to that, but Marshall agreed with Bevin that the Soviet stance on Berlin was unacceptable. He told the president that Bedell Smith had been instructed 'to include in the record a statement that all previous four-power agreements with respect to Germany continue in effect and cannot be abrogated by the unilateral assertion of the Soviet Union'. The proposed Soviet draft on Berlin was 'entirely unsatisfactory'.[9] Smith remained hopeful.

When negotiations resumed, Molotov was more accommodating than usual. At one point, Smith even felt that the foreign minister 'was prepared to accept the western position'. The devil was in the detail. The Allies wanted an end to the blockade in return for an agreement on four-power control of the Soviet mark in Berlin. Talks bogged down on Molotov's reluctance to accept that the Allies had any rights at all in Berlin, his insistence that the removal of 'all transport restrictions' applied only to those imposed after June 18th, and that quadripartite control of currency was open to an interpretation favouring Russian dominance.

In an attempt to break the deadlock, the job of resolving 'certain technical problems' was handed over to the four military governors in Germany. Their first object was to find a mutually satisfactory formula for exercising financial control. This proved to be impossible. An apparently favourable response by Stalin to the setting up of a four-power commission was dismissed by Sokolovsky as a misunderstanding. Whenever the subject was raised, Sokolovsky switched to generalisations allowing him to expand at length on western obduracy, bringing to mind the old saying about pots and kettles. To add to the difficulties, a Russian demand for exclusive control over air traffic in and out of Berlin was tacked on to the agenda.

*

The diplomatic game of bluff and counter-bluff played out behind closed doors was replicated, in brutal style, on the streets of Berlin. The tension of not quite knowing where the next meal was coming from intensified by rumour and by Soviet provocation. In Potsdamer Platz, where black-marketeers hovered around the sector boundaries, a pitched battle took place on August 19th. Ruth Andreas-Friedrich recorded her impression.

> Kidnapping across the boundary. Police raids. People being dragged into the other sector. People protest. Shots are

fired, stones are hurled. People are arrested. People are wounded. Who is the enemy?[10]

A campaign of Soviet propaganda accusing the west of preparing for a coup triggered a concerted attempt to subvert the elected Berlin Assembly where the Social Democrats had a four-to-one majority over the SED.

A favoured technique for putting pressure on city officials who were tainted with western sympathies was to submit them to interrogative meetings, often late at night. One who suffered this treatment recorded being harangued by Soviet officers for eleven hours on the need to cooperate with the SED. His wife feared he had been kidnapped.

The most prominent victim of Soviet harassment was acting mayor, Louise Schroeder. Towards the end of August she became seriously ill and was flown to a hospital in west Germany. Next in line was Dr Ferdinand Friedensburg, like Schroeder, a Christian Democrat, who joked that he 'could not afford to be sick'. Breathing down his neck and willing him to fail was the third deputy mayor, Heinrich Acker of the SED.

The Berlin Assembly met at the Neues Stadthaus (city hall) in the Soviet sector just short of the British demarcation line. SED demonstrations, often violent, were thus a double provocation, to the elected members and to the British authorities who were helpless to intervene. Hostilities began on June 23rd when SED agitation brought Assembly business to a halt. A move to tighten the rules against demonstrations close to city hall was disregarded by chief of police Paul Markgraf who reported directly to the Russian military. So confident was he of Soviet backup that he felt free to decamp to the east with his entire administration and to dismiss nearly 600 officers who were judged to be unreliable.

An attempt by the Magistrat to sack Markgraf was defeated by a Soviet veto. Instead, an alternative police force was set up in the western sectors under Markgraf's deputy, Johannes Stumm. A majority of his former colleagues elected to join him. It was a risky decision. Defectors were subject to arrest and beatings for 'illegal exercise of authority' if they strayed back across the border. Ominously, when General Kotikov, Soviet military commander, claimed Markgraf's exclusive right to exercise police authority in the east and west sectors, he signed himself Military Commander of Berlin. Markgraf's refusal to accept his reduced jurisdiction extended to a ban on the circulation in the Soviet sector of a telephone directory listing Stumm's office under Police Headquarters.

An east–west division was soon common to nearly all areas of city administration. The excuse for setting up a food office responsible solely to the Soviet military was to blame the Magistrat for allowing 'chaotic and dangerous conditions' to mar the rationing system. The response from Friedensburg was to point out that living standards in Berlin were superior to those in the east zone. The evidence could be found in statistics published by the Soviet authorities.

On July 30th, Berlin's central bank with headquarters in the east was ordered to block the accounts of the Magistrat and of all enterprises based in the west. No explanation was given. With wages unpaid and bills mounting up, the Allies had no choice but to create a new bank in the west. A short time later, the Soviet-controlled bank presented a cheque for three million marks to its branch in the British sector, claiming that the money was needed to pay employees in the Soviet sector. The cheque was refused.

While four-power negotiations were underway in Moscow, a campaign of intimidation was launched from east Berlin. On August 14th, *Neues Deutschland* ran on its front page the headline,

'Chaos in the West sectors imperils all Berlin'. A call to action came the next day. 'Not one more day in office for this government.' The Social Democrats, 'a reactionary clique', were said to be planning a coup.

It was close to midnight on August 24th when Friedensburg was summoned to a meeting to receive a note from General Kotikov accusing the Magistrat of causing 'disorganization and division' in the police by suspending Markgraf. All recent decisions of the Magistrat were declared void. Refused permission to talk directly with Kotikov, the acting mayor responded with a written refusal to accept the Soviet order. He was backed by the Allied military commanders.

The eightieth meeting of the city Assembly was scheduled for August 26th. By early afternoon, several thousand demonstrators were gathered outside city hall calling for 'direct action'. After a ten-man communist delegation regaled Friedensburg with a demand for the resignation of the Magistrat, the Assembly meeting was called off.

It was now the turn of west Berliners to take to the streets. Some 30,000 supporters of the Magistrat gathered on the square fronting the skeletal Reichstag where Reuter told the crowd: 'We Berliners have said No to communism and we will fight it with all our might as long as there is breath in us.' An attempt to convene the Assembly the following day failed when SED agitators broke down the doors and pushed their way into the chamber waving red banners and placards. Again, the speaker, Dr Otto Suhr, was forced to declare an adjournment. An appeal to Kotikov to restore order received a disingenuous response defending the free rights of Berlin's workers to petition the Assembly: 'If demonstrations are forbidden how can the working population express their grievances?' In Moscow, Frank Roberts called on Molotov to restore calm in Berlin to allow the military governors to proceed with their talks in a spirit of friendly cooperation. Molotov was unmoved. As Sokolovsky had his instructions there was no need to discuss the matter further.[11]

By early September it was clear that the military governors were at stalemate. On the 14th, the Allied ambassadors in Moscow protested that talks in Berlin had borne no relationship to the brief agreed with Stalin and Molotov. The response, four days later, supported the position taken by Sokolovsky and accused the Allies of interpreting the Moscow directive in a 'unilateral manner'.

Having started on a course of which he disapproved, Bevin was not about to say, 'I told you so'. He believed, or rather hoped, that a settlement was still within reach. But in Washington, there were feelings of despair. As under-secretary of state Lovett remarked to defence secretary Forrestal, the 'sheer duplicity' of the Soviets was beyond the experience of the state department. When, on September 7th, talks finally broke down, Murphy wrote: 'It is clear that the Soviets are making only those proposals which would give them complete control so as to make our acceptance impossible.'

Soviet pressure was building up in Berlin. With renewed threats of violence, an Assembly meeting on September 3rd was abandoned. But city hall was not left unoccupied. A gathering of the SED along with supposedly representative members of the 'democratic' parties held a session to form a 'Berlin Democratic Block' to negotiate with the Magistrat. The semblance of an alternative city government did not go unnoticed in the west.

Yet another attempt to reconvene the legitimate Assembly was planned for September 6th. Police from west Berlin volunteered to keep order. They proved to be no match for the SED demonstrators, well plied with alcohol, who arrived in trucks provided by the Russian military.

Overseen by Markgraf and other senior officers supposedly responsible for security, the mob broke into the council chamber, forcing members who were not of the SED to leave. With no prospect of regaining control, Suhr called a halt to proceedings. While the People's Police made random arrests an SED leader mounted the rostrum to denounce all opponents of the Soviet regime, and to propose a 'winter emergency programme' which was duly approved by acclamation.

As the crowd dispersed, the People's Police was active in picking out and arresting those of their colleagues who had transferred their allegiance to the west. A few were able to take refuge in the French liaison office where they remained for two days while General Ganeval secured a promise of safe conduct from Kotikov. This proved to be worthless. When the besieged emerged from their hideout they were arrested by Russian troops and handed over to the communist police. By way of excuse, French liaison officers were said to be drunk. Ganeval protested bitterly – 'I still cannot believe that your personal guarantee should have been broken in such a flagrant way' – but in vain. A later Soviet account of the day's events simply denied the evidence, adding that if there had been any disorder it had taken place in the part of Berlin not under the control of the Soviet command.

The response from west Berliners was immediate and robust. Estimates of the number of people who gathered at the Platz der Republik on September 9th vary wildly but it is likely that the crowd in front of the Reichstag was well over 200,000. Since the square straddled the British–Soviet boundary there were Allied fears of the rally getting out of hand but the popular mood was such as to defy efforts to have it postponed or moved to a more secure venue.

The first speaker was Franz Neumann who called for a minute's silence in memory of the victims of Nazism. 'These people gave their lives for freedom. The concentration camps are still the same but now the hammer and sickle waves over them.' Reuter followed with an appeal to the western powers not to settle for a 'rotten compromise'. The demonstration was intended to end with a petition to the now defunct Allied Control Council but a section of the crowd peeled off to continue their protest at the Brandenburg Gate where Russian and British guards faced each other across the boundary. A Soviet flag flew over the triumphal arch. The image, often reproduced, of victorious Soviet troops raising their flag to mark the capitulation of Berlin, spurred action. An intrepid climber tore down the symbol of Russian oppression. When someone set a match to the flag, Soviet troops fired over and into the crowd, killing a fifteen-year-old boy and injuring others. Stones were thrown and vehicles overturned. Yet above the noise of street battle came the drone of the airborne convoy that was keeping west Berlin alive. For those under siege it was a sound that inspired hope. But for how long would it last?

*

Bevin made his report to the Cabinet on the morning of September 22nd.[12] Discussion with Sokolovsky having ended in deadlock, Molotov had been told of the points at issue. His response a week later was interpreted as a move to prolong talks until the coming winter. It was agreed that a final note to the Soviet government should set out western views and ask for the blockade to be lifted. If there was no settlement by September 29th, the dispute would be referred to the United Nations.

Later in the day, Bevin spoke in the Commons, describing the blockade as 'senseless'. At his pugnacious best, he went on: 'If there is no let-up, and the worst comes to the worst, we are confident ...

that by a combination of the two air forces, augmented ... by the tremendous effort of the United States, we shall be able to see the winter through.'

Berlin took centre stage at the UN Security Council on October 4th. First to be decided was whether the Security Council was competent to take on the dispute. The challenge came from the Soviet representative, Andrei Vyshinsky, a rising star in the Kremlin who was soon to replace Molotov as foreign minister. Denying the existence of a blockade or that Berlin was threatened with starvation, Vyshinsky invoked Article 107 of the UN Charter which excluded from its jurisdiction actions of occupying powers in former enemy countries. When the Security Council decided by nine votes to two (Russia and Ukraine) that Berlin was in dispute between the occupying powers rather than between them and Germany, Vyshinsky announced that the Soviet delegation would take no further part in the proceedings. The search for a compromise was handed over to a committee of six neutral member states presided over by the Argentinian foreign minister, Dr Juan Bramuglia.

On October 22nd, they came up with what was widely judged to be a sensible resolution to the crisis – an immediate end to the blockade followed by an arrangement between the four military governors to introduce a single currency based on the eastern mark. But what looked good on paper to disinterested observers was seriously at fault with the contestants. Russia insisted on the introduction of eastern marks happening simultaneously with an end to the blockade while the western powers wanted it spelt out that a single currency required four-power control.

The reality was that both sides were playing for time.

As the Berlin crisis escalated, the moves towards sovereign status for west Germany also gathered pace. It would be wrong to suggest that the creation of the Federal Republic was entirely the result of what was happening in Berlin. But progress towards independence would have been more protracted had not Berlin provided a powerful impetus.

The foundation for self-government had come early with the setting up of citizens' advisory councils at local and regional level. These bodies were reinforced by free elections held across the three western zones in 1946. A year later, a start was made on delegating responsibilities to elected parliaments for eleven Laender (states), a federal structure that helped to calm political nerves in France where opposition to a neighbouring centralised state, liable to nationalistic overtones, was absolute. France was equally intractable when it came to building a self-supporting German economy. Marshall Aid for Germany, a halt to dismantling industrial plants and returning the Ruhr to German control were all resolutely opposed.

It was the struggle for Berlin and the accompanying fear of Russian expansionism that pushed the Allies towards an accord that met French concerns while championing a new, if divided, Germany.

On July 1st, 1948, a week after the start of the Airlift, the three commanders-in-chief called upon the minister-president of the eleven Laender to join in drawing up a democratic constitution. The response was hesitant. No German politician was willing to put his name to a strategy that implied a permanent division of the country. On the other hand, there was much to be said for some form of political interlocking that would allow for a joint approach to negotiations with the Allies.

The compromise was to set up a Parliamentary Council to work on a provisional constitution to be known as a Grundgesetz (Basic Law). Of the 65 voting members of the Council, the Christian

Democrats and its Bavarian off-shoot, the Christian Social Union (CDU/CSU) were on equal terms with the Social Democrats (SPD), each having 27 seats. On paper this left the smaller parties – the Germany Party, the Centre and the Communists (two seats each) along with the Free Democrats (five seats) in a commanding position. But since mutual animosity was all they had in common, it was left to the liberal Free Democrats to act as power-brokers. Favourably disposed to the CDU and open to blandishments (the FDP leader, Theodor Heuss, was to become federal president), a centre-right coalition in all but name had a slight edge in the Parliamentary Council. It met for its first session in Bonn on September 1st, with Dr Konrad Adenauer as chairman.

It is hard to know how much calculation there was in Adenauer's rise to prominence. This 'pale, lean German with his hard Tartar face' as a Swiss newspaper described him, carried an air of austere authority – cold but competent – that made him a natural choice for heavy committee work. But few took him seriously as a contender for high office. All else aside, age was against him. At 73, he was seen as fulfilling a caretaker role until the way was clear for one of the new political generation to take the lead.

Born in Cologne, Adenauer advanced through the rounds of local government to become mayor, an administratively powerful role, in 1917. Removed from office by the Hitler regime, he managed to keep a low profile for the duration of the war, re-emerging in 1945 to resume his mayoral duties. And Cologne is where he might well have remained had not a British brigadier taken against his assertive manner. To fill the gap in his career, Adenauer played a more active role in the wider affairs of the CDU, positioning himself as the Catholic conservative opponent to Kurt Schumacher, the charismatic leader of the SPD.

While chairing the Parliamentary Council, Adenauer had to make his mark with the occupying powers and with General Clay in particular. At first, the American was sceptical of Adenauer. In no way a glad-hander, this elderly politician was well informed and persuasive on points at issue. But his staying power had to be in doubt. Meanwhile, his chief asset for Clay was that he was easier to get on with than the touchy and truculent Schumacher, who made no secret of his disdain for American values. Schumacher was on better terms with General Robertson who was acting for a Labour government wedded to planning and welfare. Schumacher's closest advisers had spent the war years in exile in London.

In the early days of the Parliamentary Council it was Schumacher and his allies who made the running with demands for a system of government that concentrated power at the centre. This was not at all to Clay's liking. Schooled in American constitutional law, he was an advocate of state rights. His objection to 'too much centralization of authority' for legislative and financial matters won backing from his French counterpart, General Marie-Pierre Koenig. Looking to hold back on a German revival, instructions from Paris were for the widest possible delegation of powers, allowing even taxation to be a purely state affair. Prompted by Bevin, Robertson warned of 'chaos and anarchy'. Seeking compromise, Adenauer proved to be the ultimate pragmatist. As it began to evolve, the Basic Law emphasised the essential freedoms including the right to property, with the federal government having overall control, leaving the Laender to take care of education, police and other areas that could be safely delegated without impinging on the national structure.

Berlin rarely intruded on Council debates. Schumacher held out the promise of a united, neutral Germany with Berlin as its capital but few believed him. Certainly, Adenauer saw Berlin as a problem to be sorted out by the occupying powers. Any involvement on his part could only make matters worse.

But Adenauer's instinct for practical politics was reinforced by his dislike for the city. As a Rhinelander, he distrusted what he regarded as the Prussian mindset, as a Catholic he was hostile to the hedonistic image of Berlin from the years of the Weimar Republic. Moreover, as the torch-bearer of the CDU he had no wish to give advantage to a socialist stronghold. It is likely that Adenauer would have washed his hands of Berlin. Fortunately, little of this intruded on Clay and none at all on General Tunner, who remained convinced that the city could be saved for western democracy.

CHAPTER NINE

Tunner had two goals: to make the best of what he had, and to prepare the way for something better. On the first count, it was all about tightening his organisation to a point of maximum productivity. There was no romance in Tunner's dream. As he wrote in his book *Over the Hump*:

> The operation of a successful airlift is about as glamorous as drops of water on stone. There's no frenzy, no flap, just the inexorable process of getting the job done. In a successful airlift you don't see planes parked all over the place; they're either in the air or on loading or unloading ramps. Flying crews are either flying or resting up so that they can fly again tomorrow … The real excitement from running a successful airlift comes from seeing a dozen lines climbing steadily on a dozen charts – tonnage delivered, utilization of aircraft – and the lines representing accidents and injuries going sharply down. That's where the glamour lies in air transport.

A vision opened up of a mightier and super-efficient Airlift that could sustain west Berlin for years ahead. Few politicians and diplomats believed in Tunner's grandiose schemes. As Marshall told the NSC on September 9th, 1948, 'time is on the side of the Soviets'. Setting out the options, a CIA report advocated pressing ahead with the creation of a state of West Germany, the success of which would counterbalance the otherwise humiliating necessity of abandoning Berlin.[1]

The pessimism in Washington was fed through to Stalin. A Soviet delegate to the UN, basing his report on a conversation with a French press officer, gave what had become a typical view of the crisis.

> The American military say that in the approaching winter conditions flights will be very complicated and the personnel are so exhausted that great efforts have to be made to make the pilots go on flying. The *materiel* will soon be worn out. This American said that the American army command and the State Department fear that the 'air-bridge' will cease to operate in the very near future.[2]

Nothing daunted, Tunner kept up the pressure for more and bigger aircraft, a generous supply of spare parts and enhanced technology on the ground and in the air. A priority for the boffins was to make it easier for pilots to find their way across an open but not necessarily clear sky.

At the start of the Airlift, the flight to Berlin along narrow corridors was governed entirely by a series of radio beacons. The all-important one was at Fulda, otherwise distinguished as the site of a Benedictine monastery. When the signal was picked up at Fulda, it told the pilot that he was entering Soviet-held territory. Thereafter, for over 200 miles, he was dependent on whatever navigational aids he had in the cockpit until he made contact with ground control as he began his descent to Berlin. Even when there was a navigator on board, as with most RAF flights, bad weather could make it near-impossible to hold course for 40 minutes or more. One unfortunate crew, having lost direction in mist and rain, ended up in Prague. They were entertained royally by the Czech air force before hastily taking off for home when told that Russian troops were on the way.

With a new generation of direction and distance finders, pilots were better able to plot their course and to calculate, early in the flight, their arrival time in Berlin. Electronic equipment was vulnerable to jamming but Russian provocations stopped short of a serious risk to lives. Occasional buzzing by Soviet fighters was more irritating than threatening. Dickie Arscott had a simple way of coping with Russian aerobatics. 'We turned the aircraft straight in on them. They soon gave up on that game.'

The drive for efficiency touched all aspects of the Airlift. With the conversion of a squadron of B-17 Flying Fortresses to weather observation, long-range forecasting took a leap forward. At Gatow, the RAF used falcons to prey on flocks of birds that were liable to collide with their man-made brethren.

The greatest disruption to schedules was caused by the shortage of spare parts, which were gobbled up at an unprecedented rate. A stock of windscreen wipers that should have lasted six months was exhausted in a fortnight. Because there were so many landings in relation to flying time, tyres and brake drums had to be replaced more frequently than had ever been anticipated by any maintenance manual. Ready to break the rules when it suited him, Tunner took to raiding reserves of military hardware scattered across Germany. 'I needed those replacement parts and I didn't care where they came from.' But having been left to moulder, much of the purloined equipment was sub-standard or ill-suited to the latest aircraft. Tunner did better with programming aircraft maintenance. Holding to his axiom that the secret of productivity was the repetition of specific tasks, each mechanic knew precisely what he had to do, over and over again.

A coup for Tunner was to persuade Clay to let him employ German mechanics. Three years after the end of the war, this was still a sensitive issue. Those associated with the Hitler regime, however remotely and however well qualified for civilian jobs, were liable to find their careers blocked. With approval from Clay, underwritten by LeMay, Tunner put out a search for General Hans-Detlef von Rohden, formerly chief transport officer for the Luftwaffe. In addition to his engineering expertise, von Rohden spoke good English and was able to translate maintenance manuals into German. Before long he had a full team of mechanics working round the clock to support the Airlift. Tunner's original plan was to have a nine-man German maintenance crew for each squadron. Eventually, he had 85 per squadron, with more German than American and British mechanics working to strengthen the air bridge to Berlin.

The biggest single breakthrough was the installation of ground control approach radar (GCA). From pint-sized vans lined up along the runway, air traffic controllers, seated at radar screens, were able to talk directly with pilots, giving them precise instructions whatever the weather. The schedule for convoys of aircraft to land, unload and take off at predetermined intervals was now possible even when there was zero visibility. With two of the three air corridors reserved for incoming traffic, Tunner was able to have the sky at night as busy as it was throughout the day. In late August another 75 C-54 Skymasters arrived, bringing the USAF total of planes on the Airlift to close on 200. Now, there was a manpower problem to be solved.

As the Airlift intensified, aircrews were drawn increasingly from the pool of young reservists, many of whom had joined up towards the end of the war. They had little hard experience of flying and none at all with the new generation of heavy load aircraft. Time had to be given over to training, though this meant using experienced flyers as instructors and thus cutting back on the number of men and planes on the Berlin run.

The manpower shortage in the RAF was partly compensated by recruiting volunteers from the Commonwealth. Ten Australian crews checked in at Luebeck in mid-September. A month later they were joined by ten crews from South Africa and, a little later, three crews from New Zealand. Having been told that their attachment would be for a few weeks, most of them stayed for over a year. All were assigned to Dakotas already in service.

Even so, the RAF found it hard to keep up with its big brother. As the weeks passed and the USAF strength in Germany was augmented by the arrival of new aircraft, Britain's share of the Airlift was correspondingly reduced. While there were advanced transport planes such as the Handley Page Hastings at the start of the production line, the RAF had meanwhile to make do with lumbering Dakotas (the British version of the C-47) and with converted bombers such as the Lancastrian, the Halton and the York.

In the cause of greater efficiency, with perhaps more than a touch of self-aggrandisement, Tunner pressed hard for a joint Anglo-American command with himself in pole position. It made sense. With more American 'heavies' filling the sky, the older and less capacious aircraft on offer from the RAF could be pensioned off. Inevitably, this was to relegate Britain to the role of junior partner. It was a repeat of what had happened in the European war when the supreme command settled on Eisenhower as the general backed by a superiority in manpower and weaponry. But the future

US president was adept in massaging bruised egos. Tunner was not of that breed. Britain was rightly proud of its part in the Airlift and politicians as much as senior officers were quick to detect any suggestion of being sidelined. A dispatch to the embassy in Washington in which Bevin complained of being 'ordered about' by the Americans would have received a round of applause on British bases had it been circulated.

Critics accused Tunner of confusing higher standards with different standards. A lot of hard work had gone into adapting Fassberg to accommodate 65 American Skymasters and their crews. But Group Captain Biggar, who headed the British administration, received little in the way of thanks. Instead, there were loud complaints about the accommodation (too cramped) the food (unfamiliar) and the entertainment (English films). At short notice, Biggar found himself rearranging menus (ham and eggs for breakfast and not, most emphatically not, kippers) and finding movies that were more Hollywood than Pinewood.

There was another cultural clash at Burtonwood, a maintenance depot near Liverpool where Skymasters were sent for their 200-hour check-out for wear and tear. Never the most attractive posting, the facilities at Burtonwood fell way short of American expectations. Tunner described the place as 'dingy, dirty and depressing', a fair assessment but one that might reasonably have applied to much of the rest of post-war austerity Britain. Aircrews did not take kindly to short rations, hard mattresses and the absence of central heating, without apparently realising that there was not much else on offer.

*

Increasingly made aware of Britain's diminished economic standing, Bevin played a weak hand as hard as he could. But he knew, as everybody knew outside a group of diehards, that the Airlift would benefit from one man, an American, taking charge of the whole operation.

An Anglo-American agreement giving Tunner 'authority and responsibility to regulate all air traffic entering or leaving the air space utilized ... in the delivery of supplies to Berlin' was signed off in mid-October. The Combined Airlift Task Force (CALTF) was headquartered in Wiesbaden. Tunner's deputy was of the RAF. Air Commodore James Mercer, whose responsibilities were largely administrative, had his HQ at Bueckeburg. The planning officer for CALTF, Group Captain Noel Hyde, was also RAF.

The Anglo-American partnership worked best when there was a clear division of responsibilities. As luck would have it, certain tasks fell easily and exclusively within the British remit. One was the carrying of salt in Sunderland flying boats. Another was transporting liquid fuel. In the early days of the Airlift, gasoline, diesel and kerosene were carried in 55-gallon drums ill-suited to being stowed in a fuselage. They were cumbersome to load and unload and though strapped down, were liable to shift during a flight. The solution was to deploy specially designed tanker aircraft, but there were few of these anywhere in service. However, a short-term remedy was to hand. Post-war, when obsolete heavy bombers were sold off cheaply, former RAF pilots saw the chance to set themselves up as civilian contractors. Since it was the demand for liquid fuel in otherwise inaccessible places that attracted the highest profits, cargo and passenger space was adapted to hold tanks fixed to the floor of the hull. Maintenance and safety were secondary to meeting customer demand.

Seventy of these 'sky tramps' were tracked down by the Foreign Office. Combined they offered a fleet of 100 planes, half of which were tankers. With nothing in common except the buccaneering spirit of pilots who were paid well above the usual rate, civilian contractors were part of the Airlift from July 22nd.

Varying in size from Air Transport and Horton Airways each with one Dakota to the Lancashire Aircraft Corporation with thirteen Haltons, these outfits were used to long-distance assignments but none were prepared for high-density operations. Civilian crews were disinclined to take orders from the RAF. They had their own, often risky, way of doing things. Criminal carelessness was to blame when a lorry carrying ground engineers of the Lancashire Aircraft Corporation collided with a taxiing RAF Hastings. Four engineers and the German driver were killed by the propellers.

A star of this flying circus was Air Vice Marshal Donald Bennett, the Australian-born one-time commander of the Pathfinders, the planes that flew ahead of bombing missions over Germany to pinpoint and mark targets. Author of a standard textbook on navigation, Bennett had scored a long-distance world record in 1938 with his flight from Scotland to South Africa. Post-war, when he headed British South American Airways, his career took a dip with the unaccountable mid-flight disappearance over the Atlantic of two Avro Tudors. As chief operating officer, Bennett accepted responsibility and left the company. But his flying days were not over. Keeping faith with the ill-fated Tudors as one of the best long-distance carriers, Bennett used his severance pay to buy two of them while prices were rock bottom. Operating as Airflight, and having converted one of his passenger Tudors into a tanker to hold 9 tons of diesel, Bennett signed on for the Airlift. One of his early recruits was Stan Sickelmore.

> I was an ex-bomber pilot and had four-engine experience on heavy aircraft, so I wrote to him saying that I needed a job, and he said 'well, come and see me' at his private address.

We had a long chat, and he said, 'if you can pass your technical examination on the Tudor aircraft, then you've got the job.' So I went off and studied at one of the schools in London for the technical side of the aircraft, went back and said 'Here I am – god's gift to aviation!'

It was Bennett himself who flew Sickelmore to Wunstorf for his first assignment.

He was a get-up-and-goer; he did things. Nobody breathing could keep pace with him. He told me 'You've got 24 hours to settle in and then we'll get started.'

Engaged as a co-pilot, Sickelmore was soon promoted to captain. His regular sortie, repeated 226 times, was the delivery of 2,500 gallons of fuel to Gatow.

The company best prepared for the emergency had been operating since 1936. Flight Refuelling was founded by aviation pioneer Sir Alan Cobham with the aim of perfecting the art of refuelling planes in mid-flight. At the start of the Airlift, Cobham was under contract to the Ministry of Civil Aviation to provide refuelling services on long-distance runs. Relocating to an abandoned airfield in Dorset, Flight Refuelling was able to offer the services of its converted Lancaster bombers, now known as Avro Lancastrians.

Not as illustrious as Bennett or Cobham but no less determined to spread his wings was Freddie Laker, a freewheeling adventurer who used his wartime experience as a ferry pilot to sell surplus spare parts from a lock-up garage in south London. He flew a Halifax bomber, converted to carry cargo. It was barely airworthy. An eyewitness at Gatow doubted that it could survive another flight. 'After each landing, Freddie, in oily overalls would rush to put together the pieces of his flying wreck.' Thanks to the Airlift, Laker built up his fleet to twelve second-hand bombers and with the launch of Laker Skytrain in the 1970s became the first to promote cheap trans-Atlantic travel.

Scary stories are told of coping with sub-standard equipment. Stan Sickelmore again:

We all knew that the Tudor had a dodgy history. The best guess as to what had happened to the two that came down over the south Atlantic was that they had a heater or pressurisation problem, or a combination of both. Because of that we were not allowed to use the pressurisation or the heaters on the aircraft. On one occasion when I was flying with captain Gerry Parkinson it was freezing cold and we were shivering. Gerry said to me, 'shall we turn the heaters on?' So we did. The Tudor heating system worked by taking petrol from the main aircraft tank, burning it in a sealed container like a blow lamp. The air came in from outside, passed over this blow lamp and went into the aircraft. It was efficient though dangerous because you were burning neat fuel.

For a few minutes we were nice and warm, but then suddenly the flight deck filled with black smoke. We thought we'd got a fire and I was told to go back and put it out. First of all we had to lift a panel on the floor; the burner was just under the diesel tank. Smoke was pouring out, so I grabbed a fire extinguisher, but like so many companies run on a shoestring, when I pressed the trigger nothing happened. Then I realised it wasn't a fire. During loading, diesel fuel had dripped onto the casing of the heater. It would have ignited eventually but for the moment it was just evaporating, causing clouds of smoke. We turned the heater off but we couldn't even see the instruments because there was so much smoke, so we opened the side windows. That was fine because the smoke was sucked out immediately, but of course once we'd done that we were a damn sight colder than when we'd started, so we wished we hadn't bothered!

Civil aircraft were short on aids that were standard for the USAF and RAF. With the risk of icing above 6,000 feet, a plane lacking de-icing apparatus had to lose height rather too rapidly before it could be brought under control. It was the frequent experience for Halton pilots. There were delays in fitting planes with radar. Until the new year of 1949, pilots had to abide by visual flight rules.

Making do with second-best extended to taking on liquid cargo at Wunstorf and Schleswigland. Work had started on a new set of filling points at Wunstorf but at the end of the year, loading was still by thirteen portable pumps with a capacity of 100 gallons a minute and seven heavy pumps moving 350 gallons a minute. At Schleswigland there was an underground fuelling system installed by the Luftwaffe for its night fighters. Eighteen refuelling bays operated six pumps fed from ten tanks. All very efficient except that the pumps worked at different rates.

Arriving at Gatow, liquid fuel was discharged into underground tanks, then pumped into road tankers to be taken to the Havel lake. From there it was ferried by canal barges to storage plants in the city. To save fuel and time, a pipeline was laid to connect Gatow with the barges on the Havel but it was February 1949 before it started operating.

Seconded to the Airlift, Edwin Whitfield of the state-run British European Airways (BEA), an experienced manager, endeavoured to bring order to a maverick enterprise. He was hindered by loose discipline. With cheap and easily available booze, Wunstorf was notorious for heavy drinking. Accidents were commonplace but were not always self-inflicted. One of the deaths on the ground was witnessed by Sickelmore.

> For a night landing at Gatow, it took less than 30 minutes to offload the diesel, just time to get to the tea wagon for a cuppa and a bun. On the walk back across the tarmac, Captain Clement Utting was about 20 yards ahead of me and the radio officer. The airfield was lit but there were areas of darkness. Suddenly, a lorry appeared. It drove straight at Captain Utting; he must have been crushed under the wheels. When we got to him, the lorry roared off. He was badly injured so I stayed with him, holding his head and trying to comfort him, while the radio officer ran to the hangars for an ambulance. He died four hours later.

Accident or murder? Since the truck was never identified, nothing was ever proved. One theory was that Utting was mistaken for Donald Bennett, a war hero to the victors but none too popular with those whose homes he had helped to destroy. More probably it was a hit and run by a thief who had been stealing from the aircraft or a driver who just didn't look where he was going.

Bennett took the place of his dead colleague. He flew three sorties a night for two months without a break.

Recruiting civilian airlines had a mixed reaction. While a determination to pull out all the stops, invoking the Dunkirk spirit, garnered a favourable press at home and overseas, there were observers who caught a whiff of desperation, a valiant but vain attempt for Britain to keep up with the front runner. It remains an open question as to whether the civilian entry to the Airlift caused more trouble than it was worth. Maverick pilots did not make Tunner's job any easier. The military saw the whole exercise as a bit of a joke but one that could have serious consequences. For Tunner, the civilian airlines were a demonstration of incompetence and a source of frustration. With frequent breakdowns, their planes were liable to miss their slots, interrupting the smooth running of other traffic. Bill Michaels was a flight engineer on a C-54 that narrowly escaped a disastrous encounter with a tanker.

As we approached Berlin, scattered low clouds were beginning to form an almost unbroken layer at our altitude and below us. Everything was normal as we turned toward Gatow. We were on a GCA approach when we broke through the cloud layer at about 400 ft. Just as we broke through, Gatow final controller shouted, '233, 233, overshoot, overshoot, overshoot.' Immediately below and slightly ahead of us was a Lancastrian tanker that had lost its radios. It was hedge-hopping to Berlin and had not been spotted by radar until it was almost too late.

We applied full power, pulled up our landing gear and were following the checklist for a 'missed approach' when I saw that we were losing number 4 engine. Manifold pressure and oil pressure were falling and the aircraft began to yaw to the right. Number 4 was feathered and the pilot was able to maintain control at about 2,000 ft ... The co-pilot and I rushed back to the cargo bay to try to jettison the coal through the open over-wing exit hatches. I had released the tie-downs and we were getting ready to try to dump the coal when we noticed the 'No Smoking' and 'Fasten Seat Belt' signs were flashing and the pilot was waving at us to come forward. On reaching the flight deck we could see that the aircraft was trimmed level and holding altitude with the pilot's hands and feet off the controls. He told me to secure the cargo and that we were taking it home. The return to Celle was uneventful.[3]

With the unrelenting pressure to keep the show moving, there were bound to be accidents – though given the complexity, duration and sheer novelty of the Airlift, the rarity of serious mishaps is astonishing. The only mid-air collision was when two C-47s, returning from Berlin, crashed in poor visibility just short of Rhein-Main. In Berlin, the worst incident was on July 25th when a C-47 ploughed into an apartment building in the Friedenau district close to Tempelhof. In all, there were around 100 fatalities attributed to the Airlift. There are 40 British and 30 American names on the memorial at Tempelhof. Most of the deaths were caused by pile-ups on the ground. Of the British who died, 21 were of civilian airlines.

The RAF handled most of the west-bound traffic out of Berlin. To support industry and employment, anything from radio and telephone parts to books and toys were carried by air. In a typical week, industrial freight on outward flights totalled around 1,500 tons. There were also passengers, many of them sick or orphaned children. The worst moment in Flying Officer Weller's flying career came in bad weather over the Soviet zone just before Christmas 1948.

We had brought a load of children from Gatow to Luebeck. Normally there was a courier, an adult sent with the children, but my load for some reason was without this courier. It wasn't a very good day. It was instrument flying most of the way back, not rough, just murky. Everything went all right until we got into the blind approach pattern at Luebeck to make an instrument approach to the runway … We had just turned on to final approach when the aircraft started to go into a fairly violent nose-up attitude and I trimmed forward and pushed forward on the stick. I had to take a bit of power off as well. We were in cloud on instruments, not very high up, it would probably be only 1,200 feet. I shouted to the wireless operator to see what was wrong. He opened the passenger door and found that nearly all the children were clustered at the rear end of the aircraft. He gesticulated and shouted for them to come forward and they got the message. I was able to retrim the aircraft and put some power on. I had missed the runway by this time and settled down into making another instrument approach pattern to pick up the runway again. What had happened was that, getting towards the end of the journey, one child had wanted to go to the toilet and the others had made a line. Which is always the way at children's parties. But I got them down all right.

Though organisation was tight there was a limit to what could be done to account for the human factor. Nineteen-year-old Alan Johnson was on night duty at the Air Safety Centre in Berlin when crisis struck.

Everything was going smoothly when at midnight I got a call from someone who sounded very authoritative. He said fog was descending on Gatow, and I had to stop all flights … So I rang all the airfields in West Germany and told them to stop flying. Some planes were diverted back. Anyhow, after about two hours, the phone rang and a voice said 'This is vice air marshal' … (whoever he was). 'I want to know who stopped flights coming in and why.' So I told him but clearly he didn't believe me because he said, 'Get me your commanding officer.' On this particular night it was a flight lieutenant – I can't recall his name … but he had a big bristly moustache and was ex-aircrew. He was a bastard. Anyhow I rushed down to his office, banged on the door and rushed in. And there he was on one of those folding camp beds having sex with a fraulein. He looked up – I'd never seen anyone performing sex before and I thought 'well if that's it, there's not much fun in it' – it looked dreadful, anyhow he looked up, saw me and said 'get out' so I went back outside and stood to attention. He came out, tucking his shirt into his trousers and wanted to know what the hell I thought I was doing. I might have asked the same thing but instead I gave him the story. Eventually it was all smoothed over. It was a long time before I realised why but he was always a good friend of mine thereafter.

*

With Tempelhof and Gatow at the limits of their expansion and with neither suitable for intensive use by four-engined heavy aircraft, there was an urgent need for a new airport. The only open site of sufficient size was in the French sector at Tegel, a former training ground for Goering's anti-aircraft divisions. The French military was happy to go along with a proposal that was already on their drawing board, waiting to be made real when it could be afforded. The deal was sweetened by an open dollar cheque and an undertaking that the work would be overseen by USAF engineers.

The first of what was to become a 17,000-strong labour force, many of them war widows seeking means of support, signed on for heavy digging on August 5th, 1948. The scale of the enterprise was breathtaking. A five-month timetable called for a main runway with hundreds of acres of taxiways, access roads and aprons. Support buildings included a control tower, five stations and an infirmary. Foundations from two to five feet deep were made of brick rubble and crushed rock brought in from bomb sites. Ten thousand barrels of surface asphalt were flown in.

Space on the Airlift had also to be found for heavy equipment, cut into manageable sections. A team of engineers, skilled in the use of oxyacetylene torches, welded the parts back into working machinery. The height of their realised ambition was to reassemble an electrical generator which became the largest of its kind in west Berlin. But even sectioned-up equipment was a challenge for the Airlift. Food and fuel had to take priority. Tunner's contribution was to change the ground plan to allow for the runway to be parallel to runways at Gatow and Tempelhof. This was to avoid cross flight paths, a curse for air traffic control.

The first plane to land at Tegel was a Dakota carrying a mixed load of tractor tyres, cooking oil and condensed milk. That was on November 18th, well ahead of the completion date. But all was not ready. The pilot, Squadron Leader A.M. Johnson, reported that while the runway and taxiways were up to standard, the rest of the site was thick with glutinous mud. There was no one to supervise the unloading. In the end, Johnson had to take his cargo back to Luebeck. It was a disappointing start. However, by the end of the year Tegel, destined in happier days to become Berlin's main airport, was up and running.

One problem easily solved was the close proximity of two transmitting towers for the communist-controlled Berlin Radio.

They had to go. Sergeant Donald Stensrud was on duty as senior traffic controller at Tegel.

> A French sergeant came hurrying up the tower stairway to tell us we had to evacuate. It seemed that the French commandant was preparing to demolish two Russian-controlled radio towers close to the path of incoming aircraft.

Stensrud could hardly believe that such a high-risk strategy would be played out but he soon found out that the French were deadly serious. Polite requests to have the towers moved had been met with a surly refusal. A formal note from General Jean Ganeval warned that the towers would be out of use after December 15th. The next day, a call to Tegel diverted incoming aircraft while those on the ground were told to sit tight.

> We all got out of the control tower and I saw the French grab the Russian guards and prepare the dynamite. I was wishing I had a camera. It was a neat, clean job; a big bang and the radio towers were gone.[4]

Neues Deutschland protested at 'an act of barbarism'.

Berlin Radio was soon on air again, broadcasting from a station at Grunau in the Soviet zone. In an attempt to repair relations, the French handed over to Soviet control the village of Stolpe on the edge of the French sector, an arbitrary decision that took no account of the wishes of the inhabitants.

When Tegel was fully operational, the three airports in west Berlin were together handling 800 planes a day. By the end of the year the loading flank of the Airlift embraced Wunstorf, Fassberg, Celle (operational from December), Schleswigland (operational from November), Fuhlsbuettel and Luebeck, all in the British zone. The risk of ice on the Havel closed Finkenwerder. In the American zone, Wiesbaden and Rhein-Main were the dispatch points. A military backup originally numbering hundreds now ran into thousands.

*

After their early encounters, Tunner and Curtis LeMay managed to rub along. Content for his colleague to be on a loose rein, the chief of US Air Forces in Europe came to respect Tunner as 'the transportation expert to end all transportation experts'. His successor was less open-minded.

In late September, LeMay was posted to Omaha to head Strategic Air Command. In his place came General John Cannon, a pugnacious front-line fighter who had worked his way up through the ranks to earn distinction in the North African and Mediterranean campaigns. Cannon was a traditionalist who set value by the rule book and was not about to be upstaged by a know-all West Pointer who assumed the right to do things his own way. For his part, Tunner regarded his new boss as an 'aging combat man' (Cannon was ten years older) who had little to bring to the party except an over-scrupulous regard for precedent. Confrontations were frequent. It was hardly surprising. Tunner's inability to exercise tact or accept criticism was notorious.

It was some time before Tunner realised that treating people as units was not the way to get the best out of them. One of his early mistakes was to allocate jobs which cut across squadron loyalty. Had he been asked, Cannon could have set him right on the virtue of the standard air force structure in fostering camaraderie. By the same token, Tunner was slow to appreciate the importance of public relations.

When reports filtered through to headquarters of a pilot throwing down sweets to children watching the planes land at Tempelhof, Tunner assumed it a time-wasting distraction from the job in hand. He soon found that heart-warming stories helped his cause in Berlin and even more in Washington. The publicity created by Lieutenant Gail Halvorsen was to make the prematurely balding 27-year-old Mormon from Garland, Utah, a media star on both sides of the Atlantic. Halvorsen was everything a good American boy should be. With his friendly grin and easy familiarity with strangers, he identified with the Berlin children who had none of the chocolate and chewing gum that were in the pockets of every kid back home. So was born the idea of dropping candy by miniature parachutes made from handkerchiefs. Everybody knew when Halvorsen's plane was coming in; he would 'wiggle the wings' just as he had when he flew over his parents' farm in Utah to 'let them know it was me'. Before long, an ever-growing crowd of children gathered at the approach to Tempelhof to wait for Onkel Wackelfluegel (Uncle Wiggly Wings).

Taken up by the Berlin press, the story was soon in papers across the world. Halvorsen was officially adopted as a good-will ambassador while the rest of his squadron joined in what became known as Operation Little Vittles. A full-time secretary was allotted to deal with Halvorsen's fan mail, addressed to Der Schokoladen Flieger (The Chocolate Flier) or Onkel Wackelfluegel. Operation 'Little Vittles' was soon dropping 6,000 consignments of goodies a day. Parachutes were no longer needed. Boxes were simply emptied out of the cargo door. And if the public heartstrings still needed a pull, there was a copious supply of press pictures of suspiciously neat and well turned-out youngsters waving at incoming flights and playing Airlift games with model planes.

There were other good news stories attached to the Airlift. From early August to late September, the daily tonnage arriving in Berlin increased from around 3,000 tons to more than 4,500 tons, close on half of what west Berlin had consumed before the blockade. One of several notable records was scored on September 18th, US Air Force Day, when 6,987 tons of coal were flown in; the RAF contribution was 1,500 tons. Another record went to a German ground crew who unloaded 19 tons of coal in just twelve minutes.

The projection to the end of the year was for Operation Vittles to deliver between 3,100 and 4,300 tons daily with Operation Plainfare bringing in just over 1,000 tons. But success or failure hinged almost entirely on the approaching winter. If it was anywhere near as bad as the winter of 1946/47, the economy of western Europe would seize up and the Airlift would be frozen to the ground.

'I had seen troops supplied by air and knew to what a catastrophe it must lead', wrote a veteran of Stalingrad. 'I gave up hope for Berlin.'

CHAPTER TEN

A cold spell in early September 1948 raised spirits in the Soviet camp. Memories of Hitler's armies foundering in the snow encouraged Stalin to believe that 'General Winter' would see him right. All he had to do was to cross his fingers and hope that the elements would do their worst. They were slow in responding. The second half of September was milder than usual. When the figures were totted up for the month it was found that the Airlift had delivered close on 140,000 tons of cargo to Berlin, an average of over 4,600 tons a day, more than enough to meet minimum standards.

Thereafter, the scorecard was less impressive as the weather deteriorated. By late October there was a succession of target failures, mostly in coal deliveries. Tunner remained confident. But even he must have had doubts when the November fog descended. Fifteen of the 30 days were almost impossible for flying. The monthly delivery total was the lowest since July. Landing at Tempelhof in a pea-souper, Clay found how bad it was getting when 'we were unable to follow the jeep that was sent to guide us and finally reached the unloading ramp guided by an airman under each wing signalling with flashlights'.

With indelible memories of the savage winter of 1946/47, the press was full of doom-laden predictions. 'As every expert knows', opined the left-wing *New Statesman*, 'despite their immense psychological effect, aircraft cannot be relied upon to provision Berlin in the winter months.' An American pollster found that 90 per cent of west Berliners did not believe they could get through the dismal months without calling on Soviet aid.

In barnstorming mood, Clay made a flying visit to Washington on October 21st. At a meeting of the NSC he argued passionately for sending more C-54s to Germany. Of the 200 American planes in the Airlift, 160 of them were Skymasters. Clay wanted another 64 to support what he described as an 'impressive and efficient operation'. He got his way, though with a warning that 'Our present military power cannot effectively support the supply of Berlin by airlift on an indefinite basis' without putting heavy strain on 'primary national security responsibilities'.

There was more good news for Tunner in the near-completion of the new airport at Tegel, additional runways at Tempelhof and the greater efficiency achieved by combined operations. But it did not take an expert to realise that fog, snow and ice could make a mockery of delivery targets.

November 1948 turned out to be the worst month for the Airlift. On the 13th, the city was enveloped in a fog said to be 1,000 feet deep. Forecasters told Tunner it could last for weeks. On the 18th only 25 planes took off from Rhein-Main. Daily deliveries fell to under 2,500 tons. A C-54 from Frankfurt to Berlin, having failed to land, returned to Frankfurt, was refused yet again and ended up delivering 10 tons of coal to Marseille.

A British journalist who managed to get through to Gatow described the 'eerie sensation' of circling over Berlin waiting 'to plunge into the sea of dense fog'.

In the cockpit nothing could be seen but the green glow from the instrument panel; nothing was audible above the roar of the engines and the chattering of the radio. Then, abruptly, the dive into clouds of billowing obscurity, followed seconds later by a sudden blinding radiance as the sodium lights rushed up out of the darkness. A twin line of flares, each with its foggy halo, marked the path along the PSP metal runway; a clanking jolt as the heavily burdened undercarriage made contact ... Twenty minutes later the same crew would be taxiing their empty plane back through the fog to the runway, ready to take off again into the night.[1]

Heavy storms were also a hazard. Several planes suffered electrical failures, windscreens were shattered by lightning.

Relations between air and maintenance crews, both under intense pressure, deteriorated with the weather. A blame culture put at risk the streamlining beloved by Tunner, as John Holdcroft testifies.

I had to de-ice a Halton aircraft. We covered the whole lot; the fuselage, the tailfins, everything. This particular aircraft taxied round to the runway and loaded and loaded, and got behind, with a lot of time waiting for clearance. It'd been de-iced but when it eventually got clearance the pilot brought it back to the dispersal point and said the plane hadn't been de-iced. We were standing there with our de-icing fluid. I wasn't very happy. I said, 'what do you think this is, scotch mist?' There was a row and I was reported. In the end it was said that I was 50% to blame, and the pilot was 50% to blame but he wasn't – he was 100% to blame because he'd stood there on the runway for so long the plane had iced up again.

If vitamin C tablets, cod liver oil, dehydrated potatoes, tinned processed meat, dried milk and egg, tea brewed from apple peel, and ersatz coffee (known as *muckefuck*) counted as food, there was just enough to go round. What made life thoroughly miserable were the cuts in electricity and gas. One hot meal a day was the best any ordinary family could hope for and there was rarely coal or wood for the hearth. The previous winter had disposed of many of Berlin's famous linden trees and any timber left standing did not last long.

Electricity supply was restricted to four hours a day. Those whose jobs depended on a regular source of power were the worst hit by the cuts. It was accepted that families would go short of domestic fuel and would suffer power cuts, but supplies to industry could not be switched on and off capriciously. If west Berlin's economy faltered, unemployment would mount and there would be more mouths to feed out of public subsidy. Moreover, as Ernst Reuter attested: 'If the people have no work they will lose heart whether they have enough to eat or not. They will surrender to Communism.'

In the event, though Berlin's economy took a steep dive after the start of the blockade, with unemployment tripling to nearly 18 per cent, some 56,000 workers were taken on to support the Airlift. After six months only one of every twenty workers was wholly unemployed. Much credit went to the larger firms adopting work-sharing and finding ways to economise on power; also to businesses in west Germany which kept up demand for products 'made in Berlin'.

Hand-operated generators came into general use. An

enterprising dentist had his wife pedalling hard on a bicycle generator so that he could continue using his drill. Malnourished children and the elderly were the most vulnerable. Over 15,000 of the youngest Berliners became passengers of the Airlift, sent on their way to join relatives or family friends in the West. Older people who had no choice but to stay put went to neighbouring 'warming centres' where they could gather round a communal stove. A thermos flask was a precious possession; candles fetched a high price. Soap was a rarity and baths were cold. Clothing was so scarce that articles could be bought only on production of a certificate proving 'essential need'.

The city at night was scary. Doctor Wilhelm Kemner enjoyed visiting a friend in the evenings to play chess but he feared walking home afterwards. There were no street lamps and his only guides were the occasional flickering candles in blackened ruins. He kept to the middle of the wide, empty streets.

Deep wells that had survived Allied bombing allowed for an adequate water supply throughout the blockade. But with limited power for sewage disposal, the open waterways were soon heavily polluted. However, infectious diseases such as dysentery and diphtheria were kept under control, causing only a tiny fraction of the deaths reported in the year after the war.

With the need to create maximum cargo space, the science of air transport became ever more sophisticated. In the early days, dried pea soup was favoured by dieticians if not by those who had to eat it. But it was not so much the sour taste as the competition with other essential products that reduced consignments. Taking two hours to cook, thick dried soup was wasteful of precious fuel.

A programme of self-help encouraged Berliners to grow their own vegetables until it was realised that fertiliser occupied a quarter more space than dried greens. Saccharin was lighter than sugar.

To save air weight, all meat was boned. No sauces or spices were carried. Even an onion became something of a luxury.

Sunderland flying boats were carrying salt to Lake Havel up to December 14th when the risk of ice put an end to the operation. A week earlier, a full load of 10,020 lbs of salt was taken off a Sunderland in three minutes twelve seconds, marking another Airlift record.

★

Movement on the diplomatic front stalled with the approach of the US presidential election in early November. This was not how Truman wanted it. Trailing in the polls, he cast about for a grand gesture that would boost his ratings. What better than a direct appeal to Stalin to support the cause of world peace?

Holding on to the belief that Stalin was open to reasoned (American) argument if the facts were presented to him face-to-face, Truman decided to send his old friend, chief justice Fred Vinson, a former treasury secretary, to 'talk peace' with the Soviet leader. It was not a job that Vinson relished but, persuaded that he could make a difference, he accepted the mission.

Truman had not thought through the consequences. Over in Paris for the Berlin session of the United Nations, George Marshall reacted angrily to a proposal that undercut his authority as secretary of state and put at risk the Allied consensus. Others who were close to Truman joined the protest. After objections from Senator Vandenberg who assumed, rightly, that Truman's chief objective was a campaign 'shot in the arm', the president gave way. Vinson was told to stand down. That might have ended the matter, had not the *Chicago Tribune* caught on to the story. Journalistic licence suggested that Marshall was threatening to resign in protest at Truman's appeasement of communism. A strong presidential rebuttal promising no repeat of Munich was well received in Berlin where tensions were raised by any talk of a diplomatic fudge.

While in Paris, Marshall took the opportunity to sit down with Bevin and Robert Schuman, a shining light in the murky world of French post-war politics. Born in Luxembourg to Franco-German parents, Schuman's legal training and service to the Resistance heralded a rapid ascent in government. As foreign minister he sought reconciliation with a democratic Germany as part of a broader movement for European unity.

At the three-power meeting at the Quai d'Orsay on October 4th, Schuman took a stronger line than his predecessors, insisting that the blockade had to be lifted before there were further negotiations with Moscow but suggesting that a third-party mediator might be brought into play. Already bruised by the Vinson episode, Marshall was reluctant to adopt another hostage to fortune. The imminence of the presidential election and the likely sequel of a shake-out at the White House starting at the top, also favoured caution. The western position was stronger than commonly realised, said Marshall. The USAF had entered the jet age with the Lockheed F-80 Shooting Star and while he did not want to lay too much stress on the A-bomb, 'it was the atomic weapon which … enables us to discount all question of Soviet military action'.[2]

On October 25th, a Security Council resolution calling for the lifting of the blockade with the simultaneous introduction of the east mark as the sole currency in Berlin was vetoed by the Soviet Union. Stalin had no intention of ending the blockade without preconditions. Equally, the western allies rejected the proposal for reopening four-power talks while the blockade was still in place. Stalemate.

While a UN-appointed committee of experts began searching for a way to reconcile the contradictions in Berlin's finances, the

Security Council turned its attention to Palestine where Zionists had assassinated the UN mediator, Count Bernadotte. His last report to the General Assembly had urged an end to hostilities on the basis that 'a Jewish state called Israel exists in Palestine and that there are no sound reasons for assuming that it will not continue to do so'.[3]

Palestine and Berlin both featured in the presidential campaign but it was anti-communist fervour, with Berlin as its sharpener, that gave the edge to the sitting tenant in the White House.

Before the election of Donald Trump, Truman's re-election had been described as the biggest political upset in American history. No one, except Truman himself, expected him to win. There were even moves in his own party to select a candidate deemed more electable. Eisenhower was a favoured choice. The Republican hopeful was Governor Dewey of New York, a veteran campaigner who came close to winning against Roosevelt in 1944. By comparison, Truman lacked charisma, a poor speaker who distracted audiences by flapping his hands. What he did have was gritty determination. His opponents failed to appreciate his will to fight. By contrast, Dewey's laid-back style came across as patronising to ordinary voters.

Seen as more of a threat to Truman, in that he would siphon off votes leaving the field clear for Dewey, was the independent, Henry Wallace, a former vice president and latterly head of the Progressive Party. His appeal was to disaffected liberals who were disappointed at Truman's low-key domestic agenda. But, portrayed as a communist stooge, only too happy to cooperate with Moscow to bring about the downfall of democracy in Europe and Asia, Wallace the isolationist soon lost momentum. Truman played foreign policy as his strongest card, presenting himself as the leader of the western nations against the evils portrayed by the

Soviet Union. The unions and the farmers, both powerful lobbies, declared for the candidate who would stand up for America.

Right up to the wire, the pollsters were confident of a Dewey win by a substantial margin. In the event, not only was Truman triumphant by 49.5 per cent to 44.5 per cent of the popular vote, but both houses of Congress fell to the Democrats. Nowhere were the results celebrated more enthusiastically than in Berlin where, despite the privations, Soviet bribes were scorned. Extra rations from the east were on offer to all who cared to register with the communist administration. No obstacles were put in the way of anyone who wanted to change allegiance. Few took the opportunity.

Institutions that had been set up to foster cooperation between the two sides were progressively divided along ideological lines. The SED, having purged 'unreliable' elements to put a communist stamp on all its activities, increasingly alienated those in the west who had put their faith in a broad-based city administration. On November 15th, by Russian order, Ernst Reuter, already displaced as mayor, was removed from his elected post in charge of transportation and public services.

By now there were over 70 checkpoints where communist police confiscated food and other goods while detaining those who were carrying 'seditious' literature such as west Berlin newspapers. Officials who were anything but card-carrying members of the SED were labelled 'fascist warmongers' and faced dismissal or worse if they worked on the wrong side of the boundary. Schools and colleges came under pressure to conform to Soviet dictates. The first lectures at west Berlin's Free University, founded in protest at communist domination of the older establishment, were held on November 15th. No longer able to meet in its city hall, now in the hands of the communist 'Democratic Bloc', the democrat majority of the Assembly found a new home in the British sector.

With *Neues Deutschland* leading the attack on an 'irresponsible' Magistrat, the SED resolved that the city administration had 'ceased to exist'. On Tuesday, November 30th, a 'special meeting of the Assembly' was held in the state opera house in east Berlin. Representatives of communist bodies such as Free German Youth and the League of the Victims of the Nazi Regime, together with what was now called the Democratic Bloc, elected a new Magistrat with Fritz Ebert, a son of the first chancellor of the Weimar Republic, as mayor. These moves went unrecognised in the west where the three military commanders voiced their confidence in the legally elected Magistrat.

By the terms of Berlin's provisional constitution, agreed by the four powers, citywide elections were to be held before the end of the year. With an anti-communist result a foregone conclusion, the SED launched a campaign to boycott free voting while fuelling rumours that the Allies would shortly abandon Berlin. After the Soviet authorities had forced a postponement by demanding the exclusion of 'militants, fascists and warmongers', a category that embraced most western-orientated politicians, December 5th was fixed as the day when Berliners would go to the polls.

In an effort to deter voters in the east, the Soviet military administration declared election Sunday to be a normal working day. Despite this and clumsy attempts at intimidation and an appeal to voters to boycott the election, there was a record turnout. The result gave overwhelming victory to the democratic parties that took their strength from the west. The Social Democrats came out top of the landslide, increasing their Assembly representation from 63 to 76 seats. Reuter returned to his old job as mayor, heading an all-party coalition as the only workable form of city government. Meanwhile, in the east sector, a new Magistrat, with the SED in control, assumed power. There were now two mutually hostile city councils.

★

With the approach of Christmas, the well publicised deprivations of west Berlin touched hearts and opened wallets. Made famous by coast-to-coast appearances to promote the Airlift, Gail Halvorsen was the preferred agent for charitable enterprise. Lunching at a New York restaurant, the celebrity was approached by John Swersey of the American Confectioners Association. 'We are really excited about what is going on out there and want to do more. How much of our stuff can you use, Lieutenant?'

Halvorsen was lost for an answer. But a month later, a freight car loaded with 3,500 lbs of candy bars and gum turned up at Rhein-Main. Another shipment of 3,000 lbs arrived the following week. The challenge of distributing this largesse was met by the decision to hold a series of mass Christmas parties. A camel called Clarence was enlisted to help distribute thousands of gift parcels that arrived in Fassberg for Berlin children.

A seasonal morale boost for Airlift forces was provided by the legendary entertainer Bob Hope. Throughout the war, his tours had been hugely popular with troops based overseas but 1948 was his first Christmas show. It got off to a rocky start. As originally planned, he was to make two appearances, the first at USAF headquarters at Wiesbaden, a second in Berlin. Tunner was outraged. He took it as an insult that most of his task force was to be denied live festive entertainment. Hope's schedule was speedily rearranged to allow for additional performances to include Celle and Fassberg where the feeling of neglect was strongest. The comedian was accompanied by Irving Berlin who wrote a song to celebrate Operation Vittles.

When Bob Hope appeared at Tempelhof, Jean Eastham was in the audience.

> We were all ready, pressed into the wings, Irving Berlin was at the piano waiting but Bob Hope hadn't turned up – because of the airlift, it was said, he'd been detained. Then he came down the central aisle with a parachute hanging behind him. He and Irving Berlin were bantering together. Bob Hope said 'Berlin – I'd change your name if I were you – with a name like that you could be divided into four sectors!' It sounds ever so corny now, but it was so funny!

The show was recorded and retransmitted across the States. The introduction by a studio-based announcer gives the flavour of American sentiment.

> These are the boys who keep the airlift in Berlin running, the boys who gave up their Christmas to help strengthen the cause of humanity. Because of these men a child eats who might otherwise go hungry and the light of freedom looms more brightly in the world.

Prominence was given to Lever Brothers, makers of Swan Soap, who sponsored the tour.

After a dismal November for the Airlift, December was just about tolerable, a dramatic reversal of the track record of the previous year. It began to look as if Stalin might be disappointed in his expectations of General Winter. On the last day of the year, Rex Waite wrote to congratulate his colleague and Tunner's deputy, Air Commodore Mercer, on 'the magnificent effort' the Airlift Task Force had made 'during the worst of the weather'. Seen from the

Berlin end of the air bridge, the challenge was to solve the fuel crisis.

> I cannot see how further coal economies can be made without stopping all industry: the unemployment figures are pretty big already. ... But the real crux of the matter is coal for German homes. They have had roughly 50 lbs of coal and 100 lbs of wood for sixty days burning and the cold is beginning to tell on them. No one knows how long they will stick it: but they have plenty of guts, especially when the alternative is Russian domination.

The air commodore need not have worried. With a milder than expected January, more Skymasters on the rota and domestic economies, the risk of a total shutdown of west Berlin's essential services receded to near vanishing point.

CHAPTER ELEVEN

On the last day of 1948, a C-54 from Fassberg, piloted by Captain Gene Patton, landed at Tegel. He was greeted with the news that he had just completed the 100,000th flight of the Airlift. Colonel and soon to be Brigadier General Frank Hayley was jubilant. 'Everybody knew that the Airlift was a success and that the blockade had failed.'

On January 13th, the Airlift scored 755 flights into Berlin, carrying 6,677 tons of supplies, a record beaten only by the Air Force Day marathon the previous September. Throughout January 1949 the Airlift delivered a daily average of 5,547 tons of cargo with the expectation that 'even the present airlift could carry at best another thousand tons a day'. On February 18th, an RAF York landed at Gatow with the Airlift's millionth ton. By then the Russians had accepted that, for them, the winter had been a failure.

Bevin told his Cabinet colleagues: 'The Airlift is now more efficiently organised and is working better than at any time hitherto.'[1] A daily target of 5,620 tons (with Britain contributing 1,250 to 1,500 tons) was well within reach and the graph was expected to rise throughout the summer. Even the characteristically gloomy General Robertson accepted estimates of 7,000 tons a day by July, provided America could keep up the delivery of heavy planes.

The Anglo-American press joined the chorus of congratulation. Surprise, surprise. It seemed that the Airlift had hit on the secret of longevity. The *New York Times* chortled over the 'grave mistake' made by Moscow in assuming that General Winter would be the decisive ally. Other papers adopted the line pushed by General Clay, that the Airlift was cheap at the price, costing less for an entire year than a single day's conflict in the last months of the world war.

Allied confidence was boosted by reports of shortages in the eastern sector where the counter-blockade was biting. A ban on the sale of steel and semi-manufactured steel products cut across the whole of east sector industry and soon made its impact on domestic consumption. When the snow fell, there were not enough shovels to clear it away.

Washington caught the mood of growing confidence. At the Pentagon, the military planners were working on a blueprint to extend the Airlift for up to three years. The target was to raise the average daily ration to 2,100 calories and to bring in extra raw materials for industry. In all, 8,685 tons of cargo had to be flown in every day. This depended on allocating a bigger share of the defence budget to advanced heavy lift transport planes such as the four-engined Boeing C-97 Stratofreighter and the Douglas C-124 Globemaster 2.

The C-97, with a payload of up to 20 tons, had clamshell doors under its tail with a retractable ramp for driving cargo in and out. The first mass-produced transport plane to boast air pressurisation, it eased the pain of long-distance flying. Nicknamed Old Shaky, the Globemaster 2 also had clamshell doors with a hydraulic ramp. It was the only aircraft of its time that could carry heavy equipment such as a tank or bulldozer without having to break the machinery into parts.

Apart from a single C-124, neither plane was ready for action by the spring of 1949 but the promise of their early arrival in Germany came as a welcome fillip to Airlift credibility. As too did the weather forecast. By March, the sun was shining. Burtonwood in England was operating efficiently with planes being checked and repaired in record numbers. With higher standards of training, aircrews were better able to handle heavy aircraft in close formation. Morale climbed with upgraded accommodation, catering and recreation. Tonnage for the month soared to 196,161 tons on 22,163 flights, a daily average of 6,328 tons.

With the Airlift, all was looking good, almost too good in Tunner's opinion. 'It was necessary, I thought, to do something to shake up the command.' The 'something' was an all-time record-breaker. For what became known as the Easter Parade, Tunner decided to focus almost exclusively on coal, with the aim of shifting 10,000 tons over the 24 hours of Sunday, April 16th.

In the run-up, Tunner was out and about urging his crews to show the world just what an airlift could achieve. It was surely no coincidence that his boss and bête noire, General Cannon, was on leave in the US at the time.

The competitive spirit enlivened what was otherwise a dull though highly effective routine. The target was met and then some, with the final tally painted on a Skymaster's nose: Tonnage 12,941, Flights 1,383.

For the duration of the Easter Parade, a plane landed in Berlin every 63 seconds. To witness the air corridor filled with planes at perfectly spaced intervals was, said a spectator, 'a beautiful sight'.

★

Not all the problems went away. The western command was uncomfortably aware that stocks in Berlin were down to less than a month. Fog had descended in February and Berlin's airfields had to shut down for 122 hours. Russian harassment was stepped up, with pilots reporting an increase in the number of buzzing and close flying incidents. Searchlights directed on to the air corridors made night flying hazardous. Radio frequencies were deliberately overcrowded to disrupt communications. But there was comfort in noting that the Russians were holding back on upgrading the blockade, for example by doing more to restrict electricity supplies or by cutting the elevated S-Bahn links between the two sides of the city.

Berlin-watchers spotted other signs that Moscow might be moving towards compromise. A fiery anti-western speech by Colonel Tulpanov, chief of the Russian military information division, scheduled for an SED party congress in east Berlin, was cancelled without explanation. An SED press conference was also called off. A further, more positive hint of change came with a speech by SED leader Walter Ulbricht in which he redefined the status of Berlin. 'We do not consider Berlin a Soviet zone city', he declared, 'but the German capital.' He emphasised that there were no plans to incorporate Berlin into the Soviet zone.

There was even some easing of restrictions on movements between the city sectors. In November, Sokolovsky had introduced new identity cards. This was an alarm signal for workers who crossed the boundary from the west. Would they now be subject to arrest if they failed to produce the required papers? The tension was relieved on January 28th when the east Berlin police announced that the old identity cards would continue to be recognised.

But the strongest signal of rapprochement in Soviet strategy came from Stalin himself, though it took some time for the west to pick up on the message. While the Russian leader rarely gave face-to-face interviews with foreign journalists, he was not entirely uncommunicative. His chosen method for making his views public was to invite selected reporters to submit written questions to which, after due consideration, he would respond with written answers.

In late January 1949, the mantle fell on Kingsbury Smith, European manager of the International News Service. His lead question related to Berlin:

> If the Governments of the United States of America, the United Kingdom and France agreed to postpone the establishment of a separate Western German state, pending a meeting of the Council of Foreign Ministers to consider the German problem as a whole, would the Government of the U.S.S.R. be prepared to remove the restrictions which the Soviet authorities have imposed on communications between Berlin and the Western zones of Germany?

The answer came back two days later. If the creation of a west German state was postponed to allow the Council of Foreign Ministers to reconvene, 'the Soviet Government could see no obstacles to lifting transport restrictions, on the understanding, however, that transport and trade restrictions introduced by the three powers should be lifted simultaneously.'

Remarkably, no mention was made of the currency question which up to now had been the key point at issue. The recommendation of the UN Committee of Experts that the Soviet east mark should be the sole currency for Berlin having been rejected as 'totally unacceptable' to Washington, a decision was in place to adopt the same financial structure for west Berlin as for west Germany as a whole. It was surely beyond belief that Stalin had nothing to say on the imminent ruling (it came on March 20th) that the east mark was no longer a valid currency in west Berlin. Yet there was no reaction when Reuter interpreted the change from dual currency as a 'definitive recognition that Berlin belonged to the west ideologically, politically and economically'.

With its unerring capacity for missing the main story, the Anglo-American press focused on another aspect of the Kingsbury Smith Q and A only indirectly connected to Berlin. The journalist had wanted to know if Stalin was receptive to a meeting with Truman.

The Soviet leader could see no objection. Why should he? After the aborted Vinson mission in the run-up to Truman's re-election, his independent rival Henry Wallace had picked up on the idea of a peace summit. Moscow had reacted enthusiastically, not least because the proposal embarrassed Truman. From Stalin's point of view there was nothing to lose and much to gain from the unsafe assumption that if they sat down together, the world's two most powerful men could settle all outstanding questions.

Press comment favouring a summit did not go down well with the new secretary of state. (Dean Acheson took over from George Marshall on January 21st.) Like his predecessor, Acheson feared that Stalin would use the opportunity to undermine the diplomatic solid ground. He was against any direct contact with Moscow until the Berlin blockade was lifted.

The Acheson line was endorsed by Truman who added that when talks did take place, they had to be on a multilateral basis involving other interested nations, principally Britain and France. The president said he would be pleased to welcome Stalin to Washington, an invitation he was confident would be turned down.

While the press was still speculating on the chances of a summit, possibly in neutral territory, the inner circle of the state department fastened on to the apparent loss of Soviet interest in shared control of the German currency. What there was to go on supported a tentative diplomatic probing into Stalin's thinking.

The task went to the deputy chief of the US mission to the United Nations. Philip Jessup appeared to be on good personal terms with his Russian counterpart, Jacob Malik. Jessup sought an opportunity to ask, informally, if Stalin had deliberately intended that the currency question be removed from the Berlin agenda. It took Malik three weeks to come up with an answer. There had been no mistake. The view from the Kremlin was that the German currency was no longer a sticking point for discussions on the future of Germany. Jessup went on to ask about a possible lifting of the blockade. After another few days, Malik reported that a solution to the crisis might well be within sight, albeit, according to Robert Murphy, on conditions that were bound to be rejected by the West.[2]

Acheson favoured a positive response, a note to Moscow suggesting a lifting of the blockade early in April prior to a meeting of foreign ministers. Bevin and Schuman were less sanguine. A strengthening of the western alliance with the formation of NATO, though agreed in principle, was still some distance from ratification. Similarly, there was more to do before the Basic Law for west Germany was agreed by all parties. As Bevin wrote: 'Our whole programme in Western Europe and in Western Germany is beginning to take shape and … the raising of the blockade of Berlin, which could be re-imposed at any time, would be a small price for the Russians to pay to stop it.'[3]

Schuman came round to a more relaxed view. A note to Moscow agreeing to a meeting on Berlin would 'serve to contradict Soviet propaganda if, at a later stage, the negotiations came to nothing'. It would also take the wind out of the communist-led peace conference set to meet in Paris.[4]

With the warnings of his European allies in mind, Acheson advanced tentatively, instructing Jessup to make clear to Malik that any discussions on ending the stand-off in Berlin would have to take account of all restrictions imposed since March 1st, 1948 and that preparations for a government for west Germany would continue uninterrupted. On reaching a settlement on Berlin, a meeting of the Council of Foreign Ministers to consider Germany as a whole might follow at the end of June.

Bevin remained convinced that the time was not yet right for a formal approach to Moscow. It would simply hand the advantage to the Russians who 'will do all they can to get out of their present difficult situation at our expense'. In a message to Sir Alexander Cadogan, British representative at the UN, the foreign secretary predicted:

> They [the Russians] will try to get us to make proposals in writing which they can criticize and amend at their pleasure. Meanwhile, Stalin will be pleasantly optimistic about the prospects of a meeting of the Council of Foreign Ministers. When, however, the meeting takes place, all the old manoeuvres will be repeated. There will be indefinite delays and we shall find ourselves back exactly where we were last summer, with this essential difference, that we shall have lost probably for good any prospect of establishing a government in Western Germany.[5]

Bevin was right in thinking that Moscow would try to stop or at least delay a west German government but, having successfully rejected a subtle rephrasing by Moscow of the terms for the resumption of negotiations, Acheson took strength from the dramatic news that Molotov, his old adversary, had been dismissed.

Releases from Russian archives make clear that the foreign minister was carrying the blame for failing to break through in Berlin or to advance the communist cause in west Germany. Summoning Ulbricht and Pieck to Moscow, Stalin had censured them and, by implication, Molotov, for moving prematurely towards an east German state on the model of the Soviet European satellites. He derided Ulbricht for talking about a socialist role in Germany, as the SED was doing, when the party had not yet gained power. 'Discussions on how Germany is to be organized are stupid', he declared. 'First you must win.'[6]

Molotov was replaced by his deputy Andrei Vyshinsky, a legal acolyte to Stalin's purges who was adept at trimming the law to suit the wishes of his master. Vyshinsky was known in the West chiefly for his appearances at the UN when he had tried to block a debate on Berlin, though with rather more finesse than Molotov had shown. No one imagined that the new foreign minister would be an easy ride but he was not thought to be inflexible on Berlin or Germany.

Sokolovsky was also on his way, though not so much for any professional shortcomings as for Stalin's decision to make a clean sweep. The Soviet military governor was made deputy minister of defence, a job he held until 1952 when he became chief of general staff. Following in Sokolovsky's footsteps was General Vasily Chuikov, a hero of Stalingrad who had headed the Red Army offensive in Berlin. Chuikov was noted for his lack of interest in politics, an indication of a change of tone if not necessarily of substance of Soviet policy.

Bevin worried that the new Soviet pecking order would be allowed to intrude on preparations for a west German government run by west Germans. In the event, solid progress was made in the first quarter of 1949. With Adenauer holding the balance between the Land delegates who were inclined to pitch their demands on the high side and the occupying powers who were wary of giving away too much too fast, the Parliamentary Council produced a draft Basic Law which, after some trimming, found favour with the three foreign ministers.

Meanwhile, the military governors had their heads down on producing a formula for future relations between a German government and the western Allies. This was to lead to an Occupation Statute, listing reserved powers including foreign affairs, disarmament and control over the Ruhr, but with the pledge to review matters within eighteen months. In the interim, three high commissioners would take over all civilian functions from the commanders-in-chief.

With Bevin in more emollient mood, the way was clear for Jessup and Malik to resume their conversations on lifting the Berlin blockade. At a meeting of the two diplomats on April 27th, Malik pulled back on demands for a postponement of a west German constitution while conceding that restrictions on transport and communications between the two halves of Berlin might be lifted as soon as a date was set for reconvening the CFM. A provisional understanding was put into writing. Bevin still fretted. 'I am disquieted and uneasy at some aspects of the way things are going', he told Acheson. The Russians 'remain bitterly hostile to our plans for Germany and I am sure there are many difficulties and dangers for us behind their present readiness to lift the blockade and begin negotiations'.[7]

The ground was taken from under him in the first week of May when Tass, the Soviet news agency, reported on the Jessup–Malik conversations and the prospect of four-power negotiations in Germany with hints of lifting the blockade. All bets were off when the Basic Law was ratified by the west German Parliamentary Council on May 8th. But pessimism proved to be unfounded.

On the 11th, the citizens of west Berlin came out on the streets to hear the news from loudspeakers mounted on RIAS jeeps.

Agreement has been reached between the three Western powers and the Soviets regarding the raising of the Berlin blockade and the holding of a meeting of the Council of Foreign Ministers. All communications, transportation and trade restrictions imposed by both sides ... and between Berlin and the Eastern zones will be removed on May 12th ...

At dusk, in streets and in homes, a flick of the switch brought the city to life as electricity supplies from the east zone were resumed. Shortly after midnight, cars and lorries began moving out of Helmstedt on their way to Berlin. A British military train set off at 0123 hours. A new timetable allowed for sixteen freight and six passenger trains, including one for Germans, each day.

As a gift to jaded palates used to dehydrated potatoes, universally judged to be the most disgusting food on offer during the blockade, the trains were loaded with fresh potatoes. At a special meeting of the city Assembly, Mayor Reuter paid tribute to the pilots and aircrews who had died in the Airlift.

The east German press had its own take on these momentous events. Having presented the Jessup–Malik talks as a western device for saving American blushes, *Neues Deutschland* credited the end of the blockade to the communist peace campaign. On May 12th, the newspaper gave over its front page to a communist plan for a meeting of 'all democratic mass organizations in Germany'. The resumption of inter-zonal communications and business was relegated to a paragraph on an inside page.

CHAPTER TWELVE

G eneral Clay could be forgiven his moment of triumphalism. 'The Soviets', he declared, 'have now capitulated entirely.' He must have known he was overstating his case. It was true that the lifting of the blockade was a victory for the West. The simple and fundamental fact was that in an eye-to-eye confrontation, Stalin had blinked first. He had pulled back in Iran and in Greece and exercised restraint in France and Italy where his followers were poised for aggressive action. He came to realise that in Berlin he had no chance of gaining his objectives short of war with an uncertain outcome.

But what, in the end, had Stalin conceded in Berlin? As Robert Murphy pointed out, all the controls imposed by Moscow during the Airlift could be re-imposed at short notice if Stalin thought it would be to his advantage.[1] That was a risk that had to be taken and allowed for. And, indeed, though the blockade had officially ended, the Russians contrived to find ways of disrupting communications. Trains into Berlin were required to have crews vetted by Soviet authorities. Timetables were changed without notice and arbitrary restrictions imposed, such as a ban on trucks using the autobahn at night. Telephone links were cut without notice. Uniformed officials took inordinate time examining transit papers, checking them against a long list of penalties for minor infringements.

As the four foreign ministers deliberated in Paris, the workers on Berlin's Soviet-controlled Reichsbahn railway came out on strike. Their grievance was over wages, not so much the size of the pay packet as what was in it. Some 15,000 workers who lived in the western sectors but were responsible for trains in and out of the east sector were paid in east marks which bought far less than deutschmarks. Soviet denial of any problem allowed the strike to drag on to late June when the three western military commanders agreed to provide funds for 60 per cent of wages to be paid in deutschmarks, initially for three months, in effect a subsidy to the east.

With west Berlin in no state to look after itself, there was no let-up in the Airlift. The machine-like routine, 'this steady rhythm, constant as a jungle drum', as Tunner put it, with daily deliveries averaging 8,000 tons, continued into the fall of 1949. It was not until October 1st that Tunner was able to announce, 'mission accomplished'.

By then, Clay had retired from the army and was busying himself helping Eisenhower to secure the Republican nomination for the presidency. Memories of the previous May were fresh in his mind. His departure from Berlin was marked by a victory parade. Alongside a visibly exhausted but jubilant Mayor Reuter, Clay was cheered by thousands of Berliners lining the streets. On his return to America there was a ticker-tape parade in New York, an address to Congress and a fishing holiday on the Chattahoochee River. It was a satisfying end to an illustrious military career.

For the prime architect of the Airlift, the sequel was more of an anti-climax. A tireless self-promoter, General Tunner made sure that his part in the Berlin story was fully recorded. The plaudits he received for achieving what few thought was possible were fully justified. Never before had there been anything quite like the Berlin Airlift. What Tunner found hard to accept was that there would be nothing quite like it ever again. Greater carrying capacity with heavy-duty air transporters was all well and good but successful delivery depended on the absence of ground fire. The limitations on bringing in equipment and reinforcements by air were soon demonstrated, all too tragically, in Indo-China in 1954 when French forces fighting guerrilla insurgents were trapped in the village of Dien Bien Phu, 170 miles from their supply base at Hanoi. Artillery fire from the surrounding hills ruled out airborne support or any sort of rescue operation. Of a force of nearly 17,000 only 3,000 survived the siege or subsequent captivity.

In lobbying hard for bigger and faster cargo planes, Tunner came up against the military establishment who held that the USAF should focus on upgrading its bombing power. Tunner's single-minded dedication combined with an irascible personality cost him dear in the race for promotion. When the job of commanding the Military Air Transport Service fell vacant in 1951, he was passed over in favour of General Joseph Smith, his unfairly maligned predecessor in running the Airlift. Their relationship did not improve.

★

The core significance of the Airlift was that it committed America to Berlin and thus to west Germany and thus to Europe. Without the Airlift, it is unlikely that the North Atlantic Treaty Organization would have shaped up in the way it did. Embracing America and Canada with ten European nations, NATO was designed to deter Russian aggression and German revanchism.

In a typical pithy aside, Lord Ismay, Churchill's wartime chief of staff and NATO's first secretary general, gave it as his brief 'to keep the Russians out, the Americans in and the Germans down'.

Truman hailed NATO as 'the last nail in the coffin of isolationism'. It was also a nail, though not quite the last, in the coffin of the Council of Foreign Ministers. Its meetings in Paris spread over May and June 1949 deteriorated to empty rhetoric. Stalin knew that his call for a revival of the Allied Control Council for Germany with the right of national veto would go unanswered, while the Allies did not need to be told that supervised free elections across Germany were unacceptable in Moscow. An old idea of creating a military-free zone by the mutual withdrawal of forces had some traction until the West realised that it would leave Berlin more isolated and thus more vulnerable to a Soviet takeover.

When the foreign ministers went their separate ways on June 20th, it was with the unstated understanding that they would live and let live in Germany. The CFM was not to meet again for five years.

Stalin did not give up in Germany. A draft constitution for the Soviet zone was on the drawing board. Notwithstanding lobbying by Ulbricht to have it approved, Stalin held back while there was still a chance that the western consensus might fall apart. That all things were possible had been borne out in January when Peking surrendered to the People's Liberation Army. After the fall of Shanghai on the fourth day of the CFM conference, Stalin could find consolation for backtracking on Berlin in the sure knowledge that China would soon join the communist bloc. And there were other rich pickings still to be had in Asia. Korea came to mind.

But the advance of communism in Europe was on hold. A constitution for what may now properly be called West Germany or the Federal Republic was signed off by the military governors on May 12th, the very day that the Berlin blockade ended. With the transfer of power from the military to civilian government, the military governors were designated high commissioners. Clay was then succeeded by former head of the World Bank, John McCloy, while General Koenig handed over to André François-Poncet, a pre-war ambassador to Germany. General Robertson stayed on. No longer commander-in-chief, his authority came from the Foreign Office with instructions from Bevin to keep in 'close touch with McCloy and ... to establish relations which go beyond the normal, rather sporadic contact between High Commissioners'.[2] The aim was to keep a check on any inclination McCloy might have to assert American priorities over British interests.

Bevin's sensitivity was justified. The Airlift had marked a high point in Anglo-American relations. But it had shown up the weaknesses as much as the strength of the alliance. Bevin had good reason to be proud of his role in shaping events. By giving early and unreserved support to the Airlift he had ensured, as it were, that it got off the ground. NATO, in its early days, was largely an Anglo-American affair. But Bevin was less successful in challenging the American post-war impression of Britain as a spent force.

British dedication to a common cause was welcomed in Washington until it came to a point where the weaker partner tried calling the shots. Bevin reacted sharply to any hint that he might be excluded from decision-making, while he was seemingly unaware that his constant stream of exhortations to the state department to raise its act was more irritating than helpful. With their innate sense of superiority, British diplomats could be exasperating in their offer of superfluous advice.

American resentment was fed by the knowledge that, high-flown sentiments aside, Britain was unable to keep pace with its commitments. The return to great power status, promised within five years of the end of the war, was a fading vision. The real and immediate prospect was of another financial crisis.

A hard act to follow, Lewis Douglas was succeeded as US ambassador in London by Walter Sherman Gifford, a 65-year-old businessman whose knowledge of Britain was confined to a motoring tour in the 1930s. His disinclination to get involved in detail kept him apart from the day-to-day consultations Bevin had enjoyed with Douglas. But like Douglas, the latest ambassadorial incumbent recognised that Britain was 'over extended economically, politically and militarily'. He was aware of sensitivities on the Anglo-American relationship, but frustrated by the inability of the British government to get its house in order.

The continuing fuel crisis headed the list of American fault-finding. Debates on how Britain might contribute to the European Recovery Program initiated by Marshall Aid returned time and again to the need to increase coal exports. How else could Britain claim to be the dominant power in Europe? There was bold talk of 'dealing with the minority of workers not pulling their weight', even of increasing the working day by a half hour 'for a limited period', but when it came down to hard decisions the chalice was passed to the government-appointed National Coal Board which had all the responsibility for managing the industry but none of the power to raise the investment needed for modernisation.

After the disastrous winter of 1947, it was not until the snow had cleared and the ensuing floods subsided that a start was made on planning for the next winter. Informed opinion held that another fuel crisis was almost inevitable (it came in 1951) with coal consumption outstripping production for years ahead. A conversion from coal to oil advanced fitfully and it was not until 1953 that a start was made on Britain's first nuclear power station.

Among other sources of discord the British tendency to invoke

Commonwealth and Empire as justification for privileged status was particularly irksome. Of all the evils in the world, Americans regarded imperialism only a little way short of communism. The widely predicted break-up of the British Empire, following independence for India in 1947, was warmly welcomed across the Atlantic.

But it was the economic factor that weighed most heavily on the Anglo-American accord. Britain's finances were in free fall. A commitment to sterling as an international trading currency to rival the dollar put an intolerable strain on export industries that had to cope with an overvalued pound. The inevitable break came in 1949 with a devaluation of sterling by a third of its value. There was little sympathy in America for what was seen there as a self-inflicted crisis. Though it was early days, voices in Washington were heard to promote West Germany as having more in common with American values. These feelings were reciprocated. The consolidation of the Federal Republic accorded with Adenauer's dream of modelling his country on America's record of achievement and success.

The first nationwide election since Hitler came to power was held across the Federal Republic on August 14th. It turned into a presidential-style contest between Adenauer and Schumacher. As the now undisputed leader of the CDU and as a much-lauded chairman of the Parliamentary Council, Adenauer had carved out a reputation as a safety-first politician and statesman, one who could deal with the Allies on his own terms. Schumacher was more the inspirational crowd-puller who excited audiences with visions of a social renewal wedded to egalitarian ideals.

Inevitably, Schumacher was tarred with the 'red brush', a sure vote-loser in the wake of the Berlin crisis. But Adenauer was vulnerable to claims that he was too ready to go along with American-inspired policies for perpetuating the division of Germany, acceding to the loss of the Saar and to the international control of the Ruhr. Put more constructively, Adenauer's aim was to integrate the Federal Republic into the western sphere of influence, to advance his country from an 'occupied state' to 'western ally'. This required not only an accommodation with America but also reconciliation with France. Britain was important insofar as it could influence America to favour the interests of the Federal Republic.

The election was close-run. The CDU came out ahead with 139 seats, only eight ahead of the SPD. Once again, the Free Democrats and the Germany Party, mustering a total of 69 seats, were the power-brokers. Significantly, the communists ended up with a mere 6 per cent of the vote and just fifteen seats. Adenauer was only too pleased to forge a coalition with the two small centre parties. He was elected chancellor by a margin of one vote – his own, as the opposition delighted in pointing out. For Schumacher, the defeat was a blow from which he never recovered. Even the consolation prize, the federal presidency, was snatched from him.

The new government opened for business in Bonn, a small university town near Cologne which happened to be Adenauer's home ground. Known as the 'federal village', Bonn was an unlikely choice for a capital. Frankfurt and Hamburg had a far stronger claim. But since putting the Bundestag (parliament) and Bundestrat (representing the Laender) in Berlin was out of the question, it made sense not to settle anywhere that might look to be too much of a rival to Berlin.

This left west Berlin in the curious position of lacking a clear German identity except as an outpost of western democracy, a 'capitalist oasis in a communist desert' as one observer put it. The big question was whether it could be made to work. When, earlier in the year, Bevin had taken time out from the CFM for a flying visit to Berlin, he announced that at no time since 1945 had he been so optimistic about the future. West Berliners could be forgiven for holding back on a full endorsement. The Airlift, though an undoubted success within its own terms, had been all about survival, not regeneration.

Though the western half of the city had experienced a rebirth, it was still a fledgling in poor health when the Airlift ended. As Bonn was getting used to its celebrity status, the former capital was registering record unemployment. A quarter of a million, a fifth of the working population, were without jobs. A desperate housing shortage was exacerbated by the influx of refugees from the east, more than 170,000 of them in the last quarter of 1949. The smarter shops were well-stocked but were reserved for the wealthy minority.

> In the Kurfürstendamm you see the customary mixture of ruins and luxury. The upper floors of many houses are still uninhabitable but on street level you find the richest and most alluring shops in Europe – high quality products, most un-English food-stuffs, silk, jewellery and china. It is a magnificent show. … Then you see the ruins. Whole square miles are completely obliterated. You cannot see one single tree in the Tiergarten and much of the rubble has not been cleared away yet from many streets all over the city. You walk in the ruined streets for hours and suddenly a surprising phenomenon strikes you. Boards, showing the names of the former and now non-existent streets, have been put back in their old places and little posts erected at street corners; neat little number-plates mark the sites of houses

which stand no more. All this is very logical for one who is trying to find his way with the help of a map.[3]

In October, Mayor Reuter led a delegation to Bonn. He and Adenauer did not get on. Reuter was too impulsive for Adenauer and Adenauer too staid for Reuter. There was no meeting of minds on priorities. Reuter focused exclusively on the problems of Berlin while the chancellor had to remind his visitor that the Federal Republic had wider objectives. It was left to the Allied high commissioners to try to hold the ring.

Reuter's appeal for west Berlin to be accepted as a state on equal terms with the other eleven Laender was rejected, largely on French insistence, as a move that would invite Soviet retaliation. Instead, the free sector of the city was to be designated as an emergency area for which the Bonn government would take responsibility. To kick-start the economy, Berlin was to be given a generous allocation of contracts for public works, tax concessions to support production, and financial aid to help the Magistrat (now called the Senate) balance its budget. The high commissioners agreed to dollar investment in modernising the city infrastructure.

So it was that west Berlin, though integral to the Federal Republic 'in principle', remained a place apart. If its citizens wanted to resettle in another German city, they had to make formal application. To avoid infringement of four-power status, before any Federal law could be applied to west Berlin, it had first to be ratified by the city's new House of Representatives.

The developments in the Federal Republic had great import on Berlin. The first was an end to dismantling industrial plant judged to have military potential. The contradictory policy of building up the West German economy while knocking away some of the strongest foundations had long been apparent. US high commissioner, John McCloy, thought the strategy was nonsense and said so while Robertson, in his last weeks in Germany, argued forcefully for an immediate stay on dismantling. But in France and also in Britain there were commercial lobbies only too pleased for Germany's competitive edge to be blunted. A compromise agreement, reckoned to be a triumph for Adenauer, allowed for a winding down of the programme with an immediate stop on all dismantling in Berlin and a lifting of restrictions on steel output. By 1950, Siemens in Berlin was once again a major steel producer.

The second development that advantaged west Berlin as much as the Federal Republic as a whole was the appointment of Ludwig Erhard as economics minister. Erhard was a disciple of the social market economy, allowing free enterprise to thrive while providing a soft cushion for those who fell victim along the way. A recognised opponent of Nazism, this laissez-faire economist worked on currency reforms for the Bizonia administration before becoming director of the Economic Council in Frankfurt where he took it upon himself to abolish price and production controls.

Though Clay was a root and branch capitalist, he and his advisers were made nervous by this sudden release of entrepreneurial energy. In a session with Erhard, Clay told him sternly that his experts warned of an impending economic disaster. Puffing on his trademark cigar, Erhard had a straight answer: 'My experts tell me the same thing.' Bullish determination was what Clay admired most. He gave his backing to ending the elaborate system of rationing and controls except for prices of basic foodstuffs and for controls on key industries such as coal and steel. Production soared.

As economics minister, Erhard kept chipping away at what he saw as bureaucratic lumber while encouraging innovation and investment. There followed the German economic miracle;

in just three years industrial production rose to its pre-war level. Germany's share of world exports increased from 1.8 per cent to 3.5 per cent in 1950. Over 19 per cent of GDP was invested in new plant and buildings. The comparable figure for Britain was 9 per cent. There were other points of comparison unfavourable to Britain, not least the fact that Germany was able to abolish food rationing six years ahead of Britain. Soon shortages were a thing of the past. In September 1946, there were 10,000 hospital patients in the Duesseldorf area suffering from deficiencies due to hunger. In June 1952, the president of the Rhineland-Westphalia Diet announced that the seats of the chamber at Duesseldorf were to be replaced by larger ones. Having been installed six years earlier, they were no longer broad enough for the bulk of the average deputy.

*

American politicians and businessmen saw the German economy as more dynamic and efficient than the British. Regardless of the deep estrangement during the war years, American entrepreneurs were soon looking to the German market as their focus in Europe.[4]

Seven years after the end of the war that had brought Germany to the lowest point in its chequered history, that part of the country that was entrenched in the western alliance was showing all the signs of re-emerging as a major power. Although Adenauer was loath to admit it, the credit had to be shared with Berlin, a city revived by the Airlift to inspire a debilitated people to rediscover their pride in national identity.

Reading the signs, Stalin moved grudgingly towards allowing east Germany a semblance of self-government. The new framework was justified by the 'national emergency precipitated by the policy of the western powers'. From October 1949, the Soviet zone transmogrified into the German Democratic Republic (DDR or

GDR). Renaming itself as the Soviet Control Commission, the military administration was charged with responsibility for seeing that the DDR fitted into the pattern of east European Soviet satellites. Wilhelm Pieck, by now in his late seventies and in frail health, was the figurehead 'Father of German Unity'. He deferred to Otto Grotewohl as prime minister but he, in turn, took his lead from Walter Ulbricht, who, as deputy prime minister and as secretary of the Socialist Unity Party (SED) acted as the front man in dealings with Moscow.

East Berlin was excluded from the new state but became the seat of government. Admitted to the Council of Mutual Economic Assistance (COMECON), the DDR benefited from a relaxation of reparation but suffered the Ulbricht-inspired collectivisation of industry, commerce and agriculture. Said Stalin, 'The west will make west Germany their own, and we shall turn east Germany into our own state.'

What this meant in practice showed up most vividly in Berlin where the contrast between the two sectors became ever more marked.

> Just as soon as you enter the Russian Sector, you realise that you have arrived in a different world. Although East Berlin is a showpiece – the Russians know that many Western visitors go over to their sector – everything is shabby and poor. After West Berlin's exaggerated – I might almost say infuriating – luxury, the contrast cries aloud. You seem to be able to get a great many things in East Berlin, which, I am told, one cannot get in the Western zone proper, but at a high price and of very poor quality. I saw electrical appliances such as lamps in the shop windows and the thin layer of paint was falling off them before they reached the

customer. I saw black frying pans, made of the worst kind of crude iron, which looked filthy and disgusting. Shoes were appallingly badly made and ugly.[5]

CHAPTER THIRTEEN

After the triumph of the Airlift, and despite its economic straits, Britain was in prime position to take the lead in Europe. The invitation came from Washington. America looked to its wartime ally to act as the binding force for a federal structure of west European democracies, not unlike the United States. National security adviser George Kennan was an early exponent of a European customs union that would also be a vehicle for peaceful co-existence between France and Germany.

The idea was not new. As early as 1929, French foreign minister, Aristide Briand, put to the League of Nations a plan for European-wide economic collaboration. That Briand spoke with the support of his German counterpart, Gustav Stresemann, gave his proposal traction but it was brought to a halt by Stresemann's early death, the slump in the world economy and the resurgence of German nationalism.

Post-war there came a revival of interest in European unity. Churchill lectured an audience in Zurich on his vision for a united Europe where 'there would be no limit to the happiness, to the prosperity and glory which its four hundred million people would enjoy'. Soon after the European Recovery Program was underway, secretary of state George Marshall gave his backing to the unifiers.

He took care to say that America would 'avoid premature endorsement of any specific proposal' while declaring that 'we intend to encourage publicly and privately the progressively closer integration, first of free Europe and eventually of as much of Europe as possible. We feel that unless there is a progress towards unification, our efforts to re-establish the European economy will not be fully effective.'[1]

The job of the Organization for European Economic Cooperation, created in April 1948, was to coordinate economic policies, give technical assistance to industry and agriculture, sponsor research and to allocate raw materials in short supply. A political context was provided by the Council of Europe 'to achieve a greater unity between its members for the purpose of safeguarding and realizing the ideals and principles [of] their common heritage'.

In May 1948, European leaders agreed to a consultative assembly. The Council of Europe, the first official political institution of the future European Union, was based in Strasbourg. The British response was at best half-hearted. Muting his initial enthusiasm, Churchill declared: 'We are with Europe, not of it.' Bevin followed suit. Europe was 'only twenty-five per cent of our existence'. Britain's imperial reach, though destined soon to be cut off at the arm, inhibited positive thinking. A meeting of senior civil servants to discuss European cooperation started with the haughty assumption that the OEEC would break down 'unless we contrive to take the lead'. But the concept had to be 'one of limited liability'. There was no question of agreeing 'measures of cooperation which surrender our sovereignty and which lead us along paths from which there is no return'.

Much to Anglo-American surprise and to American delight, a more constructive frame of mind was adopted by France where thinking on the future of relations with Germany was undergoing a sea-change. The inspiration came from Jean Monnet, businessman, economist and close associate of Charles de Gaulle who had delegated to him extraordinary powers to restore and modernise the French economy. At its inception, the Monnet Plan assumed a takeover of German coal in the Saar and in the Ruhr. But when efforts to keep Germany down were defeated by Anglo-American resistance, Monnet reversed his position.

On the principle that if you can't beat them, join them, his policy evolved from building up his country's economic strength at Germany's expense to seeking ways in which the two nations might bind together to benefit common interests and joint security. The starting point was to create a common market in coal and steel, to invest in economies of scale and to end wasteful competition caused by national rivalries. But the chief purpose of the European Coal and Steel Community was to 'make war not only unthinkable but materially impossible'.

Monnet had a close ally in Robert Schuman who, after a failed premiership, had more success as foreign minister. Schuman's first call was to London. He and Bevin had a successful meeting in January 1949 when they agreed on overseeing a self-governing West Germany with a Ruhr regime that respected French interests. They also bowed to the American wish to ease restrictions on German industrial production and to stop dismantling industrial plants. To the delight of General Clay, who went to Paris for talks with Schuman, work started on a less restrictive occupation status.

But there were contentious issues to be settled before France and Germany could hold hands. When Schuman paid a five-day visit to Germany in January 1950, he and Adenauer engaged in many hours of what the host described as 'free and frank' discussions 'marked by mutual trust'. This was to soft-soap an agenda headed by the future of the Saar, which France had no intention of giving up, and French obstruction to returning the Ruhr mines to German control.

Even as Schuman was trying to reassure the chancellor of French good intentions, the Saar's prime minister, a puppet figurehead, was on his way to Paris to sign conventions handing over rights to Saar coal for the next 50 years. When this became public knowledge, Adenauer denounced 'the detachment of one million Germans from Germany' while SPD leader Kurt Schumacher declared that Germany could not now join the Council of Europe. The High Commission stood by helplessly as politicians racked up the tension.

Then, with perfect timing, Schuman let his rabbit out of the hat: a plan for pooling Franco-German coal and steel resources in an organisation which other European nations would be invited to join. Within days, Belgium, Luxembourg, the Netherlands and Italy announced their readiness to take up the offer. Sensing a capitalist plot, Schumacher was not persuaded, but as far as his austere countenance would permit, Adenauer was jubilant. The Schuman Plan took the sting out of the Saar controversy and made the International Ruhr Authority obsolete before it had even started, while allowing the chancellor to garner sufficient support for German participation in the Council of Europe. The response from the western Allies was to commit to accelerating the removal of the remaining occupation restrictions on German sovereignty. This happened when the Bonn Conventions were signed on May 26th, 1952. By then, the famous 'Six' were well on their way to establishing a customs union, the forerunner of the European Union.

★

Britain's up and down relationship with its European neighbours had and still has a long way to go – but the point here is that the dividend from participation in the Berlin Airlift which entitled Britain to a strong voice in Europe was squandered on unfounded optimism and complacency.

With no sense of economics or financial reality, Bevin put his faith in strategic security. If this could be fixed, all else would follow. The priority was to stick close to America, a policy mythologised as the 'special relationship'. European entanglements were a distraction and a possible threat to Britain's world roles. Or so it was said.

Bevin was losing his spark. As heart disease took its toll, he was persuaded to resign in March 1951. He died a month later. As his successor, Herbert Morrison was a poor substitute, having little grasp of or interest in foreign affairs. He lasted until the general election in October, when the Conservatives came to power with Churchill back as prime minister along with Anthony Eden as foreign secretary. Europe remained out of bounds. As Eden told an audience at Columbia University: 'Joining a European federation is something we know in our bones we cannot do.'

What Britain did feel able to do was to increase defence expenditure by 50 per cent, the better to support American forces in their efforts to reverse a Russian- and Chinese-sponsored invasion from North into South Korea. Part of the commitment was a substantial increase in American air power based in Britain. Moreover, the latest heavy bombers were most definitely equipped to deliver A-bombs. Under the 'double key system', the consent of the country hosting the nuclear weapons was needed before they could be used. But, practically, how was this possible? As ambassador in Washington, Sir Oliver Franks worried that the Pentagon might 'call me up some night and say, "Our planes are taking off in five minutes from your fields, do you mind?"'

Though never openly admitted, it was obvious that the much-vaunted national sovereignty that had to be protected at all costs against European encroachment had already been surrendered to Washington. In the Labour government's last year in office there was something like panic in London when the story got around that Truman was contemplating using the A-bomb to support the roll-back of communist insurgents in Korea. Attlee flew over to Washington to put the counter-argument. Beyond the ruminations of armchair strategists there is no evidence to suggest that Truman was anywhere near ready to press the button but, at home, Attlee was widely credited with having stayed the hand of an impetuous president. The prime minister gave himself a pat on the back. Britain, he told Bevin, 'had been lifted out of the European queue and treated as partners, unequal no doubt in power but equal in counsel'.[2] On such flimsy structures are illusions built.

The American military boost in Britain had its equivalent in West Germany where there were fears that what was happening in Korea would be replicated in Europe. Ulbricht raised the stakes when he predicted that the Federal Republic would soon fall. Nerves were strained in Berlin, now once again in the very front of the front line. But Ulbricht did not speak for Stalin, who was disinclined to break the status quo in Germany. A change of policy would have to wait on a change of leader.

CHAPTER FOURTEEN

Stalin died on March 5th, 1953. With no plans for departing the scene, he left a power vacuum which sucked in rivals for the succession. In the strongest position to inherit was Lavrentiy Beria, head of the NKVD secret police and deputy premier from 1946. A sadistic brute, responsible for the Soviet network of slave labour camps, he was also intelligent and astute. With Stalin gone, Beria moved quickly to take command of the regular as well as the secret police. He looked to be impregnable. But he reckoned without elements in the Soviet empire that were beyond his immediate control.

Soon after Stalin's death, East Germany sprang back into political life. Oppression and intimidation combined with widespread poverty brought a backlash, starting in Berlin. On the morning of June 16th, workers on a building site in Stalinallee downed tools in protest against revised 'production norms' which demanded more work without more pay. The strike spread until there were more than 5,000 demonstrators on the streets calling for free elections and an end to Soviet rule.

The insurrection soon spread to other parts of the GDR. Ulbricht panicked. An appeal was made to Moscow for Russian troops to restore order. Acting the strong man who had no fear of leaving the Kremlin to its customary infighting, Beria flew to Berlin to oversee the suppression of 'anti Marxist' tendencies and to fling back the 'fascist agents' who were said to have infiltrated from west Berlin.

The job was soon done. A spontaneous uprising with no discernible leaders or objectives, beyond vague hopes for making things better, was no match for trigger-happy Volkspolizei supported by Soviet weaponry. Secret police (Stasi) files reveal savage reprisals. Some 300 died in street fighting and of the 4,000 or so arrested, 200 were executed and some 1,400 were handed down life sentences.

But this mini-revolution was not without far-reaching results. By revealing to all the shoddy life that was the lot of most citizens of the GDR, it built up resentment against Ulbricht and his cohorts. In the year of the uprising more than 300,000 fled to the West, most of them via Berlin. They included the brightest and best of the young people who had been educated to lead an economic recovery that had receded yet further into the distance.

For Beria, the consequences were fatal. His absence from Moscow had allowed his enemies to muster their strength. Leading the pack was Nikita Khrushchev, an arch-plotter who had managed to keep in with Stalin. When Beria heard that a Presidium meeting had been called in his absence, he hurried back to a hostile reception. He was arrested on June 26th and executed soon after. Power now rested with Khrushchev. Molotov came back as foreign minister.

There were high hopes of a fresh start in Berlin. No one imagined that Khrushchev would be sympathetic to the West but as a practical politician, argued Reuter, he must surely recognise that Ulbricht was incompetent and that the GDR was a drag on the Soviet economy. A deal on Berlin could well presage a settlement covering all Germany.

This was not a vision that had much traction in Bonn where Adenauer had his mind set on making West Germany an integral part of the western alliance. Berlin was an unnecessary distraction and German unity a mirage. Adenauer's success in gaining western legitimacy for his government neutralised opposition. His political enemies were dropping away. Schumacher died in late 1952. A year later in elections across the Federal Republic, Adenauer and the CDU were delivered a crushing victory. Near full sovereignty for the Federal Republic was granted when the Bonn–Paris Conventions were signed on May 26th, 1952. Adenauer was happy for west Berlin to remain under the protection of the Allies who also held on to hypothetical rights to be involved, some time in the speculative future, in reuniting the two Germanys.

Ratification of the Conventions was held over on the question of German rearmament. If the member countries of NATO were serious in their commitment to defend western Europe they had to decide what Germany's contribution should be. From Washington, the message was explicit: West Germany had to have its army.

In Paris, the opposite view prevailed – as, indeed, it did among a large part of the German citizenry, young and old, who were made sick by the prospect of again taking up arms. Reuter was a vocal opponent of rearmament. The French solution which seemed to offer a mutually acceptable compromise was for German rearmament to be encompassed within a European Defence Community (EDC), governed by the same kind of institutional framework as the European Coal and Steel Community (ECSC).

But public opinion in France was sharply divided and, as with the ECSC, Britain was suspicious of any arrangement that might detract from its links with Commonwealth and Empire. Already facing up to opposition at home to any form of militaristic revival, Adenauer had to accept that there was to be no European army.

The final rites were held in the French National Assembly in August 1954 with a decisive vote against the EDC.

Britain came up with an alternative plan, an enlargement of the Brussels Treaty organisation to bring in Germany and Italy. This would ease the way for West Germany to become a member of NATO. The proposal was appraised at a nine-power conference in London on September 28th, 1954. The problem of the Saar was to be settled by plebiscite. The following year the Saar voted for reunification with Germany.

The Bonn–Paris Conventions were ratified in May 1955. The Western European Union was consolidated on the 7th. Two days later West Germany was presented at a NATO conference, almost exactly ten years after the fall of the Third Reich.

★

The advance of the Federal Republic towards full independence raised pressure on Berlin. The DDR's arbitrary increase in auto-bahn tolls, ostensibly to pay for road maintenance, the interruption without warning of bus and tram traffic, even the cutting of tele-phone links played on the nerves of west Berliners. But all this was as nothing compared to the fury in the DDR at the welcome signs for refugees who continued to arrive in west Berlin at a rate of a thousand or more a day. The total since 1945 was close on 4 million.

Whatever his limitations as a popular leader, it was Ulbricht who faced up to Khrushchev with a stark warning of impend-ing disaster if the status quo in Berlin was allowed to continue. Khrushchev would not be hurried. Decisions had to wait on yet another Council of Foreign Ministers, this in Berlin, where Molotov reprised his appeal for a pacifist neutral Germany, reunited on fed-eral lines. What this would mean in practice was exposed when discussions bogged down on the question of free elections, judged by the West to be the essential prerequisite for true independence.

The stalemate set Ulbricht thinking on how he might tighten the screws on Berlin, the 'malignant tumour' as he called it. After Reuter's death in September 1953, Otto Suhr stood in as mayor until elections in 1957 put in place Willy Brandt, Reuter's long-time assistant. Brandt had to cope with a plethora of petty restrictions imposed for no intelligible reason. Persons who were deemed 'undesirable' were given a hard time, while the definition of what was said to infringe DDR sovereignty grew ever wider. In 1957 new passport laws imposed swingeing prison sentences on those who made unauthorised journeys outside the DDR. Even so, in that year alone, over 260,000 East Germans chose to defy the law to escape to the West. West German citizens had to apply for a permit to enter east Berlin.

Khrushchev's remedy for clearing what he described as 'a bone that stuck in my throat' was to eliminate the western powers' right to be in Berlin. To this end, he announced an impending peace treaty with the DDR that would override four-power status in Berlin, implying this would leave the way clear for East German forces to take over the western sector and for Berlin to become a 'Free City'. The response from the Bonn government, orchestrated by the western Allies, declared Berlin to be inseparably connected with the German question as a whole. And there the matter rested – for the moment.

It was not until 1961 that Khrushchev judged the timing to be favourable for another diplomatic offensive. In January, the youngest president in American history was propelled on to the world stage. Following two terms of Dwight Eisenhower's laid-back brand of Republicanism, the 43-year-old John F. Kennedy was elected on a platform of 'getting America moving again'.

What this meant in terms of American–Soviet relations was unclear. Anti-communist sentiment in America required a tough president but one who could achieve his aims while stopping well short of war. There was a contradiction here that was pointed up in Berlin. Kennedy was on record, pledging 'no sacrifice of the freedom of the people of Berlin, no surrender of principle'. But what were the alternatives to appeasement? There were some 11,000 Allied troops in Berlin. They were outmatched by a 350,000-strong Soviet force in East Germany. Yet there was no getting away from the fact that Berlin headed the list of differences in Soviet–German relations. The advice from London was for Kennedy to move cautiously, a marked change of emphasis from the days when Bevin was the cheerleader for action. After the disastrous Suez War of 1956 when, without trans-Atlantic consultation, Britain and France in collusion with Israel had invaded Egypt in a vain attempt to stop the nationalist takeover of the Suez Canal, Britain had to work its passage back into American favour. It did so by adopting an avuncular approach that suited the patriarchal prime minister Harold Macmillan and his mild-mannered aristocratic foreign secretary, Alec Douglas-Home.

Macmillan wanted a great power summit in which he could perform as the reconciler and the arbiter of peace. Meanwhile, leading to general disarmament, nothing must be done to cause unnecessary stress in Moscow. In the event of a re-imposition of a blockade in Berlin, the Allies should start up again with the Airlift.[1] This did not appeal to Washington, where, having stood down at the end of Truman's second term, Dean Acheson had re-emerged as the chief foreign affairs adviser.

Acheson was scornful of another Airlift. It was, he believed, an unacceptably weak response of the sort that had led to the Korean War. Instead, he fell back on the strategy mooted by

General Clay when the Berlin crisis first broke. This was to send an armed convoy to reopen the way to Berlin, by force, if necessary. The objections were familiar to anyone who had taken part in the Airlift. All the Russians had to do was to allow the convoy to get well on its way before bringing it to a stop by detonating the road at the front and rear.[2] Kennedy was urged to pursue 'quiet diplomacy'.

Hopes of that foundered on the coral reefs of Cuba. In an operation as ill-conceived and as incompetent as the Suez debacle, Kennedy gave half-hearted approval to a CIA-sponsored invasion of Cuba in April 1961 by opponents of the communist regime of Fidel Castro. The fighting was over in three days with Castro boasting a glorious victory.

Krushchev, who would later send Russian missiles to Cuba in support of Castro, was eager to push his advantage following the disastrous US invasion of the island. He looked forward to the face-to-face meeting with Kennedy suggested by the American president earlier in the year. The summit was held in Vienna in early June 1961. Berlin was top of the agenda.

The untutored and untried Kennedy did not quite know what to make of Khrushchev, a self-made man of the type who stopped short of finishing the job. Of formidable intelligence, he could be charming and accommodating, then arrogant and vulgar with barely a pause in between. While he earned grudging respect for introducing a lighter touch into domestic politics and for denouncing his late master for excesses to which he, Khrushchev, had contributed, his tactics followed the Stalinist tradition of probing for weaknesses in the western alliance, the better to consolidate the power of the eastern bloc and to extend the Soviet reach.

Kennedy had no defence against the hectoring tone adopted by the Soviet leader, who pushed hard at what he saw as the American weak spot – a fear of nuclear war. Time and again Khrushchev returned to the Berlin question. If there was failure to agree a peace treaty with Germany that would remould Berlin's status, Moscow would act alone and end all post-war Soviet commitments. Kennedy temporised; though he pledged to fight for a just cause it was noted subsequently on both sides of the Iron Curtain that he spoke only of *west* Berlin as if he was not concerned with agreements that were supposed to cover the city as a whole.

In early August, at a gathering of Warsaw Pact* leaders in Moscow, Ulbricht took the chance to impress on Khrushchev the dire consequences not just for East Germany but for the entire eastern bloc, if free access from east to west Berlin was allowed to continue.

Social unrest was endemic, with persistent food shortages and frequent breakdowns in industrial output. Migration intensified the crisis which, in turn, persuaded more citizens to flee. The only way to break the vicious circle, Ulbricht argued, was to close the escape route in Berlin. Khrushchev got the message. After a bombastic warning to the West not to intervene – he even summoned the British ambassador to his box in the Bolshoi to conjure up images of a nuclear wipe-out of his country – the order was given to seal the border. The peace treaty with East Germany could wait.

On Sunday, August 13th, 1961 at a few minutes past midnight, the East German news agency put out a Warsaw Pact communiqué accusing the NATO powers of undermining East Germany's economy. Action was demanded to 're-establish order'. Within the hour, armoured cars rolled up to the border. Police and soldiers sealed all but twelve of the 80 crossing points and by morning

---

* The Warsaw Pact was the military equivalent of COMECON, a mutual defence treaty for the Soviet Union and its satellite states.

sprawling spirals of barbed wire had cut the city in two. Two days later, a start was made on strengthening the barrier with concrete blocks up to six feet high.

The West's response was not immediate. When it came it was weak. On Sunday afternoon, Dean Rusk, American secretary of state, said that western rights were unaffected, but that a protest would be made. There was no demand that the measures be halted or reversed. Both he and Kennedy agreed nothing should be done to aggravate the situation.

Willy Brandt reacted angrily. Addressing himself to the three western commandants, he called for retaliation against an aggressive act which had destroyed the city's four-power status. Expectations in west Berlin were of demonstrations of American strength equivalent to the 1948 Airlift. Thousands gathered on the border to shout their protests as the barricade thickened. But short of sending in the tanks, a risk too far for Washington to contemplate, there was not much to be done except to authorise a modest strengthening of the American garrison.

A formal protest to Moscow was ignored. Postal and telephone links were cut and vehicles from west Berlin were turned back if they did not have a permit to cross into the east. Soviet protests at Allied 'misuse' of the air corridors suggested that other impediments to traffic flow could be expected.[3] The British ambassador to Bonn reported that Berliners 'have been shaken to a greater extent than at any time since 1948'.[4]

On Wednesday the 16th, a crowd of 250,000 gathered at west Berlin's city hall. A much-photographed placard read, 'Munich 1938, Berlin 1961'. When Brandt spoke it was to announce that he was demanding action from Kennedy. In an open letter to the president he warned of a severe 'crisis of confidence' if the western powers remained 'inert and strictly on the defensive'.

Washington was not best pleased at this outburst. There was an aggrieved sense of Brandt getting above himself. But with a federal election in which Brandt was the SPD candidate for the chancellorship just a month ahead, he was intent on establishing his credentials as a national politician, contrasting his youthful energy (he was 48) with the fading powers of the 85-year-old Adenauer.

The chancellor recognised the danger. He resisted pressure to visit Berlin or to give a television address, excusing himself by saying that he had no wish to incite unrest or encourage false expectations. It was ten days after the border closed before Adenauer put in an appearance. It was a hard-headed decision but in avoiding what would have looked to be an endorsement of Brandt, his instincts served him well. The voters gave him another term as chancellor, a job he held for two more years until, as part of a coalition deal, he stepped down in October 1963.

Kennedy showed scant appreciation of the essentials of German politics, just as he had failed to recognise Khrushchev's strength of purpose. Weakened by his less than impressive performance in Vienna, he felt himself adrift, not knowing which way to turn. To add to his discomfort, some German students sent him a black umbrella, symbolising Chamberlain and his policy of appeasement.

But there was consolation. While Ulbricht and Khrushchev in concert had appeared to score a trick in Berlin it might be argued that they had in fact made a tactical retreat. Instead of blockading the west as in 1948, they had sealed off the east. Was this not a confession of failure? Kennedy could see the chance of recovering prestige by defending what Khrushchev had already conceded, the inviolability of west Berlin.

Aiming at maximum publicity, vice president Lyndon Johnson was sent off on a glad-handing visit to west Berlin. With him went

General Clay, the hero of the Airlift. Johnson did not relish his assignment but changed his mind when he arrived to an emotional reception. On a drizzly Saturday afternoon, half a million people lined the streets. Johnson told them: 'We are with you in the determination to defend your liberty and the holy cause of human freedom.' The American visitors went home after the weekend but Clay was soon back as the president's personal representative in Berlin. With no troops to command, his role (much resented by his military colleagues) was that of public figurehead on display to help boost confidence.

One public relations success deserves another. Doubtless reflecting on the glowing reception fed back by his vice president, Kennedy decided that he too would make the pilgrimage to Berlin. He did so on June 27th, 1963. Adenauer and Brandt were at Tegel to greet him. Their motorcade, with Kennedy standing and waving from the back seat of an open convertible, was cheered all the way along the 35-mile route.

After a turn of the city that took in Checkpoint Charlie and a walk along a section of the Wall, the president mounted a podium outside city hall where a massive crowd, reckoned to be over 300,000 strong, was waiting to hear him. By now he was totally smitten by the emotional power pressing in on him on all sides. His speech was magnificent. Played with perfect timing, the message he gave out was no less than the ordination of Berlin as the mecca of democracy.

> There are many people in the world who really don't understand, or say they don't, what is the great issue between the free world and the Communist world. Let them come to Berlin. There are some who say that Communism is the wave of the future. Let them come to Berlin. And there are

some who say in Europe and elsewhere we can work with the Communists. Let them come to Berlin.

And he added the unforgettable personal endorsement:

All free men, wherever they may live, are citizens of Berlin and, therefore, as a free man, I take pride in the words, 'Ich bin ein Berliner'.

There could be no backing off. Kennedy's declaration left no room for misunderstanding. American commitment to west Berlin was total. It followed that American commitment to the Federal Republic and to the rest of western Europe was also total. Kennedy basked in his popularity at home and abroad; he had beaten Khrushchev at his own game and had graduated as a world statesman.

*

Berlin was Kennedy's epitaph – in the remaining months of his life there were no further opportunities to test his mettle.

Skip lightly over the years. In October 1963, Adenauer ended his reign in Bonn as part of the coalition deal that had kept him in power after the 1961 elections. Brandt still had his eye on the chancellorship, an ambition that had to wait until 1969 to be realised. Meanwhile, as mayor of Berlin he mounted a programme of regeneration that saw the bombsites disappear and the emergence of a flourishing economy. If Kennedy had given Berlin confidence, Brandt gave it optimism.

The showcase of the western world attracted over a million visitors a year, many of them making the pilgrimage to the Wall where, standing on wooden platforms, they could view the derelict buildings and guard posts that cordoned off the grey façade of east Berlin.

Brandt was not a hard-liner. Though holding firm to the western alliance he gave himself room to build on relations across the east–west divide. This was not easy to achieve. Understandably nervous of unfavourable comparisons, Ulbricht was suspicious of Brandt who, indeed, held to the view that the exposure of communism to western values would enhance the attractions of democracy. Brandt's task was made easier when, less than a year after the Kennedy assassination, Khrushchev was ousted by the Politburo. At the very least Brandt was able to claim that his policy of 'Ostpolitik' lightened what he called 'the ordeal of coexistence'.

Ulbricht managed to hang on until May 1971 when he was replaced by Erich Honecker, another politician from the Stalinist mould but one who could see the advantage in encouraging trade between the two Germanys and the two Berlins. What he was unable to see was that the Soviet Union was already beginning to crumble at the edges. With the rise of Mikhail Gorbachev to head of the Soviet state in 1988, the fulfilment of George Kennan's prophecy – that communism had within it the seeds of its own decay – looked to be imminent.

Honecker despised glasnost – the policy of openness – and blamed Gorbachev for the unrest across eastern Europe. But there was little he could do to hold back the pace of reform and the end of one-party rule. He was deposed a month before the infamous Wall he had masterminded as a loyal servant of the Ulbricht regime came tumbling down.

The end bordered on farce. As first secretary in east Berlin, Guenter Schabowski was the front man for explaining decisions made behind closed doors and for disguising the panic that was gripping the SED establishment as the refugee flight over East Germany's now open border with Czechoslovakia gathered pace.

On the evening of November 9th, 1989, Schabowski with three colleagues 'in cheap grey suits with party pins in their lapels' faced the press. Someone asked about freedom of travel. The question took him by surprise. All he had to help him was a note handed to him by Egon Krenz, the new East German leader. It suggested, without spelling out the details, that all citizens of the DDR were entitled to leave the country. A laborious process of visa application and approval was envisaged but Schabowski was not aware of any conditions. When pressed to say when the new rule would come into play, he searched his papers fruitlessly for an answer. For once, his response had to be spontaneous. 'Sofort', he said. 'Immediately.' Reporters rushed from the room. In that moment Schabowski knew that East Germany was finished.

> On the night of November 9th he [Schabowski] went to the border crossing at Bornholmer Strasse, the first to open. For once he was unnoticed. Honecker's hundred-year Wall was being merrily smashed down. Among the jubilant crowds, some in their night-clothes, vodka was being passed round with chunks of the Wall replacing ice; shards of it were flying through the air. And the thought must have crossed his mind: 'Did I do this?'[5]

The next day, the destruction of the Wall began in earnest.

> People with pickaxes began to take chunks out of its painted sides while more visitors climbed up on to the wide platform by the Brandenburg Gate. On the second day the infamous Glienicke Bridge was opened; East Germans

began to come from beyond Berlin in their Trabbis. Tens of thousands crossed on the U- and S-Bahns, or simply walked over the border. On that first weekend over 800,000 East German shoppers and revellers crossed into West Berlin to go on an impromptu spending spree. They were given a tremendous welcome and everything from free hot soup, hamburgers, chocolate, fruit and Sekt, and the days were punctuated by small acts of generosity. I saw people handing out money to complete strangers and guiding them around the city; the Senate printed free street maps, there was free public transport, free beer, free football matches, free souvenirs and even free accommodation.[6]

The end of the Berlin Wall was also the end of the Cold War. In 1990 the two Germanys and the two Berlins were reunited. The following year, Berlin was reconstituted as a capital city. The story had come full circle.

POSTSCRIPT

O f the post-war events that shaped the future of Berlin, none was more critical than the Airlift. And not just Berlin. As a close adviser to Bevin and as a Russian expert, Frank Roberts gave credit to the Airlift on three counts.

> First and foremost, it had changed the Western role in Berlin and therefore in the Federal Republic as a whole from occupation to protection, without which we would not have built up so successfully a new relationship with Germany as a pillar of the European Community and of NATO. Secondly, it convinced other countries in Europe that Soviet pressures were dangerous and had to be resisted. And thirdly, it showed that the West was capable of resisting them diplomatically, without risk of war, even when the geography seemed all against us.[1]

To which Robert Murphy added:

> The Russians inadvertently gave us an outpost one hundred miles inside the Iron Curtain, where the inadequacies of the Communist system show up more conspicuously

than anywhere else, in full view of everybody in the world.[2]

Memories of the Airlift are kept alive in Berlin. A potent reminder is the memorial sculpture outside Tempelhof. Displaying the names of those who died in the Airlift, the monument has three west-pointing arcs symbolising the three air corridors. Berliners call it the Hungerknolle (hunger claw) or Hungerharke (hunger rake). It was unveiled on July 10th, 1951.

The Americans took over Tempelhof in 1945 and stayed there until 1993. They left behind a leisure centre, complete with a basketball court in one of the upper storeys of the terminal. Neglected but heavy with memories, it features on conducted tours of the building.

Tempelhof was closed to air traffic in October 2008. Though ideally placed for a city airport, its runways were too short for big passenger aircraft. The airfield is currently a refugee camp. Long-haul flights use Tegel, with Schoenefeld, the one-time airbase for the Soviet sector, scheduled to take more heavy traffic.

Gatow is now the Luftwaffe Museum.

Where once there was an American forces cinema and library on Clayallee there is the Allied Museum (Alliierten Museum) with exhibitions of the Allied role in Berlin between 1945 and 1994. Among the displays is one of the original guardhouses from Checkpoint Charlie.

At the actual site of Checkpoint Charlie is a replica guardhouse, a favourite for tourists who want a selfie alongside an actor dressed as an Allied military policeman.

Of the Berlin Wall, little remains except for three sections, one of which, at Bernauer Strasse, is the closest representation of the original.

When the days of the Airlift were long over, *Der Abend*, a Berlin evening newspaper, invited readers to record their memories. Many spoke of the comfort in trying times of hearing the aircraft overhead.

> For me it became a habit before I went to bed, first to look out of the window in order to see in the sky the unswerving position lights of the aircraft roaring over us. Then, reassured, I went to bed …

And from another correspondent:

> Early in the morning, when we woke up, the first thing we did was to listen to see whether the noise of the aircraft engines could be heard. That gave us a certainty that we were not alone, that the whole civilized world took part in the fight for Berlin's freedom.

THE FINAL TALLY[1]

The Berlin Airlift ran from 26th June, 1948 to 12th May, 1949

Total delivered:	2,325,809 tons
US (Operation Vittles):	1,783,573 tons
UK (Operation Plainfare):	541,936 tons
Number of flights:	USAF 189,960 (92,000,000 miles)
	RAF 65,860 (24,000,000 miles)
USAF deliveries incl:	1,421,119 tons of coal
	296,319 tons of food
	66,134 miscellaneous
RAF deliveries incl:	164,910 tons of coal
	240,386 tons of food
	136,640 miscellaneous
UK civilian:	92,282 tons liquid fuel
	21,680 flights
US:	76.7 per cent of total
UK:	23.3 per cent of total

Deaths caused by the Airlift

RAF: Eighteen airmen including one Royal Australian Air Force pilot and one South African Air Force flying officer

USAF: 31 airmen
German: Thirteen civilians

100 million gallons of aviation fuel was consumed by the Airlift

The total Airlift labour force came to 70,000, of whom 20,000 were classed as highly skilled

Planes on the Airlift

Douglas Dakota (C-47) or Skytrain: Two-engined, a stalwart of the Second World War, it was used by the USAF, RAF and civil air companies. Maximum speed, 229 mph; Airlift cruising speed, 150 mph; payload, 3 tons

Douglas Skymaster (C-54): Four-engined. The most heavily used plane on the Airlift. Maximum speed, 274 mph; Airlift cruising speed, 170 mph; payload, 9 to 10 tons

Avro York: Standard RAF transport developed from the Lancaster bomber. Also used by civil airlines. Maximum speed, 310 mph; Airlift cruising speed, 185 mph; payload, 7 to 8 tons

Handley Page Hastings: Four-engined. Designed to replace the Avro York. Only one squadron used on the Airlift. Maximum speed, 354 mph; Airlift cruising speed, 185 mph; payload, 8.5 tons.

Bristol Freighter: Two-engined. Used for back loading big freight out of Berlin. Maximum speed, 224 mph; Airlift cruising speed, 150 mph; payload, 5 tons

Handley Page Halton: Four-engined. A civil conversion of the Halifax bomber. Maximum speed, 320 mph; Airlift cruising speed, 185 mph; payload, 6 tons

Avro Lancastrian: Four-engined. A conversion of the Lancaster bomber. Maximum speed, 315 mph; Airlift cruising speed, 185 mph; payload, 6 tons

Fairchild Packet (C-82): Two-engined. Used by the USAF for bulk freight. Maximum speed, 248 mph; Airlift cruising speed, 170 mph; payload, 5.5 tons

Avro Tudor: Four-engined. Used as liquid fuel tankers. Maximum speed, 346 mph; Airlift cruising speed, 185 mph; payload, 8 tons

Short Sunderland: Four-engined. Flying boat flown by Coastal Command. Maximum speed, 213 mph; Airlift cruising speed, 165 mph; payload, 5.5 tons

Globemaster (C-74): With a payload of 25 tons, and a top speed of 328 mph, the largest transporter of the USAF was Tunner's pride and joy. But only one was used on the Airlift and that sparingly since it was hard to fit in to flight schedules and was too heavy for the standard runways. But seven Globemasters flew cargo from the US to Rhein-Main.

BIBLIOGRAPHY

Ahonen, Pertti, *After the Expulsion: West Germany and Eastern Europe, 1945–1990*, 2003

Ambrose, Stephen, *Eisenhower and Berlin, 1945*, 2000

Andreas-Friedrich, Ruth, *Battleground Berlin*, 1990

Arnold-Forster, Mark, *The Siege of Berlin*, 1979

Backer, John H., *Winds of History. The German Years of Lucius DuBignon Clay*, 1983

Backer, John H., *Priming the Germany Economy. American Occupational Policies 1945–48*, 1971

Barnett, Correlli, *The Lost Victory. British Dreams, British Realities, 1945–1950*, 1995

Behrman, Greg, *The Most Noble Adventure. The Marshall Plan and the Reconstruction of Post-War Europe*, 2007

Berghahn, Volker R., *American Big Business in Britain and Germany. A Comparative History*, 2014

Best, Gary Dean, *Herbert Hoover: The Postpresidential Years, 1933–64*, 1983

Beugel, Ernst Hans van der, *From Marshall Aid to Atlantic Partnership*, 1966

Botting, Douglas, *In the Ruins of the Reich*, 1985

Brandt, Willy, *My Road to Berlin*, 1960

Browder, Robert Paul and Smith, Thomas G., *Independent: A Biography of Lewis W. Douglas*, 1986

Bullock, Alan, *Ernest Bevin: Foreign Secretary, 1945–51*, 1983

Burner, David, *Herbert Hoover. A Public Life*, 1978

Carr, Albert H.Z., *Truman, Stalin and Peace*, 1950

Charles, Max, *Berlin Blockade*, 1959

Charmley, John, *Churchill's Grand Alliance. The Anglo-American Special Relationship 1940–57*, 1995

Clare, George, *Berlin Days, 1946–47*, 1989

Clarke, Sir Richard, *Anglo-American Economic Cooperation in War and Peace, 1942–49*, 1982

Clay, Lucius D., *Decision in Germany*, 1950

Collier, Richard, *Bridge Across the Sky: The Berlin Blockade and Airlift, 1948–1949*, 1978

Connell, Brian, *Watcher on the Rhine. A Report on the New Germany*, 1957

Davison, W. Phillips, *The Berlin Blockade. A Study in Cold War Politics*, 1958

Deighton, Anne, *The Impossible Peace. Britain, the Division of Germany and the Origins of the Cold War*, 1990

Dennett, Raymond and Johnson, Joseph E., *Negotiating with the Russians*, 1951

Douglas, R.M., *Orderly and Humane: The Expulsion of the Germans after the Second World War*, 2012

Edwards, Ruth Dudley, *Victor Gollancz: A Biography*, 1987

Ferrell, Robert, *Harry S. Truman*, 1991

Frank, Matthew, *Expelling the Germans. British Opinion and Post-1945 Population Transfer in Context*, 2007

Gaddis, John Lewis, *We Now Know: Rethinking Cold War History*, 1997

Gere, Edwin, *The Unheralded. Men and Women of the Berlin Blockade and Airlift*, 2003

Gimbel, John, *The American Occupation of Germany. Politics and the Military, 1945–1949*, 1968

Gimbel, John, *The Origins of the Marshall Plan*, 1976

Gollancz, Victor, *Leaving Them to Their Fate: The Ethics of Starvation*, 1946

Gori, Francesca and Pons, Silvio (ed.), *The Soviet Union and Europe in the Cold War, 1943–53*, 1996

Gottlieb, Manuel, *The German Peace Settlement and the Berlin Crisis*, 1960

Grosser, Alfred, *Western Germany, From Defeat to Rearmament*, 1955

Haydock, Michael D., *City Under Siege: The Berlin Blockade and Airlift, 1948–49*, 1999

Hathaway, Robert M., *Ambiguous Partnership. Britain and America, 1944–1947*, 1981

Helmer, Stephen D., *Hitler's Berlin: The Speer Plans for Reshaping the Central City*, 1985

Ienkin, Louis, *The Berlin Crisis and the United Nations*, 1959

Hiscocks, Richard, *Democracy in Western Germany*, 1957

Hitchcock, William I., *The Struggle for Europe. The Turbulent History of a Divided Continent, 1945–2002*, 2003

Hoffmann, Stanley and Maier, Charles, *The Marshall Plan: A Retrospective*, 1984

Hogan, Michael J., *The Marshall Plan. America, Britain, and the Reconstruction of Western Europe, 1947–1952*, 1987

Horner, Arthur, *Incorrigible Rebel*, 1960

Howley, Frank, *Berlin Command*, 1950

Innes, Hammond, *Air Bridge*, 1951

Jackson, Robert, *The Berlin Airlift*, 1988

Jay, Douglas, *Change and Fortune. A Political Record*, 1980

Kempe, Frederick, *Berlin 1961. Kennedy, Khrushchev, and the Most Dangerous Place on Earth*, 2011

Kennan, George F., *American Diplomacy, 1900–1950*, 1951

Kirkpatrick, Ivone, *The Inner Circle. Memoirs of Ivone Kirkpatrick*, 1959

LaFeber, Walter F., *America, Russia and the Cold War, 1945–1975*, 1976

Leahy, Fleet Admiral William D., *I Was There*, 1950

Leffler, Melvyn P., *For the Soul of Mankind: The United States, the Soviet Union, and the Cold War*, 2007

Leonhard, Wolfgang, *Child of the Revolution*, 1957

Lochner, Louis P., *Herbert Hoover and Germany*, 1960

MacDonogh, Giles, *After the Reich*, 2008

Mallalieu, William Cassell, *British Reconstruction and American Policy, 1945–55*, 1956

Mann, Anthony, *Comeback: Germany, 1945–1952*, 1980

Mayer, Herbert C., *The German Recovery and the Marshall Plan*, 1969

Mayhew, Christopher, *A War of Words: A Cold War Witness*, 1998

Mayne, Richard, *The Recovery of Europe. From Devastation to Unity*, 1970

Meehan, Patricia, *A Strange Enemy People. Germans under the British, 1945–1950*, 2001

Mikes, George, *Uber Alles: Germany Explored*, 1953

Miller, Roger G., *To Save a City: The Berlin Airlift, 1948–1949*, 2008

Milward, Alan S., *The Reconstruction of Western Europe, 1945–51*, 1984

Miscamble, Wilson D., *Harry S. Truman, the Berlin Blockade and the 1948 Election*, 1980

Morgan, Roger, *The United States and West Germany, 1945–1973. A Study in Alliance Politics*, 1974

Morris, Eric, *Blockade: Berlin and the Cold War*, 1974

Mosley, Leonard, *Marshall: Hero for our Times*, 1982

Murphy, David E., Kondrashev, Sergei A., and Bailey, George, *Battleground Berlin: CIA Versus KGB in the Cold War*, 1997

Murphy, Robert, *Diplomat Among Warriors*, 1964

Naimark, Norman M., *The Russians in Germany: A History of the Soviet Zone of Occupation, 1945–1949*, 1995

Offner, Arnold A., *Another Such Victory: President Truman and the Cold War, 1945–53*, 2002

Padover, Saul, *Psychologist in Germany*, 1946

Parrish, Thomas, *Berlin in the Balance, 1945–1949. The Blockade, the Airlift, the First Major Battle of the Cold War*, 1998

Pelling, Henry, *Britain and the Marshall Plan*, 1988

Pennacchio, Charles, *The East German Communists and the Origins of the Berlin Blockade Crisis*, 1995

Peterson, Edward N., *The American Occupation of Germany: Retreat to Victory*, 1977

Peterson, Maurice, *Both Sides of the Curtain: An Autobiography*, 1950

Pimlott, Ben, *The Political Diary of Hugh Dalton*, 1986

Prittie, Terence, *The Velvet Chancellors: A History of Post-War Germany*, 1979

Radzinsky, Edvard, *Stalin: A Biography*, 1996

Reeves, Richard, *Daring Young Men: The Heroism and Triumph of the Berlin Airlift, June 1948–May 1949*, 2010

Richie, Alexandra, *Faust's Metropolis: A History of Berlin*, 1998

Roberts, Frank, *Dealing with Dictators: The Destruction and Revival of Europe, 1930–70*, 1991

Robertson, Alex J., *The Bleak Midwinter, 1947*, 1987
Rodrigo, Robert, *Berlin Airlift*, 1960

Schrader, Helena P., *The Blockade Breakers: The Berlin Airlift*, 2008
Sebestyen, Victor, *1946, The Making of the Modern World*, 2014
Shinwell, Emanuel, *I've Lived Through It All*, 1973
Sichel, Peter, *The Secrets of My Life*, 2016
Skidelsky, Robert, *John Maynard Keynes*, 2003
Slayton, Robert A., *Master of the Air: William Tunner and the Success of Military Airlift*, 2010
Smith, Walter Bedell, *Moscow Mission, 1946–1949*, 1950
Smyser, W.R., *From Yalta to Berlin: The Cold War Struggle over Germany*, 1999
Strang, Lord William, *Home and Abroad*, 1956
Sutherland, Jon and Canwell, Diane, *The Berlin Airlift. The Salvation of a City*, 2007

Taylor, Frederick, *The Berlin Wall*, 2007
Tusa, Ann and Tusa, John, *The Berlin Airlift*, 1988

White, Philip, *Churchill's Cold War: The Iron Curtain Speech that Shaped the Post-War World*, 2012
Williams, Francis, *A Prime Minister Remembers*, 1961
Williamson, David G., *A Most Diplomatic General: Life of Lord Robertson of Oakridge*, 1996
Windsor, Philip, *Berlin in the Cold War*, 1964
Windsor, Philip, *City on Leave: A History of Berlin, 1945–1962*, 1963

NOTES

Chapter One

1. Lord Strang, *Home and Abroad*, 1956; p. 207.
2. Stephen Ambrose, *Eisenhower and Berlin, 1945*, 2000; p. 97.
3. Wolfgang Leonhard, *Child of the Revolution*, 1957; p. 41.
4. Saul Padover, *Psychologist in Germany*, 1946; p. 211.
5. Melvyn P. Leffler, *For the Soul of Mankind: The United States, the Soviet Union, and the Cold War*, 2007; p. 41.
6. Mark Arnold-Forster, *The Siege of Berlin*, 1979; p. 27.
7. Giles MacDonogh, *After the Reich*, 2007; p. 255.
8. Alfred Grosser, *Western Germany, From Defeat to Rearmament*, 1955; p. 89.
9. Willy Brandt, *My Road To Berlin*, 1960.
10. George Clare, *Berlin Days*, 1989; p. 16.
11. Peter Sichel, *The Secrets of My Life*, 2016; p. 157.
12. Giles MacDonogh, *After the Reich*, 2007; p. 251.
13. Marianne Beier, *Duesseldorf Historisches Archiv*.
14. Lucius D. Clay, *Decision in Germany*, 1950; pp. 25, 26.
15. Frank Howley, *Berlin Command*, 1950; p. 52.

Chapter Two

1. William Leahy, *I Was There*, 1950; p. 442.
2. Anthony Mann, *Comeback: Germany 1945–1952*; p. 117.
3. Arnold Offner, *Another Such Victory: President Truman and the Cold War, 1945–53*, 2002; p. 127.

4. Victor Sebestyen, *1946: The Making of the Modern World*, 2014; p. 321.

5. Melvyn P. Leffler, *For the Soul of Mankind: The United States, the Soviet Union, and the Cold War*, 2007; p. 49.

6. John Lewis Gaddis, *We Now Know: Rethinking Cold War History*, 1997; p. 21.

7. Minutes of Defence Committee, March 8th and 18th, 1946; DO46.

8. Robert Ferrell, *Harry S. Truman*, 1991; p. 235.

9. Philip White, *Churchill's Cold War: The Iron Curtain Speech that Shaped the Post-War World*, 2012; p. 200.

10. The National Archives UK, PREM 8/26, May 1st, 1946.

11. Victor Gollancz, *The Ethics of Starvation*, 1946.

12. Charles Pennacchio, 'The East German Communists and the Origins of the Berlin Blockade Crisis', *East European Quarterly*, Vol. 29, No. 3, 1995.

13. George Clare, *Berlin Days*, 2007; p. 42.

14. Alexandra Ritchie, *Faust's Metropolis: A History of Berlin*, 1998; p. 646.

Chapter Three

1. Willy Brandt, *My Road To Berlin*, 1960.

2. Ruth Andreas-Friedrich, *Battleground Berlin*, 1990; pp. 146–7 (Monday, December 30th, 1946).

3. Robert Skidelsky, *John Maynard Keynes*, 2003; p. 783.

4. Ben Pimlott (ed.), *The Political Diary of Hugh Dalton*, 1986; p. 384 (Dalton to Bevin, October 3rd, 1946).

5. Report of the Technical Committee on Coal Mining, 1945.

6. The National Archives UK, PREM 8/516, January 1st, 1946.

7. Ibid.

8. David G. Williamson, *A Most Diplomatic General: Life of Lord Robertson of Oakridge*, 1996; p. 97.

9. Arthur Horner, *Incorrigible Rebel*, 1960; pp. 183, 190.

10. Coal Advisory Council on Industry report, November 1946; BT171/185.

11. Alex J. Robertson, *The Bleak Midwinter*, 1987; p. 61.

12. Robert Paul Browder and Thomas G. Smith, *Independent: A Biography of Lewis W. Douglas*, 1986; p. 284.

13. Ibid; p. 254.

14. The National Archives UK, PREM 8/703.

15. Robert Paul Browder and Thomas G. Smith, *Independent: A Biography of Lewis W. Douglas*, 1986; p. 257.

16. The National Archives UK, PREM 8/449.

17. Emanuel Shinwell, *I've Lived Through It All*, 1973; p. 195.

18. Ben Pimlott (ed.), *The Political Diary of Hugh Dalton*, 1986; p. 390 (February 6th, 1947).

19. Ibid; (February 10th, 1947).

Chapter Four

1. Berlin to Foreign Office, 10 August, 1948; CAB 6531.

2. The National Archives UK, CAB 129/19; July 5th, 1947.

3. Robert Paul Browder and Thomas G. Smith, *Independent: A Biography of Lewis W. Douglas*, 1986; p. 270.

4. Ibid; p. 266.

5. Interview with E.H. van der Beugel, secretary to Dutch delegation at the first Paris conference on the Marshall Plan; by Philip Brooks, June 1st, 1964.

6. Robert Paul Browder and Thomas G. Smith, *Independent: A Biography of Lewis W. Douglas*, 1986; p. 270.

7. The National Archives UK, PREM 8/449.

8. Inverchapel to Attlee, March 10th, 1947; PREM 8/703.

9. March 23rd, 1947; PREM 8/703.

10. Report to Economic Planning Board by Sir Oliver Franks; CAB 129.22; December 22nd, 1947.

11. John Lewis Gaddis, *We Now Know: Rethinking Cold War History*, 1997; p. 116.

Chapter Five

1. Charles Pennacchio, 'The East German Communists and the Origins of the Berlin Blockade Crisis', *East European Quarterly*, Vol. 29, No. 3, Autumn 1995.

2. The National Archives UK, CAB 129/23, January 4th, 1948.

3. The National Archives UK, CAB 129/25, March 3rd, 1948.

4. Oral History interview with Harriman by Richard D. McKinzie and Theodore A. Wilson, 1971; Truman Library.

5. Berlin telegram 49, January 10th, 1948; C218/3/18.

6. Anthony Mann, *Comeback: Germany 1945–1952*, 1980; p. 48.

7. Mikhail Novinsky, *The USSR and the Berlin Crisis 1948–49*. Quoted by Roger G. Miller, *To Save a City: The Berlin Airlift, 1948–1949*, 1998; p. 1.

8. Berlin to Foreign Office, April 2nd, 1948; telegram 519; CAB 2543.

9. Telegram 652, April 1st, 1948; CAB 24273/18.

10. Foreign Office, March 18th, 1948.

11. Foreign Office minute: Strang to Bevin, April 24th, 1948; C3580/3/18.

12. Anthony Mann, *Comeback: Germany 1945–1952*, 1980; pp. 126, 127.

13. Michael M. Narinskii, 'The Soviet Union and the Berlin Crisis 1948–49', *The Soviet Union and Europe in the Cold War 1945–53* (ed. Francesca Gori and Silvio Pons), 1996; p. 66.

14. Ibid; p. 66.

15. Berlin telegram 1180, June 25th, 1948; CAB 5001/3/18.

16. Telegram 1162, June 24th, 1948; CAB 4921.

17. Conversation between the secretary of state and the United States ambassador; CAB 5031/3/G.

18. Ivone Kirkpatrick to Major-General L.C. Hollis; Foreign Office, June 26, 1948; C5015.

Chapter Six

1. Cabinet Committee of Ministers on Germany, June 29th, 1948.

2. Foreign Office telegram 1230, June 30th, 1948.

3. From Foreign Office to Paris, No. 1966, June 28th, 1948.

4. Cabinet Minutes (48), 44th Conclusions, June 28th, 1948.

5. Norman Reddaway oral interview, Liddell Hart Centre for Military Archives; GB99 KCLMA.

6. Willy Brandt, *My Road To Berlin*, 1960.

7. Hammond Innes, *Air Bridge*, 1951; p. 133.

8. George Newman, in charge of Electrical and Mechanical Workshops at Gatow at the time of the Airlift; lecture in Berlin, April 15th, 2004.

9. Ibid.

10. Ruth Andreas-Friedrich, *Battleground Berlin*, 1990.

Chapter Seven

1. 'Wochenschau – der Augenzeuge', Nr. 115, 1948.
2. 'Wochenschau – der Augenzeuge', Nr. 117, 1948.
3. The National Archives UK, CAB 129/23, January 4th, 1948.
4. Anthony Mann, *Comeback: Germany 1945–1952*, 1980; p. 140.
5. Robert A. Slayton, *Master of the Air: William Tunner and the Success of Military Airlift*, 2010; p. 45.
6. Ibid.
7. David Murphy, Sergei Kondrashev, George Bailey, *Battleground Berlin: CIA Versus KGB in the Cold War*, 1997; p. 62.
8. Oral history interview with Clay, July 16th, 1974, Richard McKinzie; Truman Library.

Chapter Eight

1. Robert Paul Browder and Thomas G. Smith, *Independent: A Biography of Lewis W. Douglas*, 1986; p. 297.
2. Despatch 1105 to Washington, July 26th, 1948; CAB 6207/3/18.
3. Roberts to Strang; CAB 6546/3/18.
4. Walter Bedell Smith, *Moscow Mission 1946–1949*, 1950; p. 23.
5. Foreign Office to Moscow, August 8th, 1948; telegram 1625; C 6423/3/18.
6. Berlin to Foreign Office, August 10th, 1948; telegram 1596; C 6531/3/18.
7. The National Archives UK, CAB 6531, August 11th, 1948.
8. Foreign Office to Washington; telegram 8758, August 9th, 1948; MOD B/C/165.
9. State Department, August 11th, 1948; Truman Library.
10. Ruth Andreas-Friedrich, *Battleground Berlin*, 1990; diary entry for August 22nd, 1948.
11. Foreign secretary's minute to prime minister, August 24th, 1948; PM/48/69.
12. The National Archives UK, CAB 128/13, September 22nd, 1948.

Chapter Nine

1. CIA to president on Moscow breakdown, September 28th, 1948; Truman Library.
2. Michael M. Narinskii, *The Soviet Union and Europe in the Cold War* (ed. Francesca Gori and Silvio Pons), 1996; p. 72.
3. William Michaels, unpublished memoir; Army Education Centre, Aurora, Colorado.
4. Edwin Gere, *The Unheralded*, 2003; p. 86.

Chapter Ten

1. Anthony Mann, *Comeback: Germany 1945–1952*, 1980; p. 137.
2. Report of meeting at Quai d'Orsay, October 4th, 1948; Truman Library.
3. Cmd 7530, progress report of the UN mediator on Palestine, September 16th, 1948.

Chapter Eleven

1. Foreign secretary's report to committee of ministers on Germany. February 4th, 1949; GEN 241/4.
2. Robert Murphy, *Diplomat Among Warriors*, 1964; p. 392.
3. Telegram 3638 to Washington, April 2nd, 1949.
4. The National Archives UK, Foreign Office, 371/7681, C3267/23/18.
5. Telegram 1524 to New York, April 20th, 1949.
6. Charles Pennacchio, 'The East German Communists and the Origins of the Berlin Blockade Crisis', *East European Quarterly*, Vol. 29, No. 3, 1995.
7. Telegram 4671 to Washington, April 29th, 1949.

Chapter Twelve

1. Robert Murphy, *Diplomat Among Warriors*, 1964; p. 393.
2. David G. Williamson, *A Most Diplomatic General: Life of Lord Robertson of Oakridge*, 1996; p. 142.
3. George Mikes, *Uber Alles: Germany Explored*, 1953; pp. 81, 82.

4. Volker R. Berghahn, *American Big Business in Britain and Germany. A Comparative History*, 2014.
5. George Mikes, *Uber Alles: Germany Explored*, 1953; p. 89.

Chapter Thirteen
1. Secretary of state, August 30th, 1948.
2. Attlee to Bevin, 10th December, 1950; FO 800/517.

Chapter Fourteen
1. Berlin contingency planning, March 13th, 1961; FO 371/160485.
2. British embassy in Bonn to Foreign Office, May 26th, 1961; FO 371/160486.
3. Cabinet memo, September 1st, 1961; CAB 129/102.
4. Berlin telegram, August 16th, 1961; FO 371/160510.
5. Guenter Schabowski obituary, *Economist*, November 7th, 2015.
6. Alexandra Richie, *Faust's Metropolis*, 1998; p. 837.

Postscript
1. Frank Roberts, *Dealing with Dictators: The Destruction and Revival of Europe, 1930–70*, 1991; p. 137.
2. Robert Murphy, *Diplomat Among Warriors*, 1964; p. 395.

The Final Tally
1. Truman Library, 'The Berlin Airlift: A USAF Summary', 1949.

ACKNOWLEDGEMENTS

The inspiration for this book came from Air Vice Marshal Sir John Curtiss, a great friend who was remarkably tolerant of my lack of aeronautical knowledge and who set me right on many factual details. Sir John's death before the book was finished was a cause of much sadness for the many who admired his courage and trusted his judgement.

I am greatly indebted to Das AlliiertenMuseum (Allied Museum) Berlin, the Truman Library, the National Archives UK, Landesarchiv Berlin and the London Library but, most particularly, to those veterans of the Airlift who were prepared to share their memories.

I have had valuable support from Nicola Varns who conducted many of the interviews, from Jill Fenner for helping to shape up the manuscript and from my agent, Michael Alcock, who was the voice of calm when it all seemed a bit too much. I owe a particular debt to my eagle-eyed publisher and editor, Duncan Heath.

INDEX